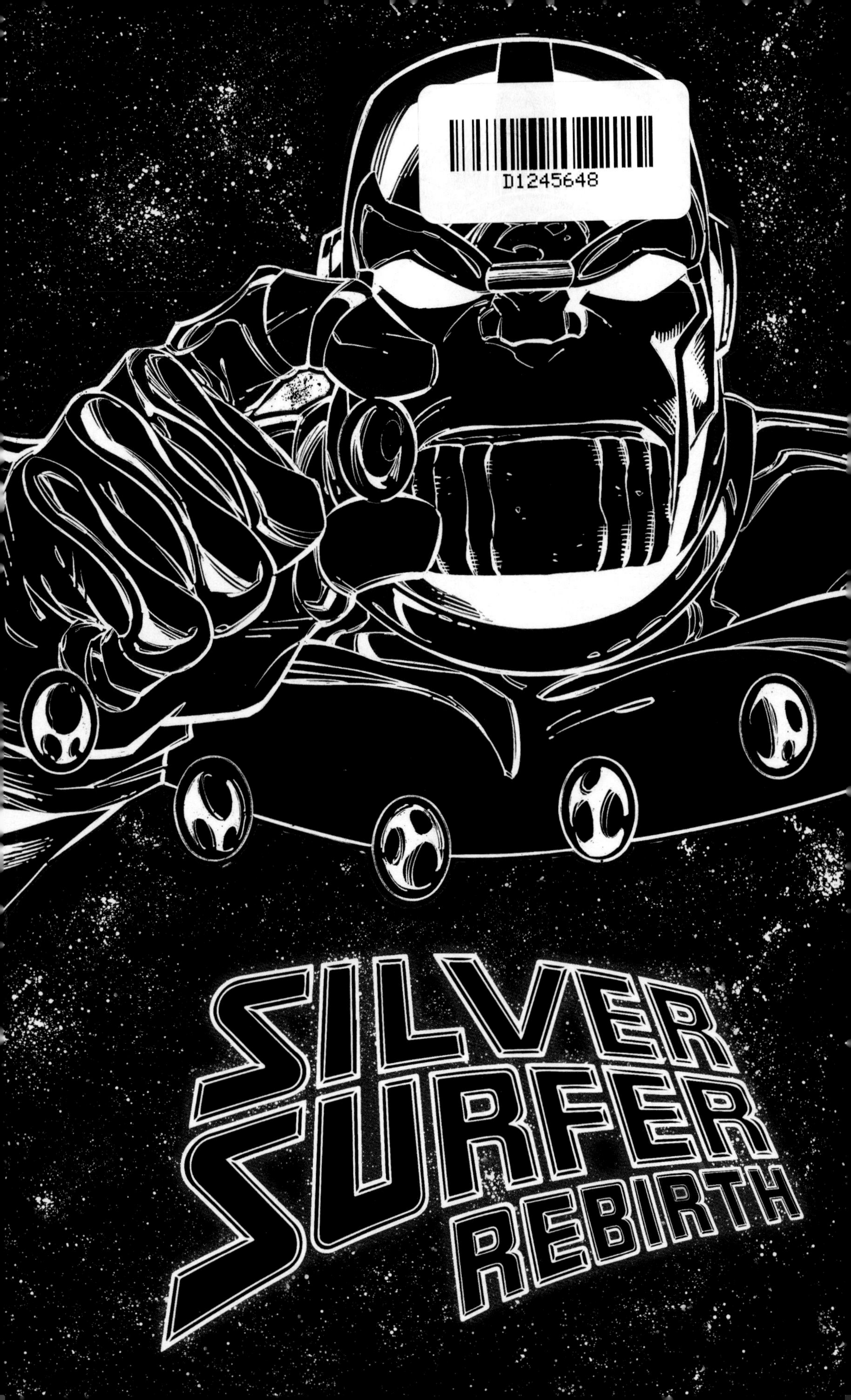
SILVER
SURFER
REBIRTH

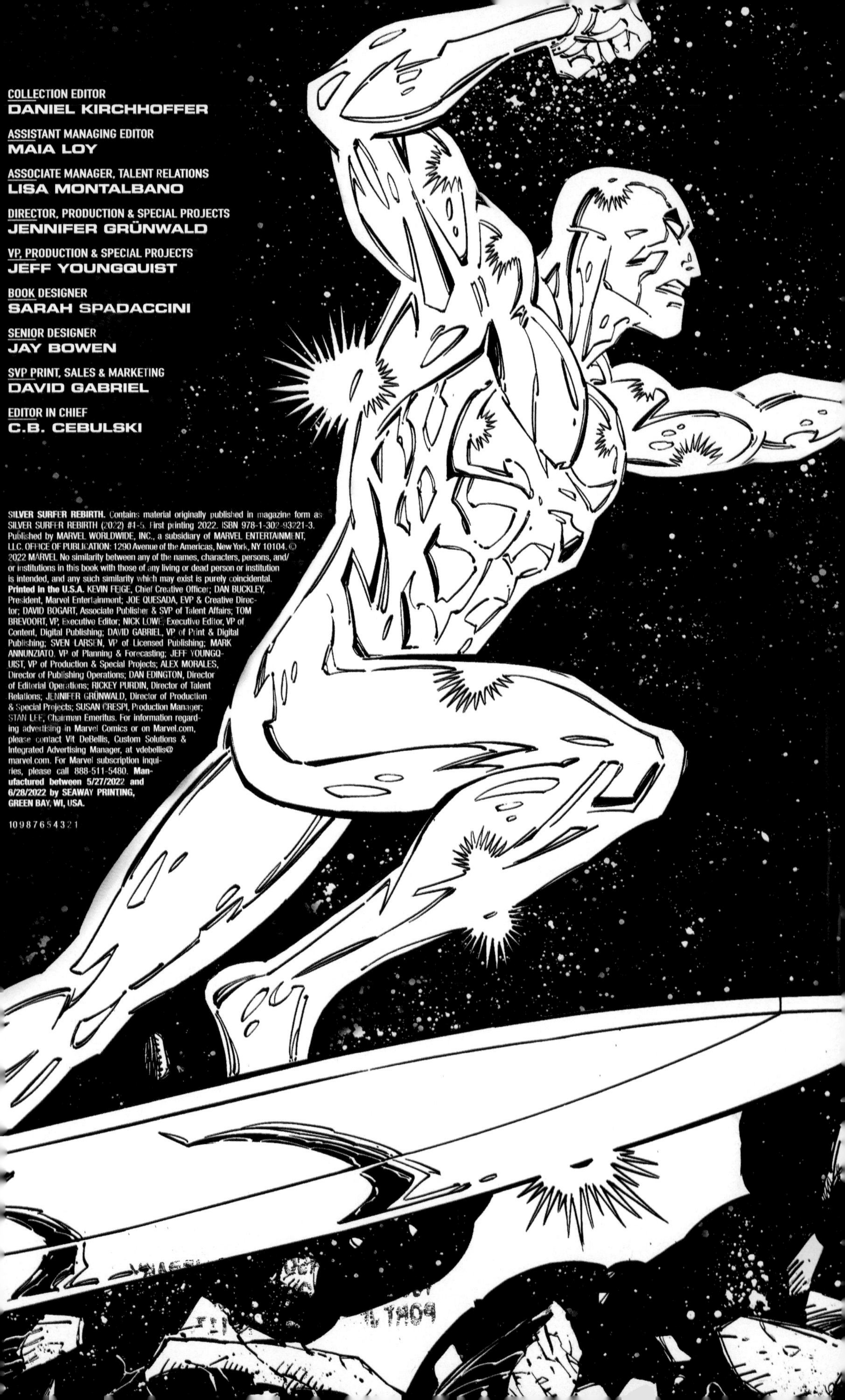

COLLECTION EDITOR
DANIEL KIRCHHOFFER

ASSISTANT MANAGING EDITOR
MAIA LOY

ASSOCIATE MANAGER, TALENT RELATIONS
LISA MONTALBANO

DIRECTOR, PRODUCTION & SPECIAL PROJECTS
JENNIFER GRÜNWALD

VP, PRODUCTION & SPECIAL PROJECTS
JEFF YOUNGQUIST

BOOK DESIGNER
SARAH SPADACCINI

SENIOR DESIGNER
JAY BOWEN

SVP PRINT, SALES & MARKETING
DAVID GABRIEL

EDITOR IN CHIEF
C.B. CEBULSKI

SILVER SURFER REBIRTH. Contains material originally published in magazine form as SILVER SURFER REBIRTH (2022) #1-5. First printing 2022. ISBN 978-1-302-93221-3. Published by MARVEL WORLDWIDE, INC., a subsidiary of MARVEL ENTERTAINMENT, LLC. OFFICE OF PUBLICATION: 1290 Avenue of the Americas, New York, NY 10104.

Printed in the U.S.A. KEVIN FEIGE, Chief Creative Officer; DAN BUCKLEY, President, Marvel Entertainment; JOE QUESADA, EVP & Creative Director; DAVID BOGART, Associate Publisher & SVP of Talent Affairs; TOM BREVOORT, VP, Executive Editor; NICK LOWE, Executive Editor, VP of Content, Digital Publishing; DAVID GABRIEL, VP of Print & Digital Publishing; SVEN LARSEN, VP of Licensed Publishing; MARK ANNUNZIATO, VP of Planning & Forecasting; JEFF YOUNGQUIST, VP of Production & Special Projects; ALEX MORALES, Director of Publishing Operations; DAN EDINGTON, Director of Editorial Operations; RICKEY PURDIN, Director of Talent Relations; JENNIFER GRÜNWALD, Director of Production & Special Projects; SUSAN CRESPI, Production Manager; STAN LEE, Chairman Emeritus. For information regarding advertising in Marvel Comics or on Marvel.com, please contact Vit DeBellis, Custom Solutions & Integrated Advertising Manager, at vdebellis@marvel.com. For Marvel subscription inquiries, please call 888-511-5480. **Manufactured between 5/27/2022 and 6/28/2022 by SEAWAY PRINTING, GREEN BAY, WI, USA.**

10 9 8 7 6 5 4 3 2 1

SILVER SURFER REBIRTH

RON MARZ
WRITER

RON LIM
PENCILER

DON HO
INKER

ISRAEL SILVA
COLOR ARTIST

VC's JOE SABINO
LETTERER

RON LIM, DON HO & ISRAEL SILVA
COVER ART

KAT GREGOROWICZ
ASSISTANT EDITOR

DARREN SHAN
EDITOR

SILVER SURFER CREATED BY
STAN LEE & JACK KIRBY

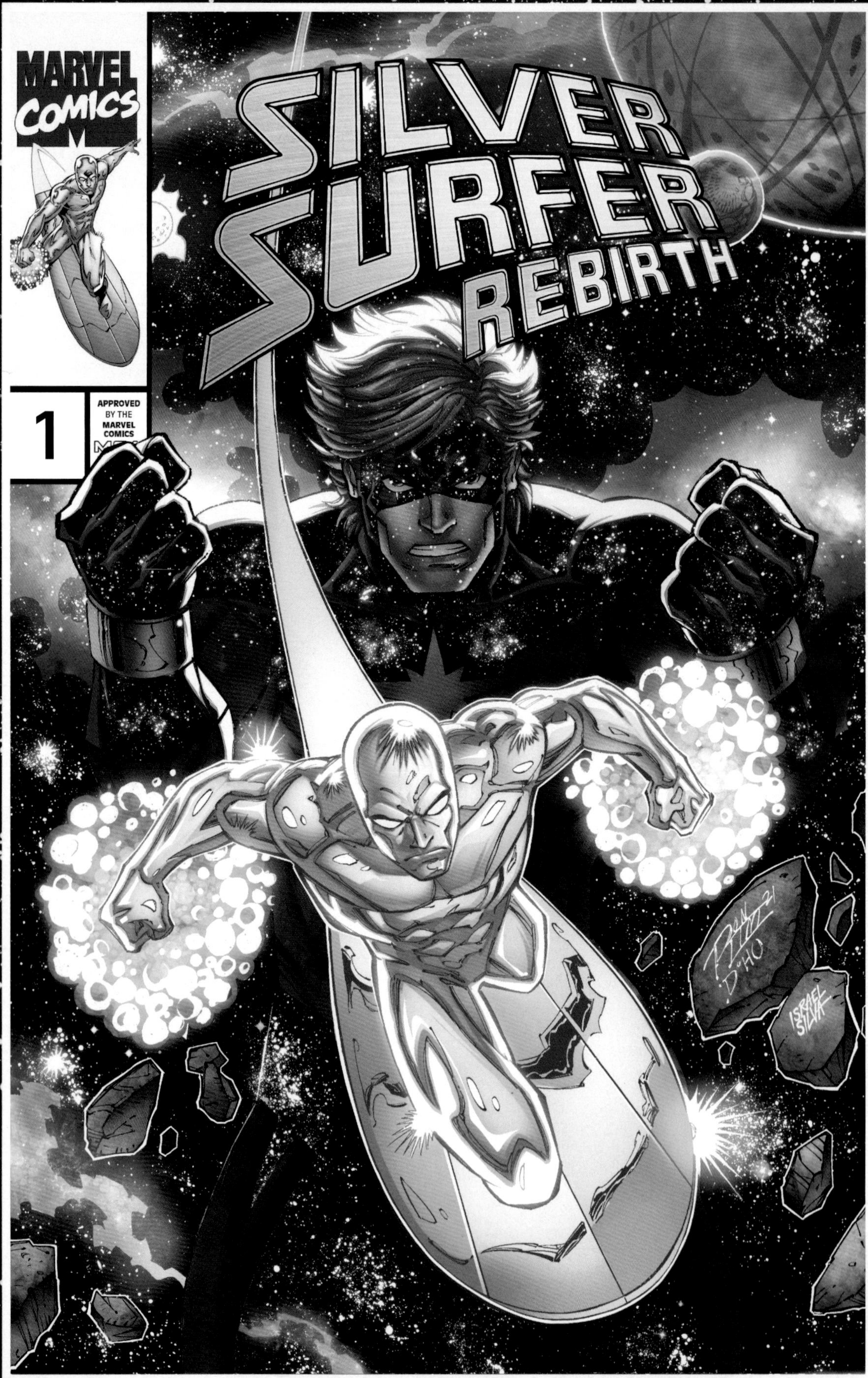

MARVEL COMICS
SILVER SURFER
REBIRTH
1
APPROVED BY THE MARVEL COMICS

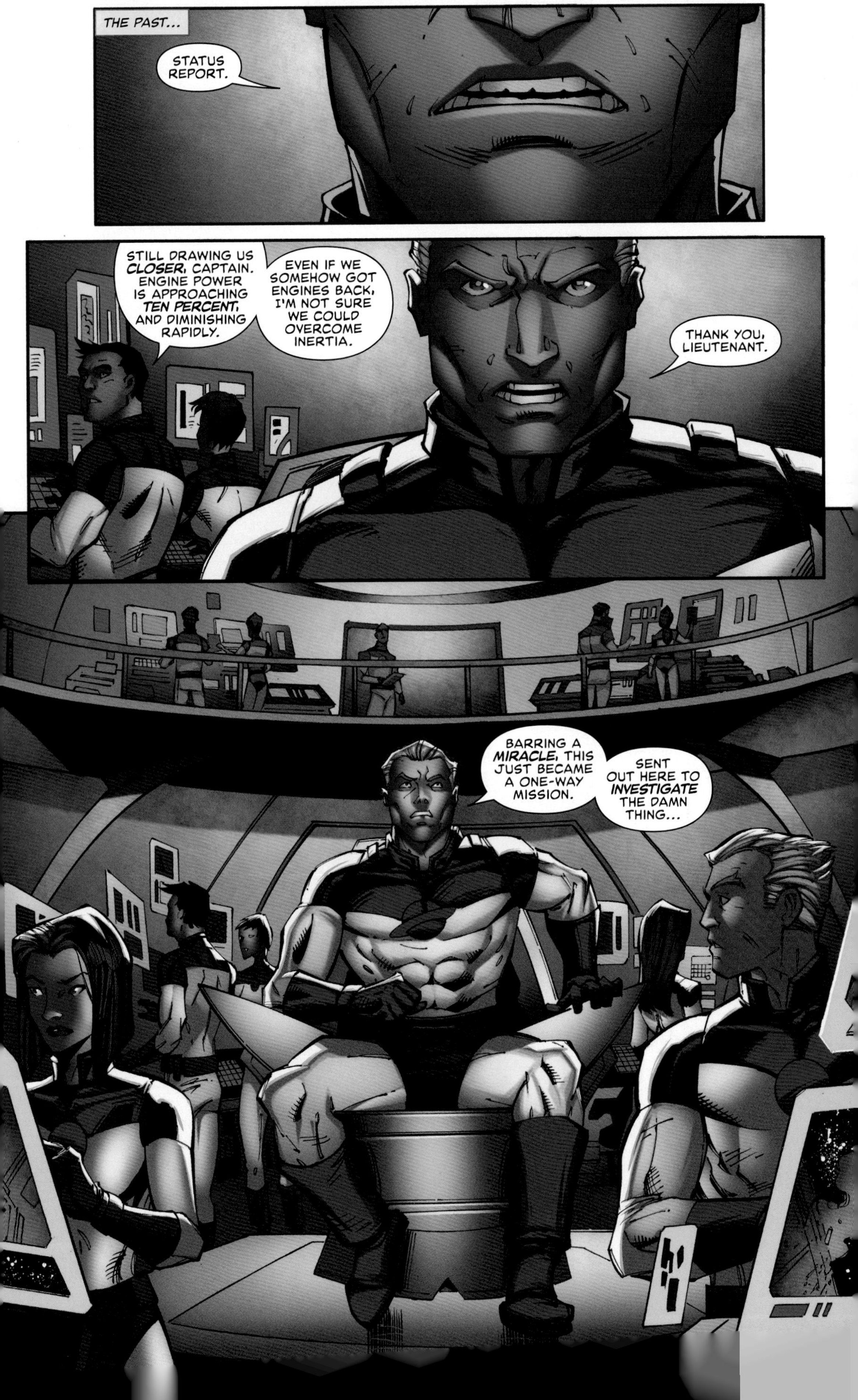
THE PAST...
STATUS REPORT.
STILL DRAWING US CLOSER, CAPTAIN. ENGINE POWER IS APPROACHING TEN PERCENT, AND DIMINISHING RAPIDLY.
EVEN IF WE SOMEHOW GOT ENGINES BACK, I'M NOT SURE WE COULD OVERCOME INERTIA.
THANK YOU, LIEUTENANT.
BARRING A MIRACLE, THIS JUST BECAME A ONE-WAY MISSION.
SENT OUT HERE TO INVESTIGATE THE DAMN THING...

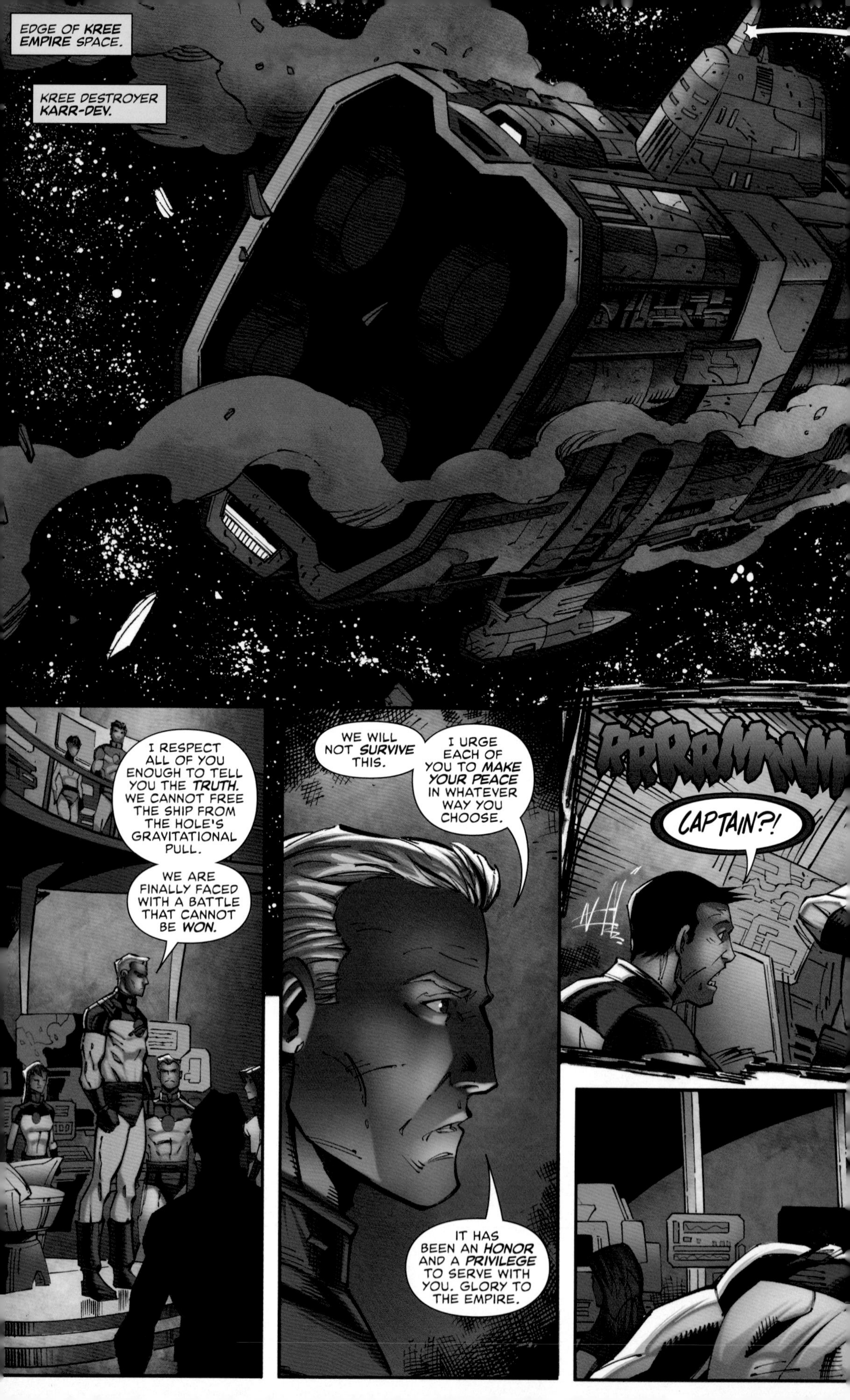
EDGE OF KREE EMPIRE SPACE.
KREE DESTROYER KARR-DEV.
I RESPECT ALL OF YOU ENOUGH TO TELL YOU THE TRUTH. WE CANNOT FREE THE SHIP FROM THE HOLE'S GRAVITATIONAL PULL.
WE ARE FINALLY FACED WITH A BATTLE THAT CANNOT BE WON.
WE WILL NOT SURVIVE THIS.
I URGE EACH OF YOU TO MAKE YOUR PEACE IN WHATEVER WAY YOU CHOOSE.
IT HAS BEEN AN HONOR AND A PRIVILEGE TO SERVE WITH YOU. GLORY TO THE EMPIRE.
RRRRMMM
CAPTAIN?!

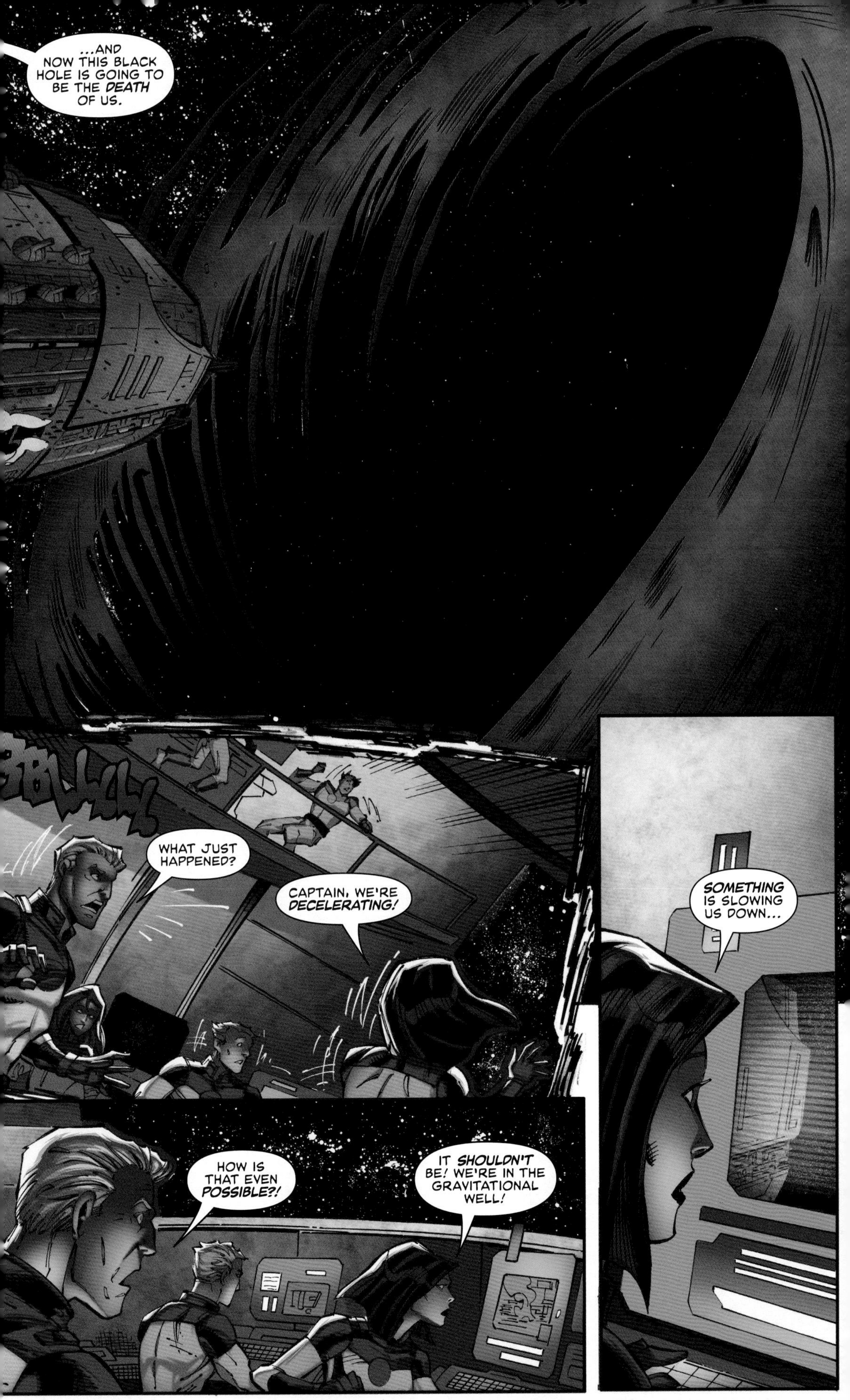

...AND NOW THIS BLACK HOLE IS GOING TO BE THE DEATH OF US.
WHAT JUST HAPPENED?
CAPTAIN, WE'RE DECELERATING!
SOMETHING IS SLOWING US DOWN...
HOW IS THAT EVEN POSSIBLE?!
IT SHOULDN'T BE! WE'RE IN THE GRAVITATIONAL WELL!

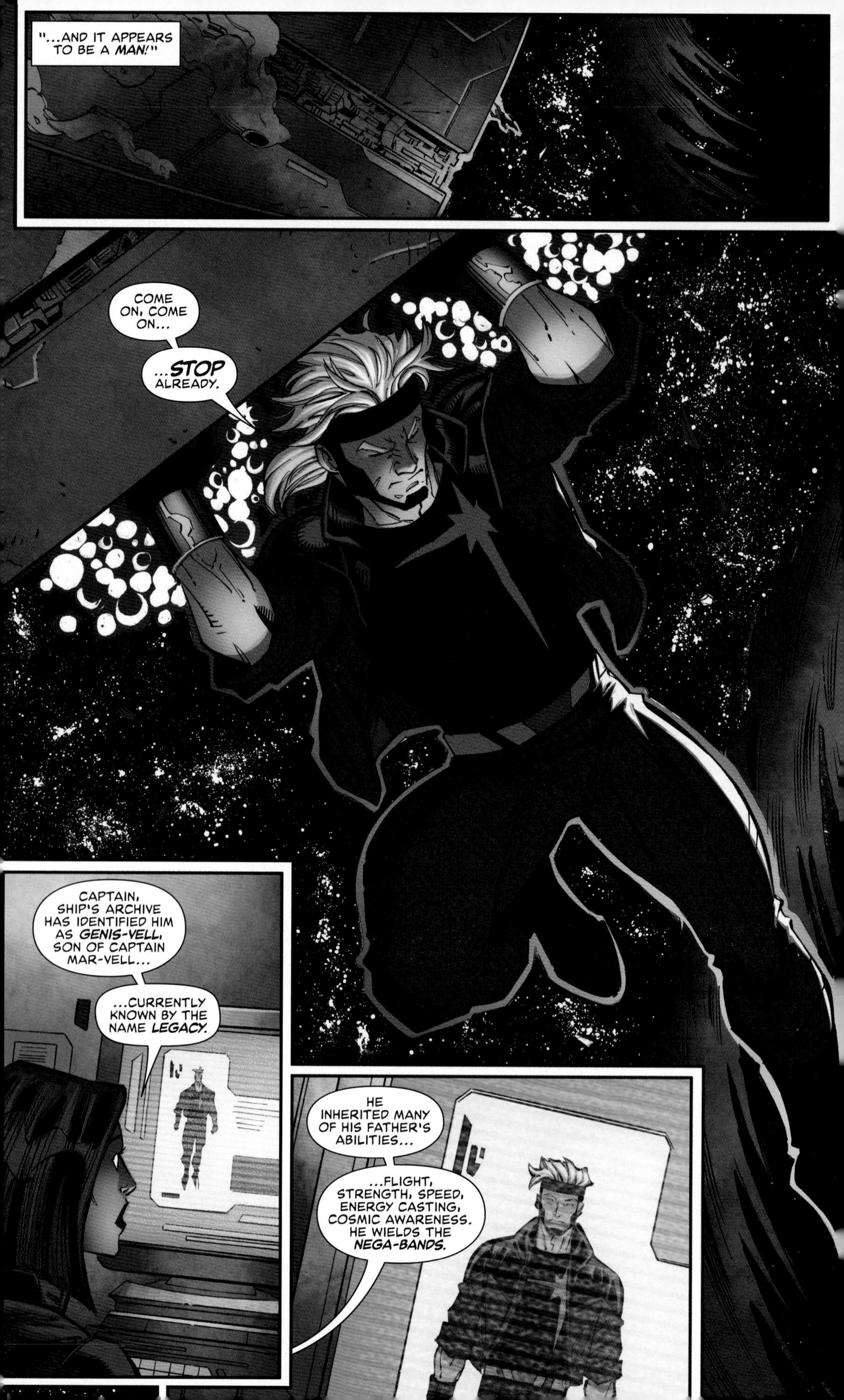
"...AND IT APPEARS TO BE A MAN!"
COME ON, COME ON...
...STOP ALREADY.
CAPTAIN, SHIP'S ARCHIVE HAS IDENTIFIED HIM AS GENIS-VELL, SON OF CAPTAIN MAR-VELL...
...CURRENTLY KNOWN BY THE NAME LEGACY.
HE INHERITED MANY OF HIS FATHER'S ABILITIES...
...FLIGHT, STRENGTH, SPEED, ENERGY CASTING, COSMIC AWARENESS. HE WIELDS THE NEGA-BANDS.

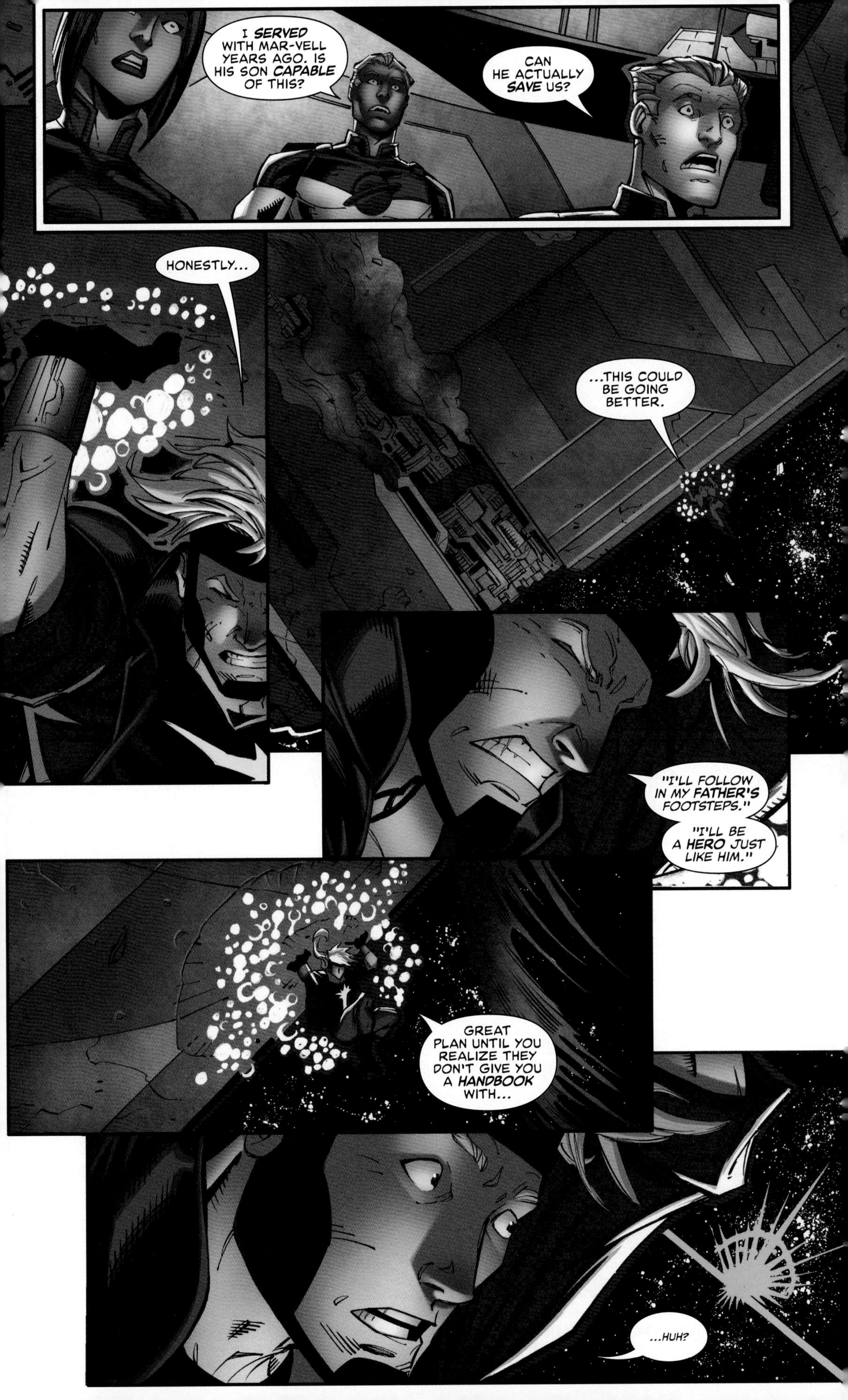

I SERVED WITH MAR-VELL YEARS AGO. IS HIS SON CAPABLE OF THIS?
CAN HE ACTUALLY SAVE US?
HONESTLY...
...THIS COULD BE GOING BETTER.
"I'LL FOLLOW IN MY FATHER'S FOOTSTEPS."
"I'LL BE A HERO JUST LIKE HIM."
GREAT PLAN UNTIL YOU REALIZE THEY DON'T GIVE YOU A HANDBOOK WITH...
...HUH?

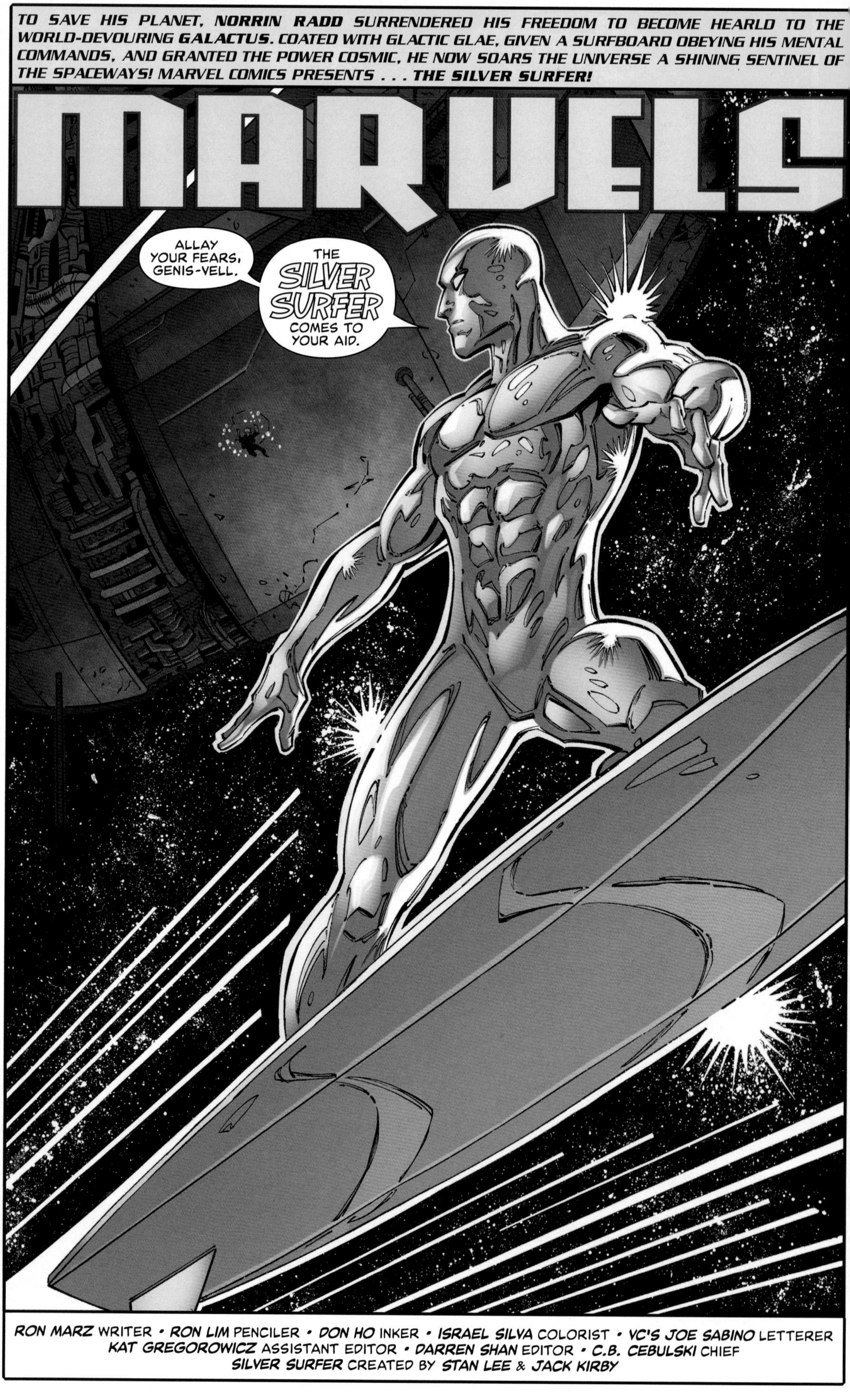
TO SAVE HIS PLANET, NORRIN RADD SURRENDERED HIS FREEDOM TO BECOME HEARLD TO THE WORLD-DEVOURING GALACTUS. COATED WITH GLACTIC GLAE, GIVEN A SURFBOARD OBEYING HIS MENTAL COMMANDS, AND GRANTED THE POWER COSMIC, HE NOW SOARS THE UNIVERSE A SHINING SENTINEL OF THE SPACEWAYS! MARVEL COMICS PRESENTS . . . THE SILVER SURFER!
MARVELS
ALLAY YOUR FEARS, GENIS-VELL.
THE SILVER SURFER COMES TO YOUR AID.
RON MARZ WRITER • RON LIM PENCILER • DON HO INKER • ISRAEL SILVA COLORIST • VC'S JOE SABINO LETTERER
KAT GREGOROWICZ ASSISTANT EDITOR • DARREN SHAN EDITOR • C.B. CEBULSKI CHIEF
SILVER SURFER CREATED BY STAN LEE & JACK KIRBY

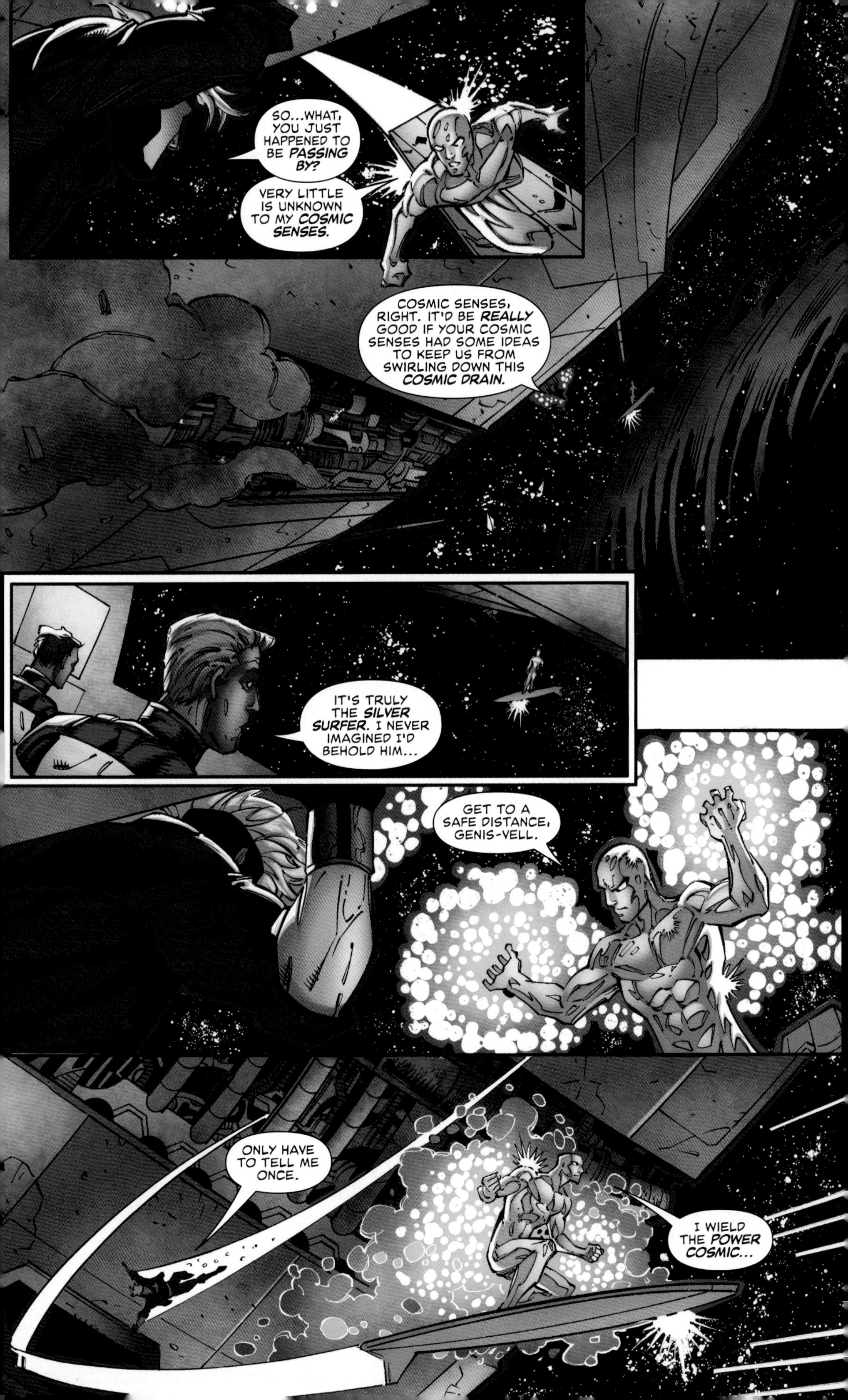
SO...WHAT, YOU JUST HAPPENED TO BE PASSING BY?
VERY LITTLE IS UNKNOWN TO MY COSMIC SENSES.
COSMIC SENSES, RIGHT. IT'D BE REALLY GOOD IF YOUR COSMIC SENSES HAD SOME IDEAS TO KEEP US FROM SWIRLING DOWN THIS COSMIC DRAIN.
IT'S TRULY THE SILVER SURFER. I NEVER IMAGINED I'D BEHOLD HIM...
GET TO A SAFE DISTANCE, GENIS-VELL.
ONLY HAVE TO TELL ME ONCE.
I WIELD THE POWER COSMIC...

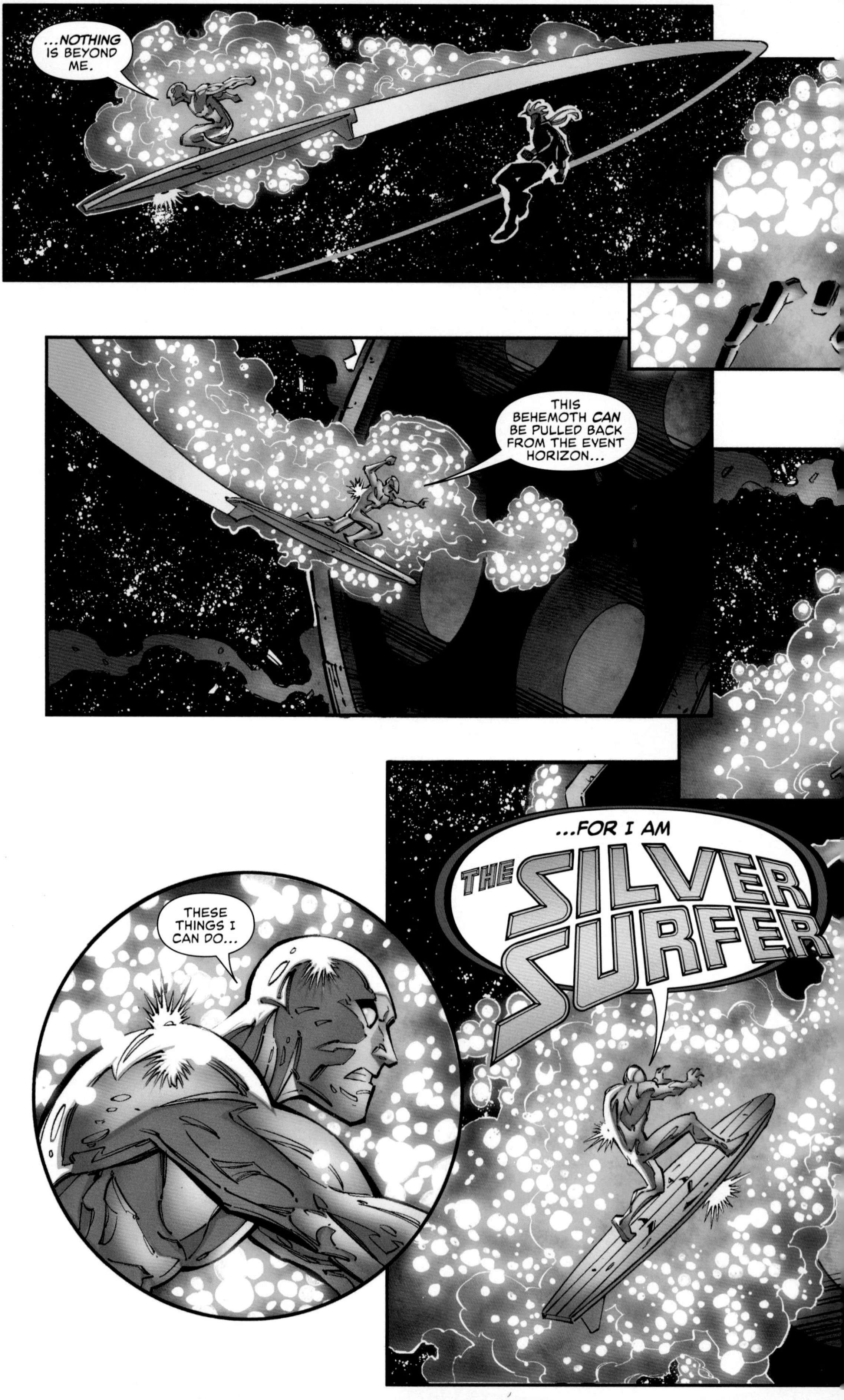
...NOTHING IS BEYOND ME.
THIS BEHEMOTH CAN BE PULLED BACK FROM THE EVENT HORIZON...
THESE THINGS I CAN DO...
...FOR I AM THE SILVER SURFER

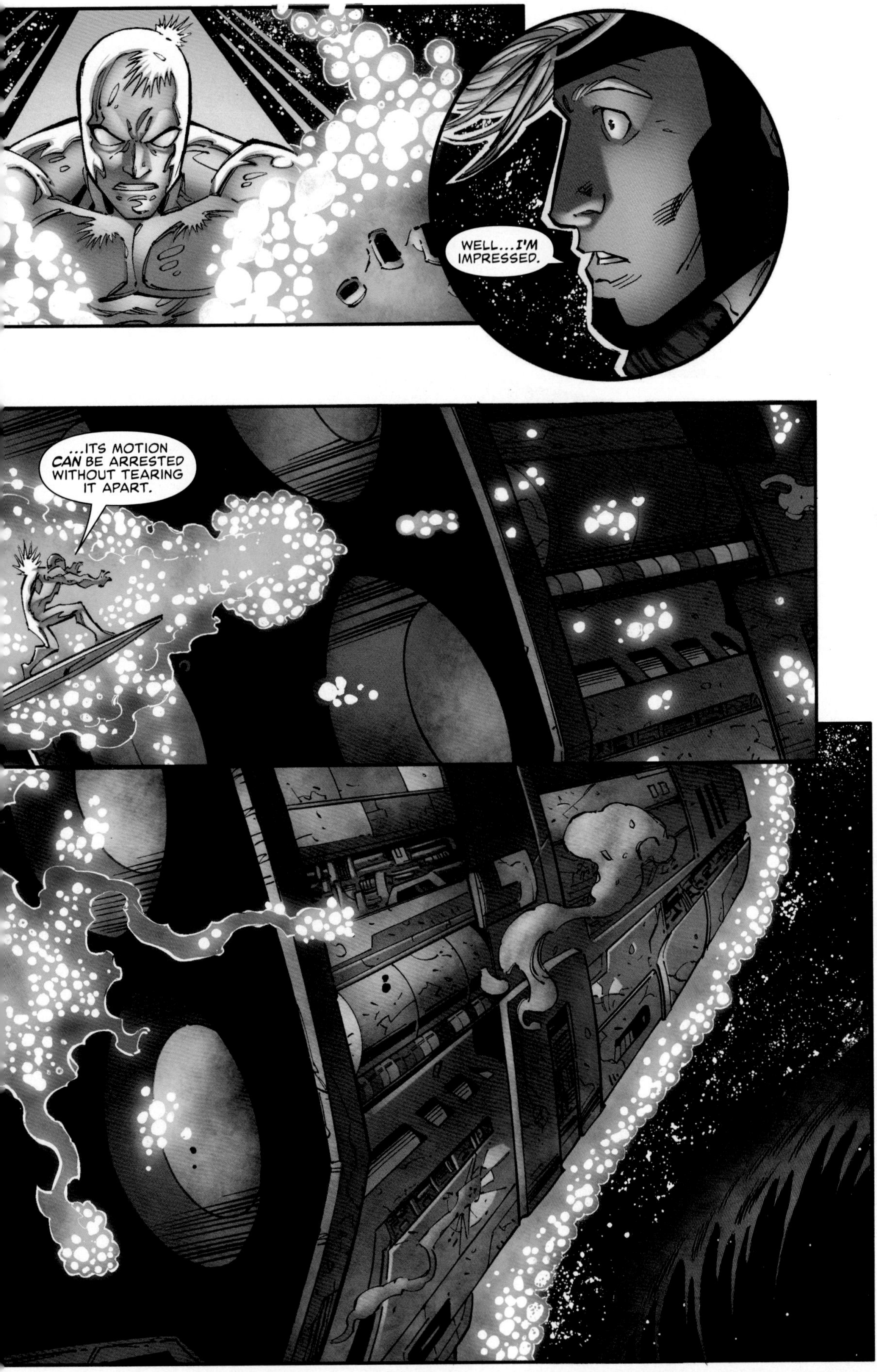
WELL...I'M IMPRESSED.
...ITS MOTION CAN BE ARRESTED WITHOUT TEARING IT APART.

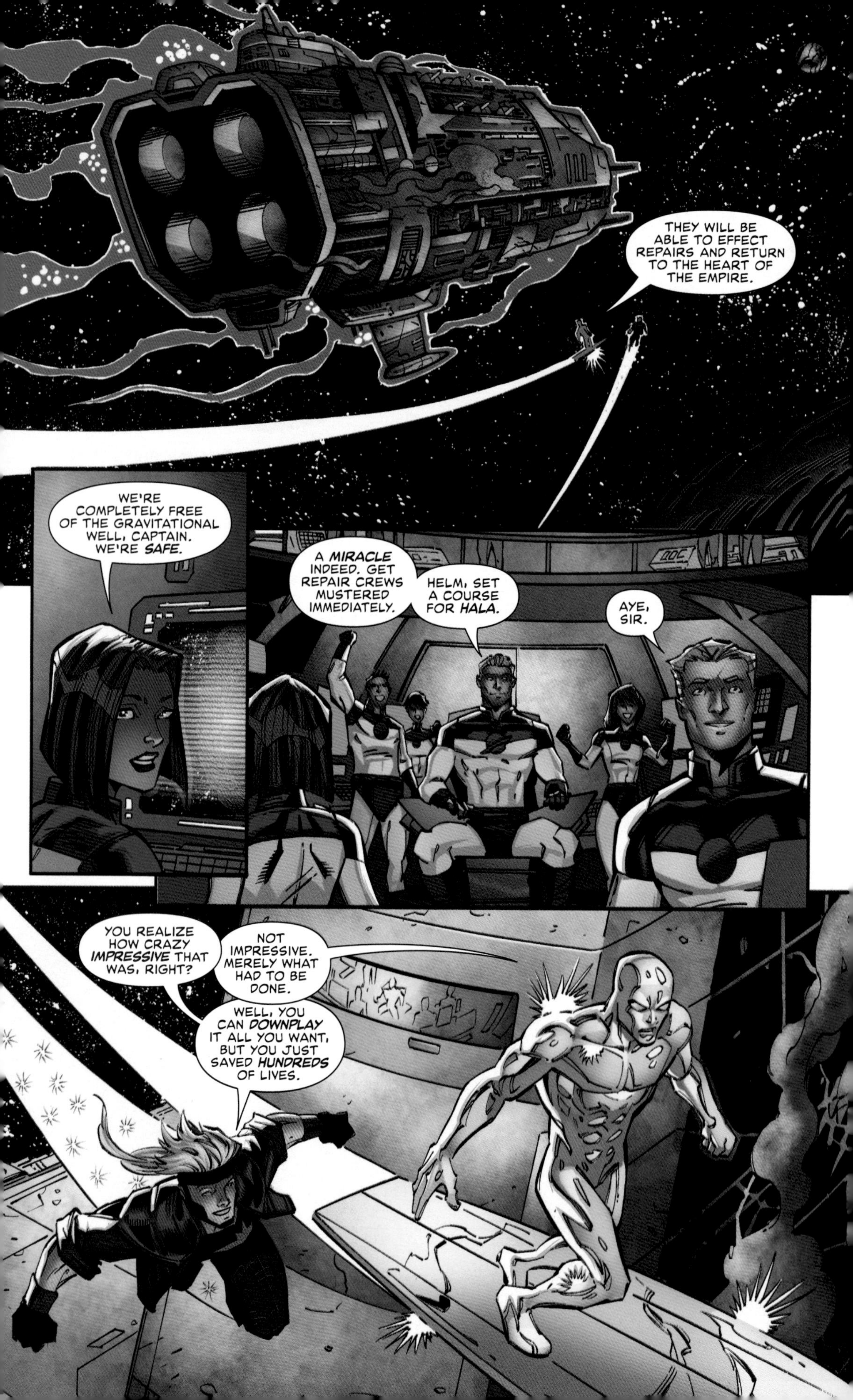
THEY WILL BE ABLE TO EFFECT REPAIRS AND RETURN TO THE HEART OF THE EMPIRE.
WE'RE COMPLETELY FREE OF THE GRAVITATIONAL WELL, CAPTAIN. WE'RE SAFE.
A MIRACLE INDEED. GET REPAIR CREWS MUSTERED IMMEDIATELY.
HELM, SET A COURSE FOR HALA.
AYE, SIR.
YOU REALIZE HOW CRAZY IMPRESSIVE THAT WAS, RIGHT?
NOT IMPRESSIVE. MERELY WHAT HAD TO BE DONE.
WELL, YOU CAN DOWNPLAY IT ALL YOU WANT, BUT YOU JUST SAVED HUNDREDS OF LIVES.

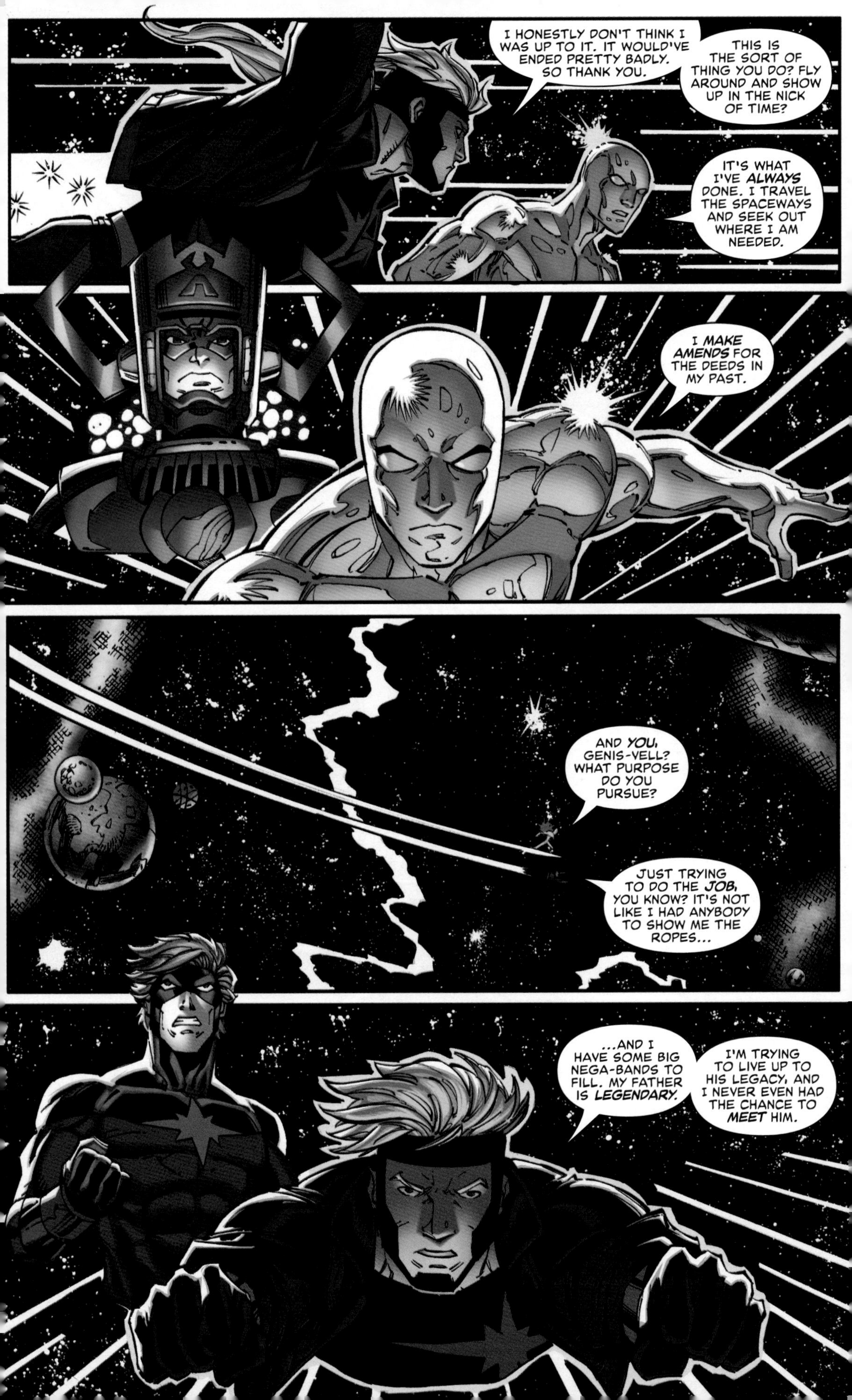
I HONESTLY DON'T THINK I WAS UP TO IT. IT WOULD'VE ENDED PRETTY BADLY. SO THANK YOU.
THIS IS THE SORT OF THING YOU DO? FLY AROUND AND SHOW UP IN THE NICK OF TIME?
IT'S WHAT I'VE *ALWAYS* DONE. I TRAVEL THE SPACEWAYS AND SEEK OUT WHERE I AM NEEDED.
I *MAKE AMENDS* FOR THE DEEDS IN MY PAST.
AND *YOU*, GENIS-VELL? WHAT PURPOSE DO YOU PURSUE?
JUST TRYING TO DO THE *JOB*, YOU KNOW? IT'S NOT LIKE I HAD ANYBODY TO SHOW ME THE ROPES...
...AND I HAVE SOME BIG NEGA-BANDS TO FILL. MY FATHER IS *LEGENDARY*.
I'M TRYING TO LIVE UP TO HIS LEGACY, AND I NEVER EVEN HAD THE CHANCE TO *MEET* HIM.

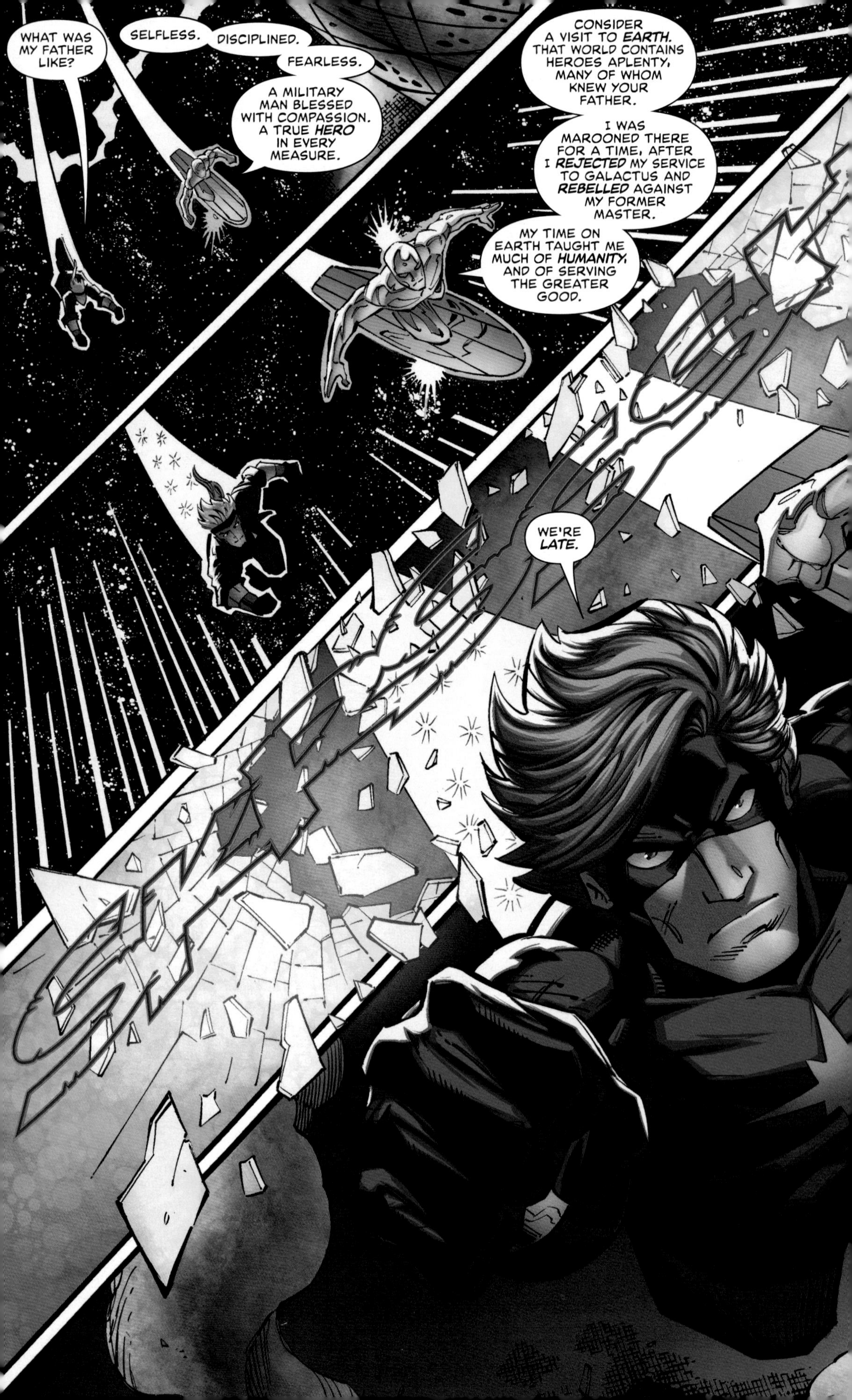
WHAT WAS MY FATHER LIKE?
SELFLESS.
DISCIPLINED.
FEARLESS.
A MILITARY MAN BLESSED WITH COMPASSION. A TRUE HERO IN EVERY MEASURE.
CONSIDER A VISIT TO EARTH. THAT WORLD CONTAINS HEROES APLENTY, MANY OF WHOM KNEW YOUR FATHER.
I WAS MAROONED THERE FOR A TIME, AFTER I REJECTED MY SERVICE TO GALACTUS AND REBELLED AGAINST MY FORMER MASTER.
MY TIME ON EARTH TAUGHT ME MUCH OF HUMANITY, AND OF SERVING THE GREATER GOOD.
WE'RE LATE.

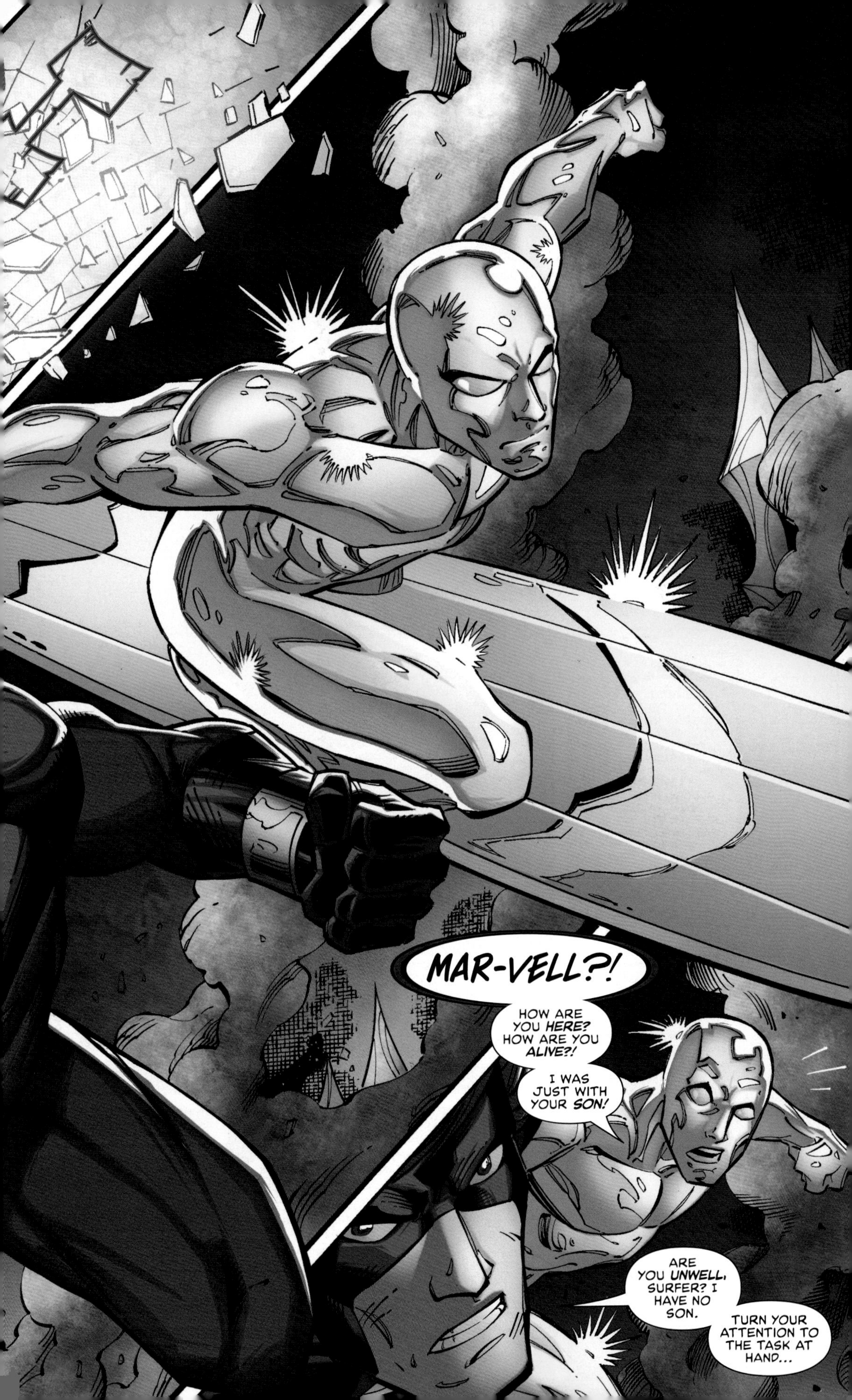
MAR-VELL?!
HOW ARE YOU HERE? HOW ARE YOU ALIVE?!
I WAS JUST WITH YOUR SON!
ARE YOU UNWELL, SURFER? I HAVE NO SON.
TURN YOUR ATTENTION TO THE TASK AT HAND...

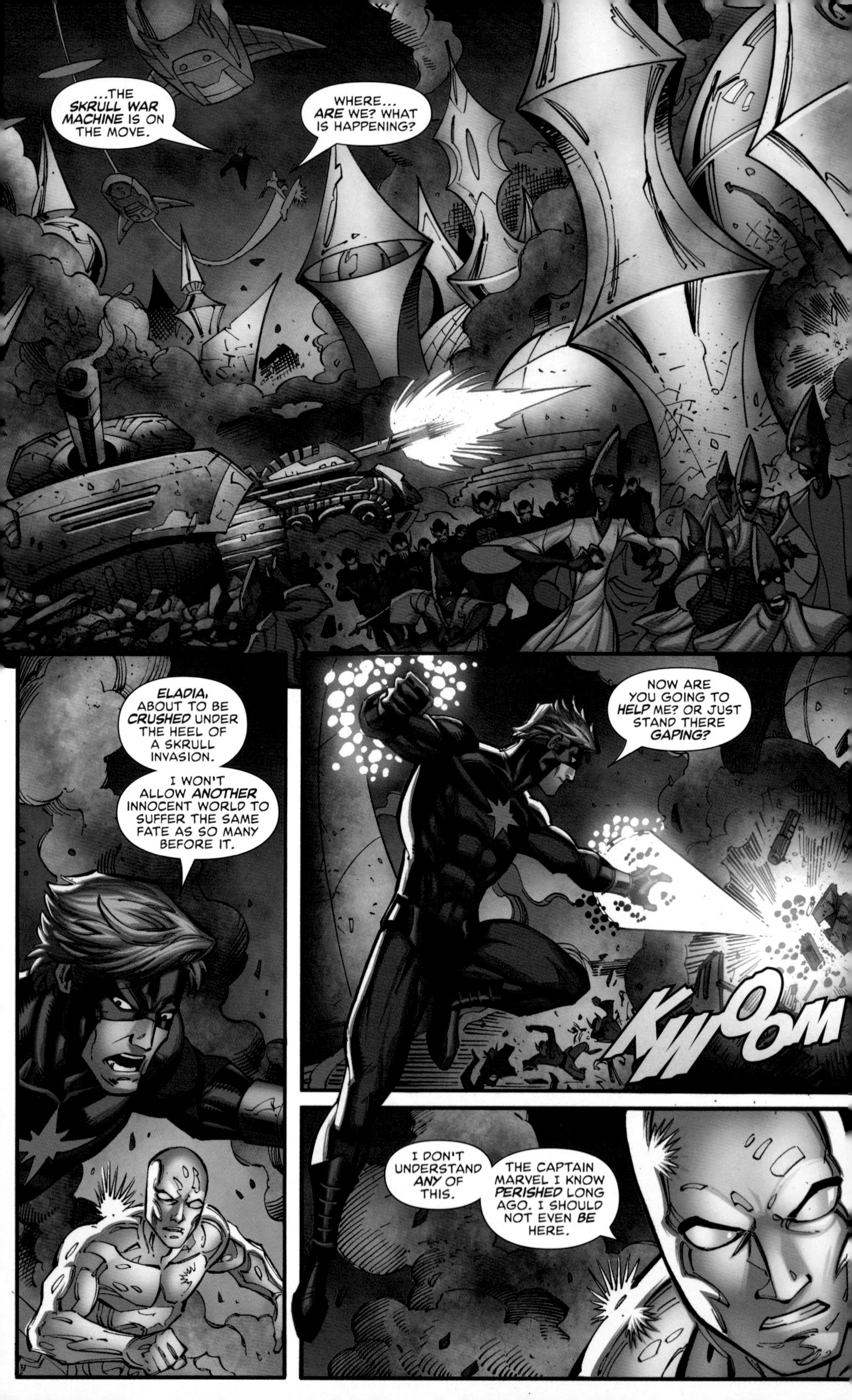
...THE SKRULL WAR MACHINE IS ON THE MOVE.
WHERE... ARE WE? WHAT IS HAPPENING?
ELADIA, ABOUT TO BE CRUSHED UNDER THE HEEL OF A SKRULL INVASION.
I WON'T ALLOW ANOTHER INNOCENT WORLD TO SUFFER THE SAME FATE AS SO MANY BEFORE IT.
NOW ARE YOU GOING TO HELP ME? OR JUST STAND THERE GAPING?
KWOOOM
I DON'T UNDERSTAND ANY OF THIS.
THE CAPTAIN MARVEL I KNOW PERISHED LONG AGO. I SHOULD NOT EVEN BE HERE.

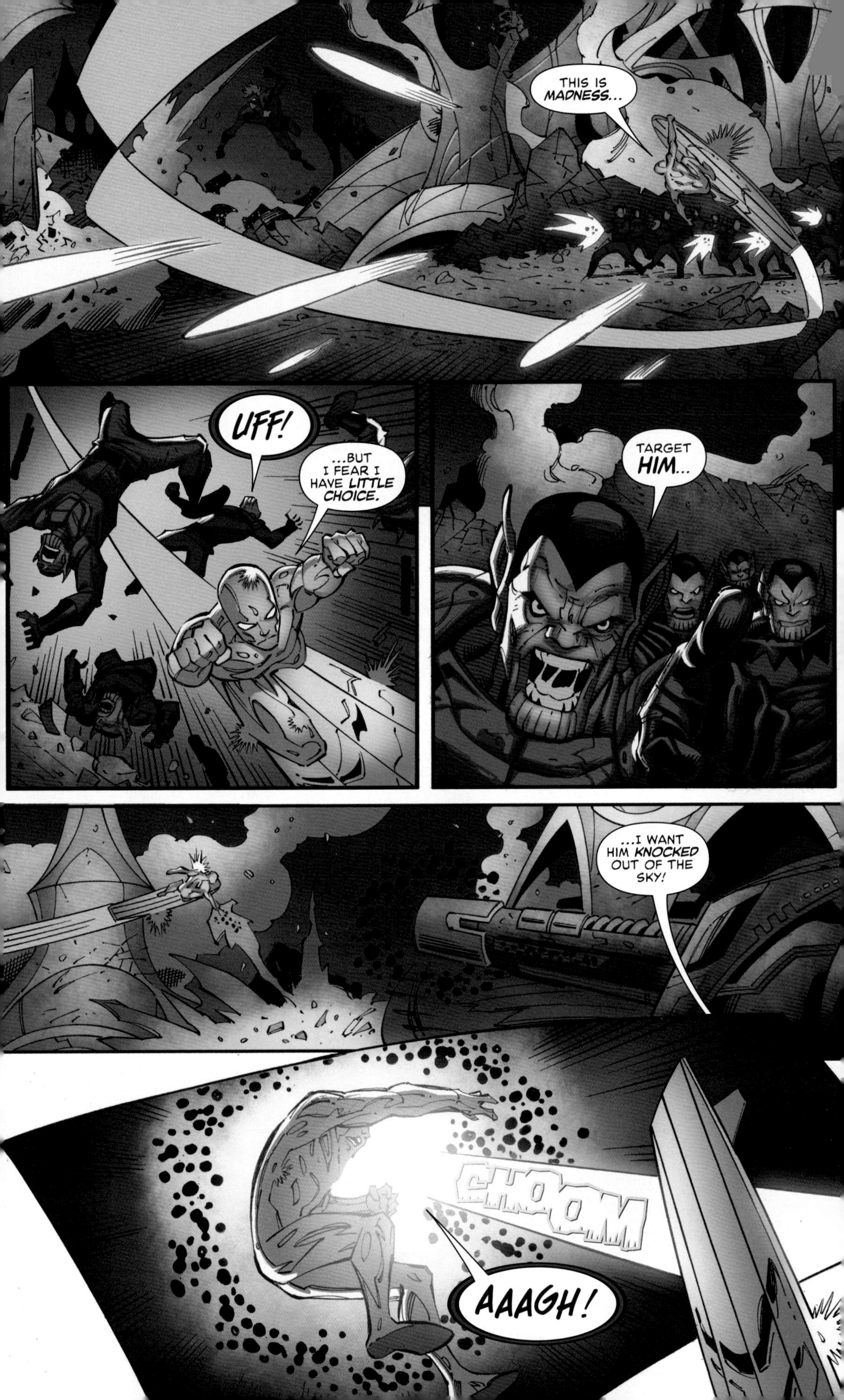
THIS IS MADNESS...
UFF!
...BUT I FEAR I HAVE LITTLE CHOICE.
TARGET HIM...
...I WANT HIM KNOCKED OUT OF THE SKY!
CHOOM
AAAGH!

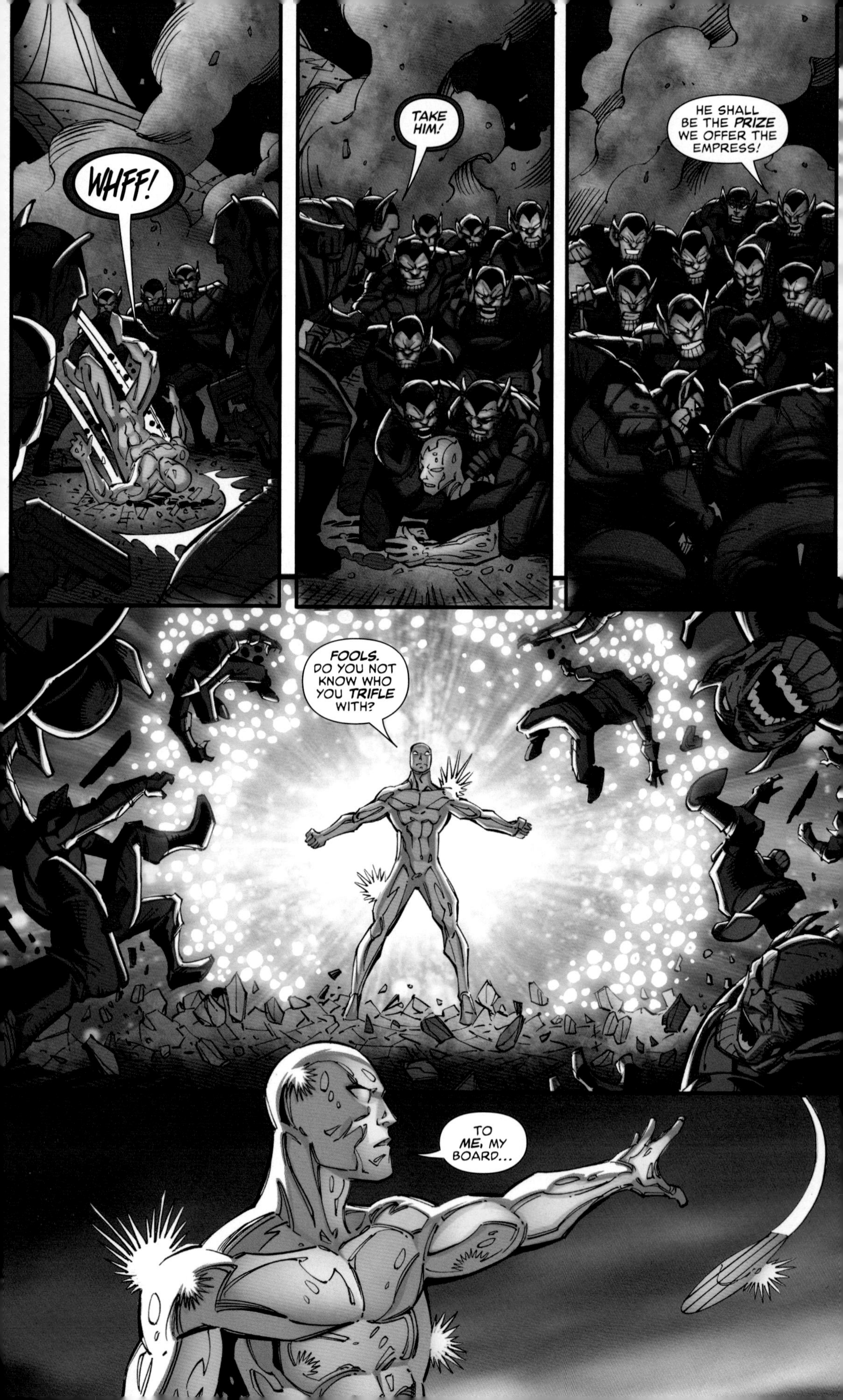
WHFF!
TAKE HIM!
HE SHALL BE THE PRIZE WE OFFER THE EMPRESS!
FOOLS. DO YOU NOT KNOW WHO YOU TRIFLE WITH?
TO ME, MY BOARD...

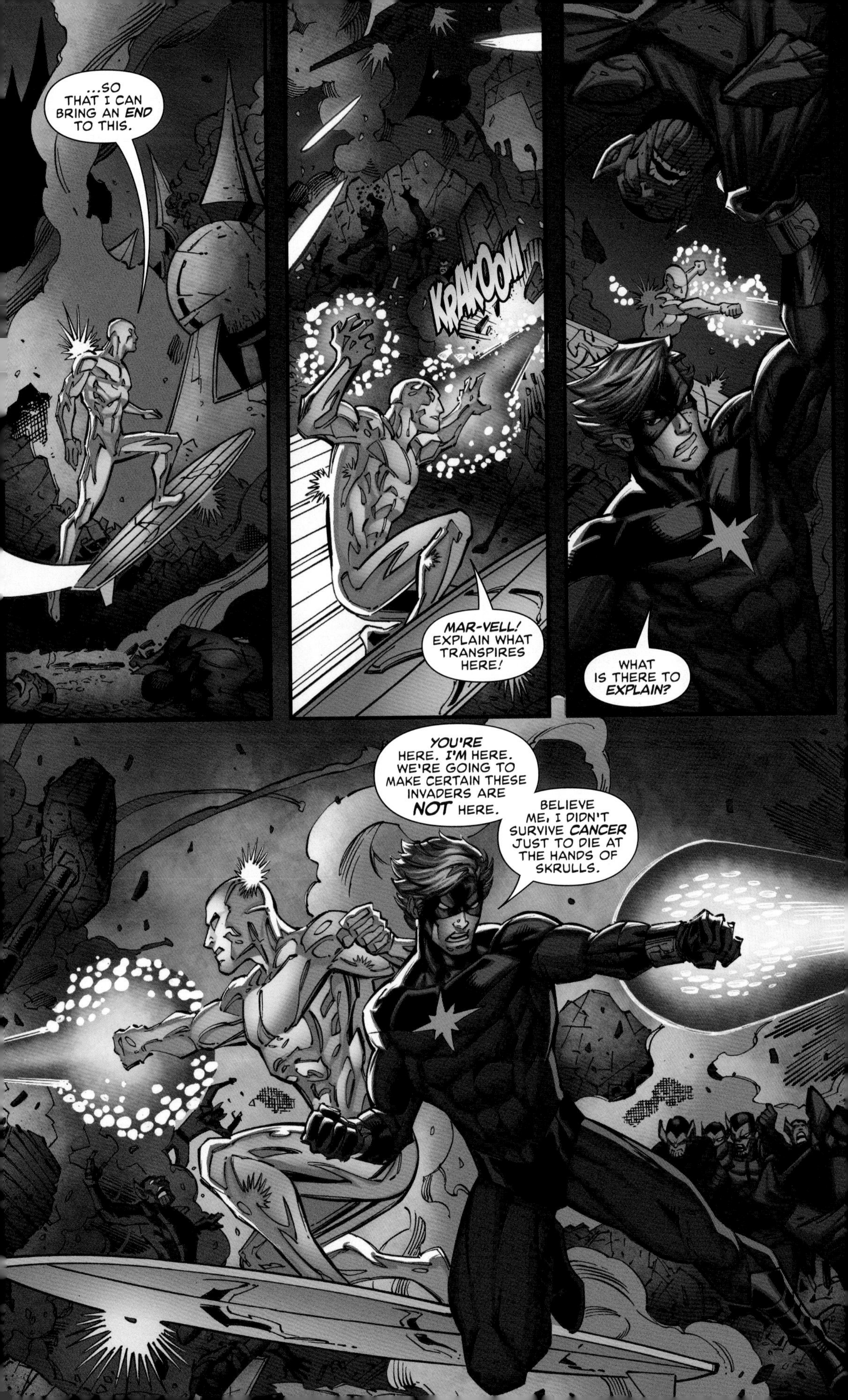
...SO THAT I CAN BRING AN END TO THIS.
KRAKOOM
MAR-VELL! EXPLAIN WHAT TRANSPIRES HERE!
WHAT IS THERE TO EXPLAIN?
YOU'RE HERE. I'M HERE. WE'RE GOING TO MAKE CERTAIN THESE INVADERS ARE NOT HERE.
BELIEVE ME, I DIDN'T SURVIVE CANCER JUST TO DIE AT THE HANDS OF SKRULLS.

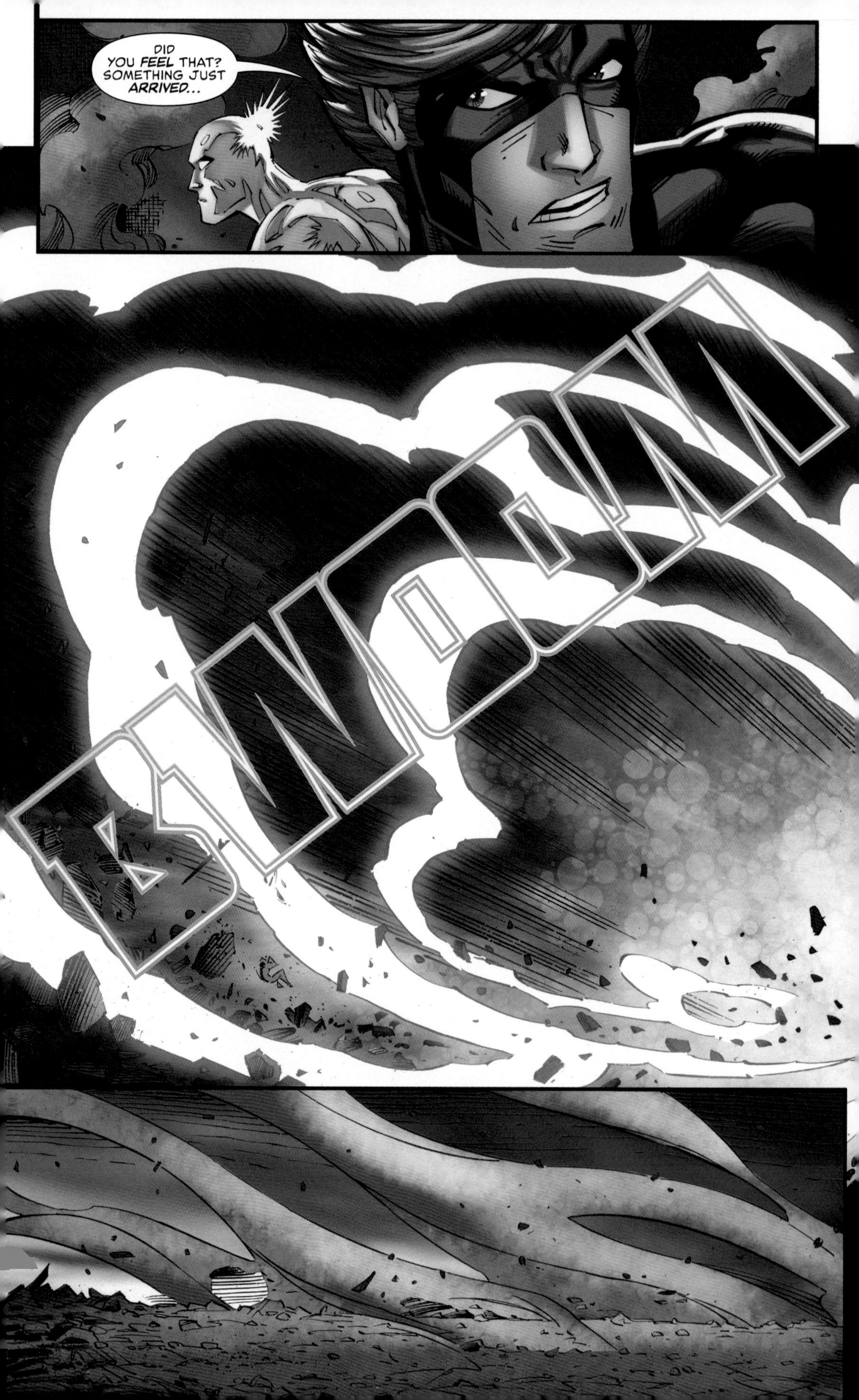
DID YOU FEEL THAT? SOMETHING JUST ARRIVED...
BWOOM

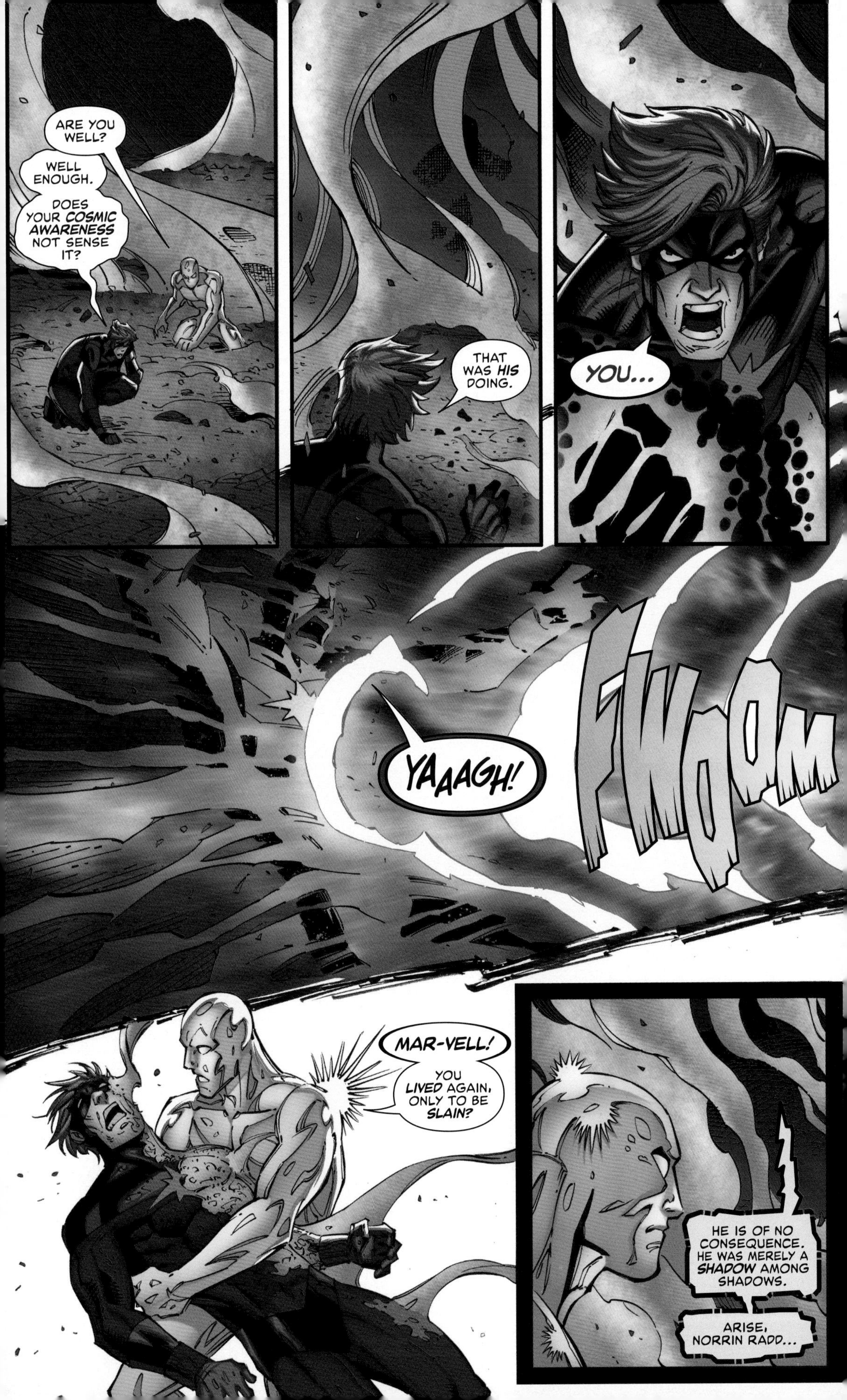

ARE YOU WELL?
WELL ENOUGH.
DOES YOUR COSMIC AWARENESS NOT SENSE IT?
THAT WAS HIS DOING.
YOU...
YAAAGH!
FWOOOM
MAR-VELL!
YOU LIVED AGAIN, ONLY TO BE SLAIN?
HE IS OF NO CONSEQUENCE. HE WAS MERELY A SHADOW AMONG SHADOWS.
ARISE, NORRIN RADD...

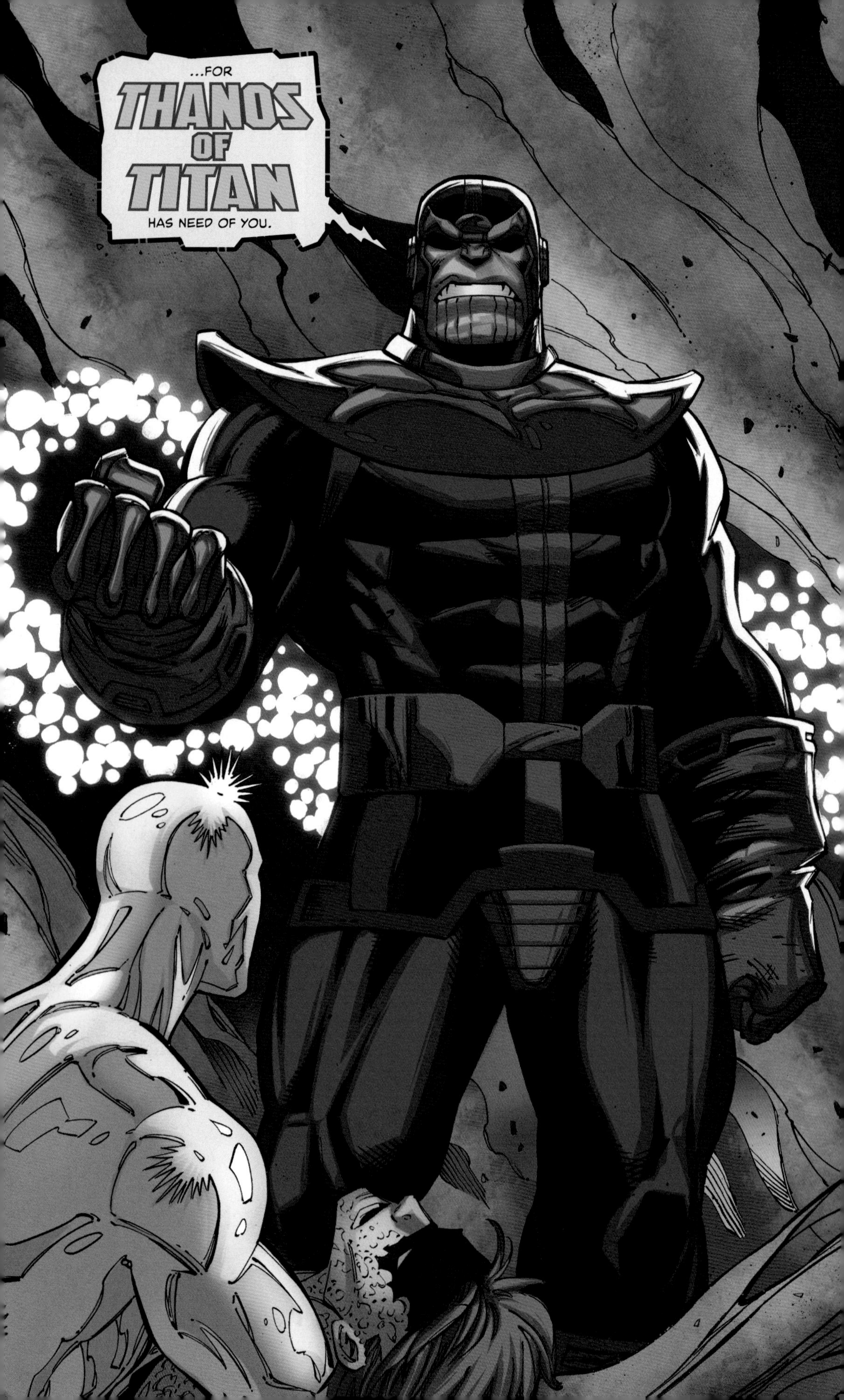
...FOR THANOS OF TITAN HAS NEED OF YOU.

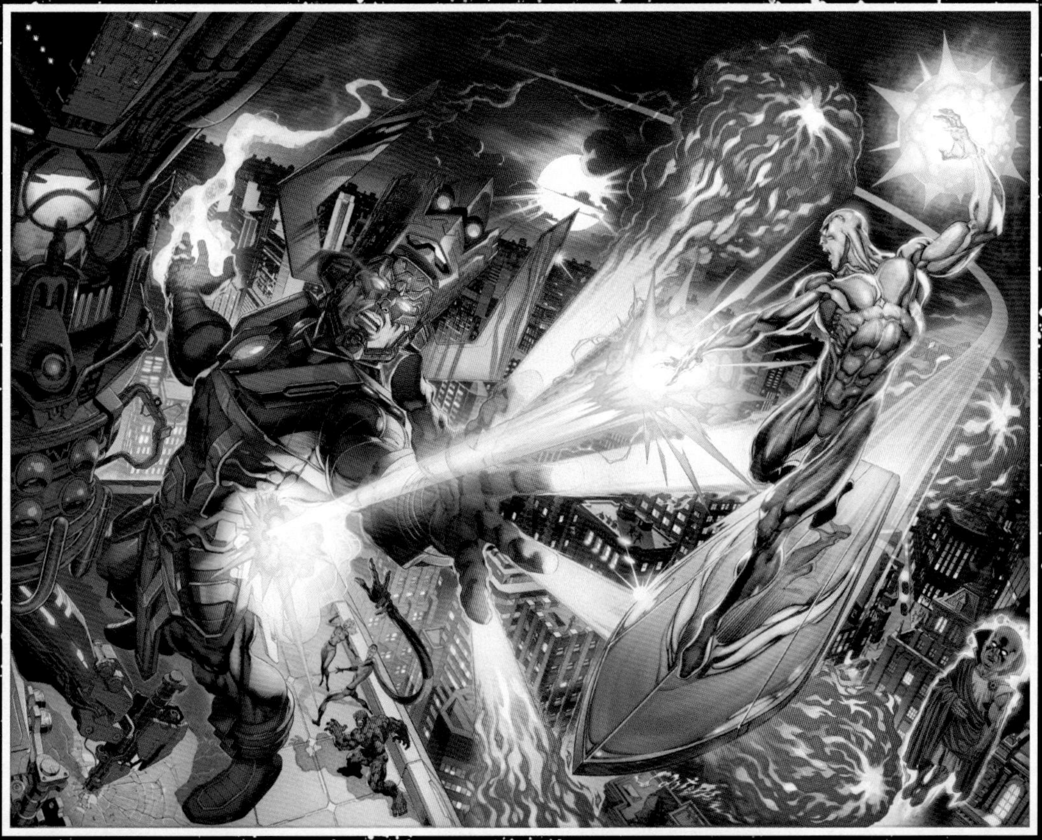

#1 WRAPAROUND VARIANT BY
CLAUDIO CASTELLINI & ROMULO FAJARDO JR.

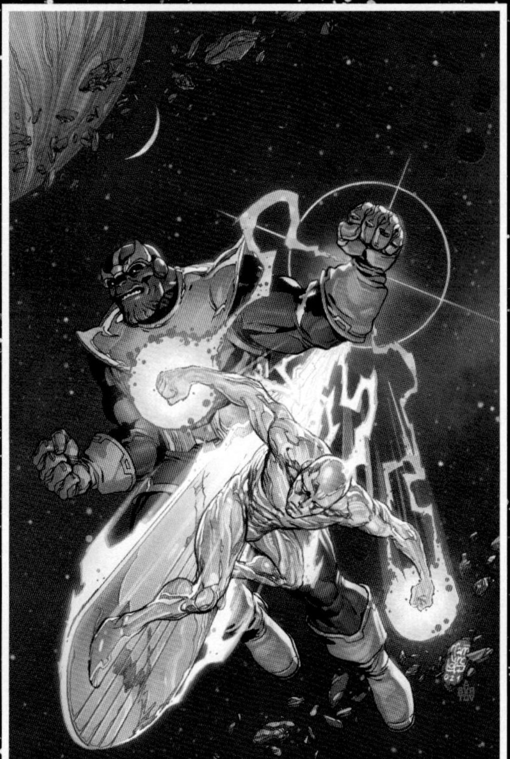

#1 VARIANT BY
GIUSEPPE CAMUNCOLI & JESUS ABURTOV

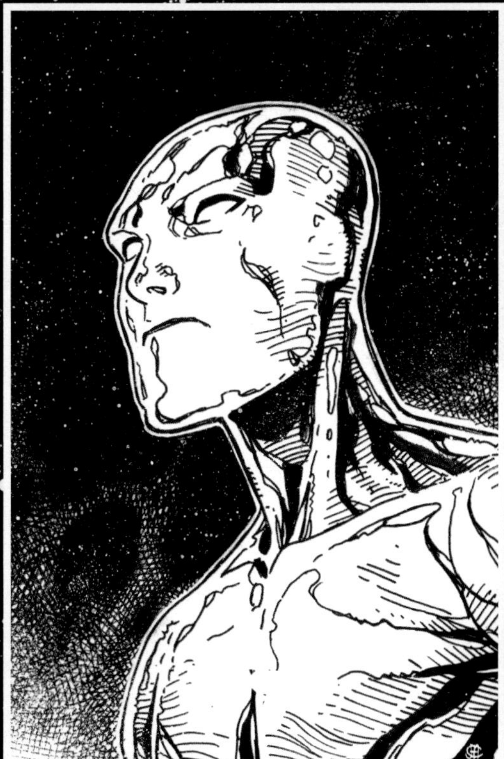

#1 HEADSHOT SKETCH VARIANT BY
JIM CHEUNG

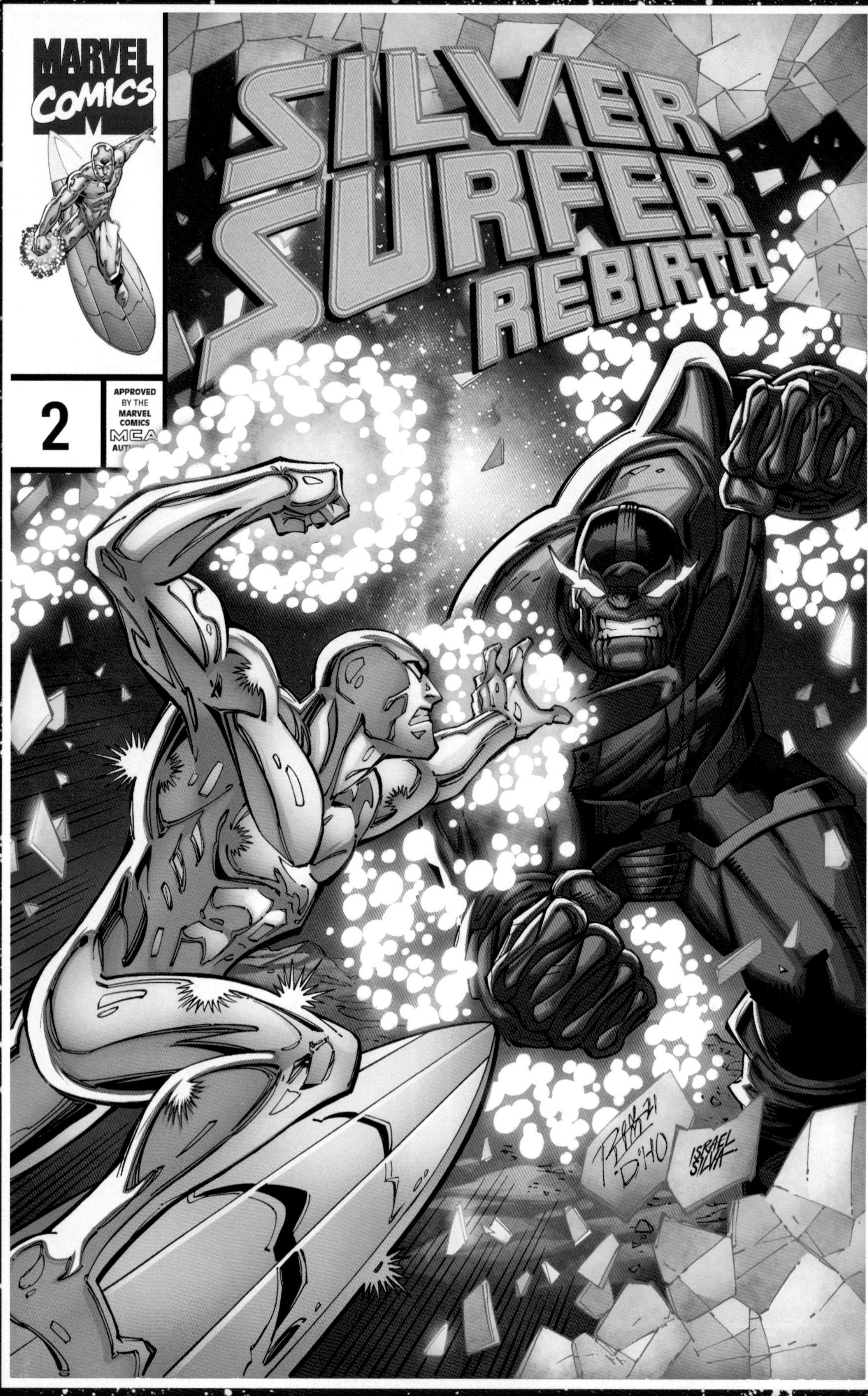
MARVEL
COMICS
SILVER SURFER
REBIRTH
2
APPROVED BY THE MARVEL COMICS
ISRAEL SILVA

TO SAVE HIS PLANET, NORRIN RADD SURRENDERED HIS FREEDOM TO BECOME HERALD TO THE WORLD-DEVOURING GALACTUS. COATED WITH GALACTIC GLAZE, GIVEN A SURFBOARD OBEYING HIS MENTAL COMMANDS, AND GRANTED THE POWER COSMIC, HE NOW SOARS THE UNIVERSE A SHINING SENTINEL OF THE SPACEWAYS! MARVEL COMICS PRESENTS . . . THE SILVER SURFER!

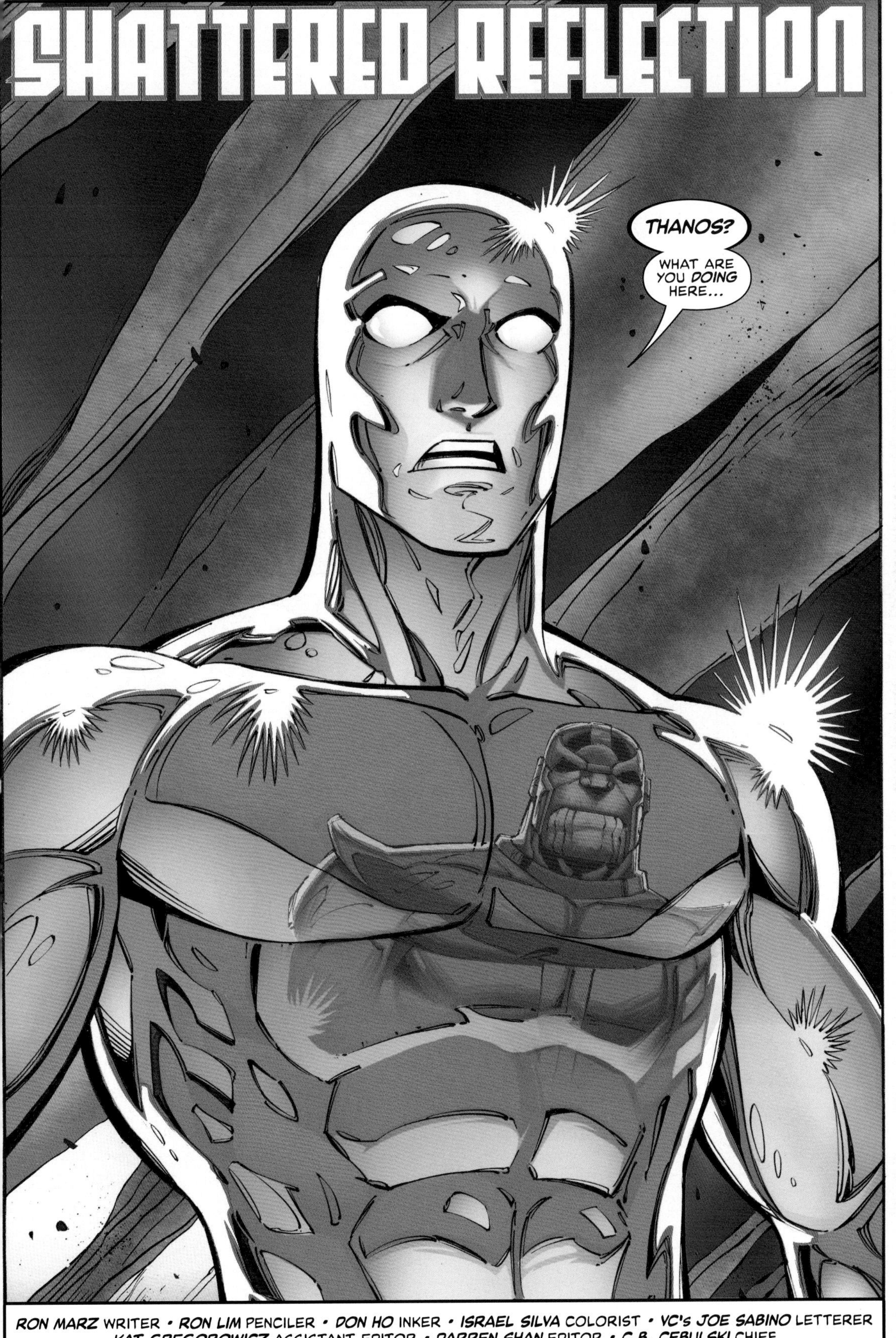
SHATTERED REFLECTION
THANOS?
WHAT ARE YOU DOING HERE...

RON MARZ WRITER • *RON LIM* PENCILER • *DON HO* INKER • *ISRAEL SILVA* COLORIST • *VC's JOE SABINO* LETTERER
KAT GREGOROWICZ ASSISTANT EDITOR • *DARREN SHAN* EDITOR • *C.B. CEBULSKI* CHIEF
SILVER SURFER CREATED BY *STAN LEE* & *JACK KIRBY*

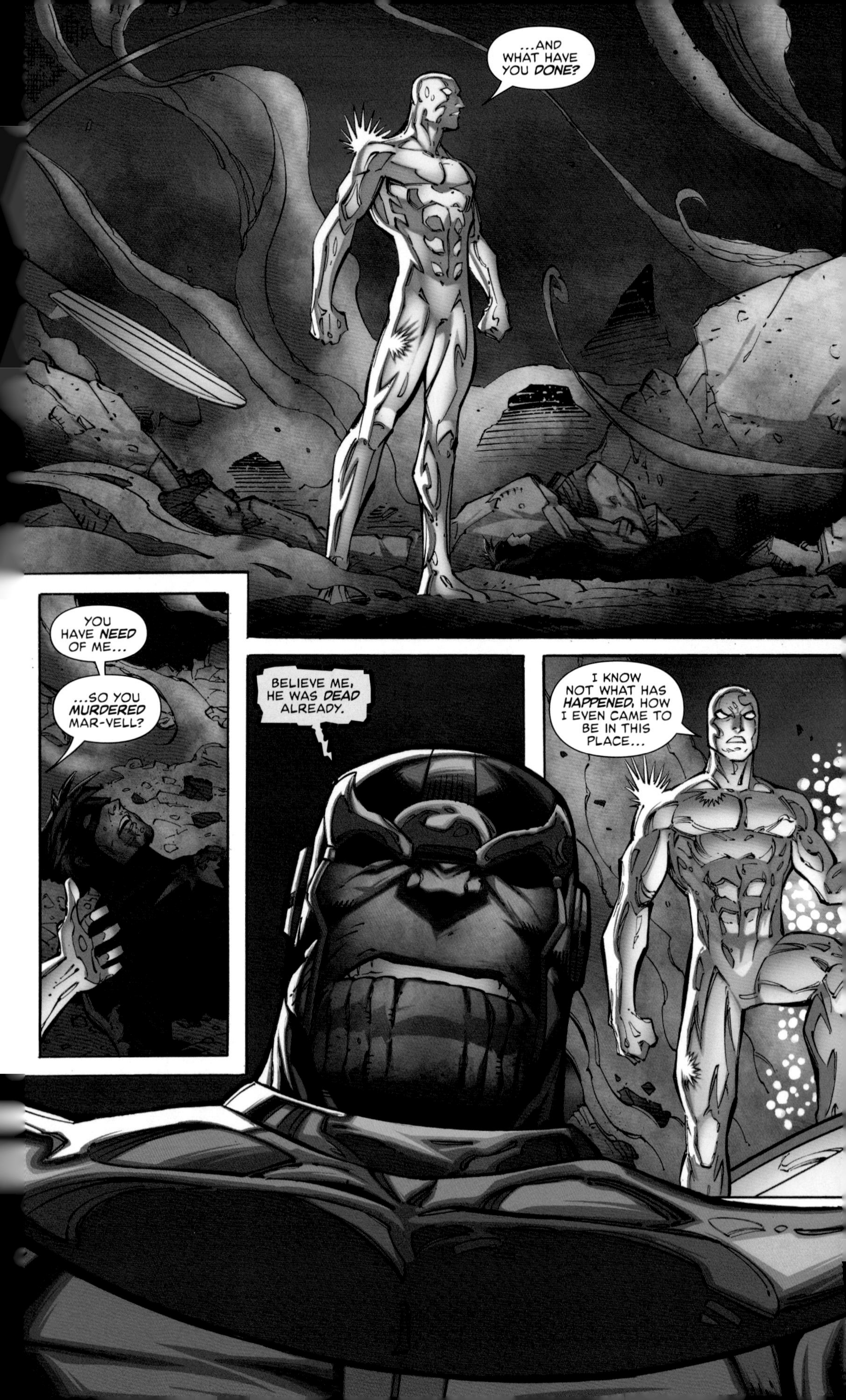
...AND WHAT HAVE YOU *DONE?*
YOU HAVE *NEED* OF ME...
...SO YOU *MURDERED* MAR-VELL?
BELIEVE ME, HE WAS *DEAD* ALREADY.
I KNOW NOT WHAT HAS *HAPPENED,* HOW I EVEN CAME TO BE IN THIS PLACE...

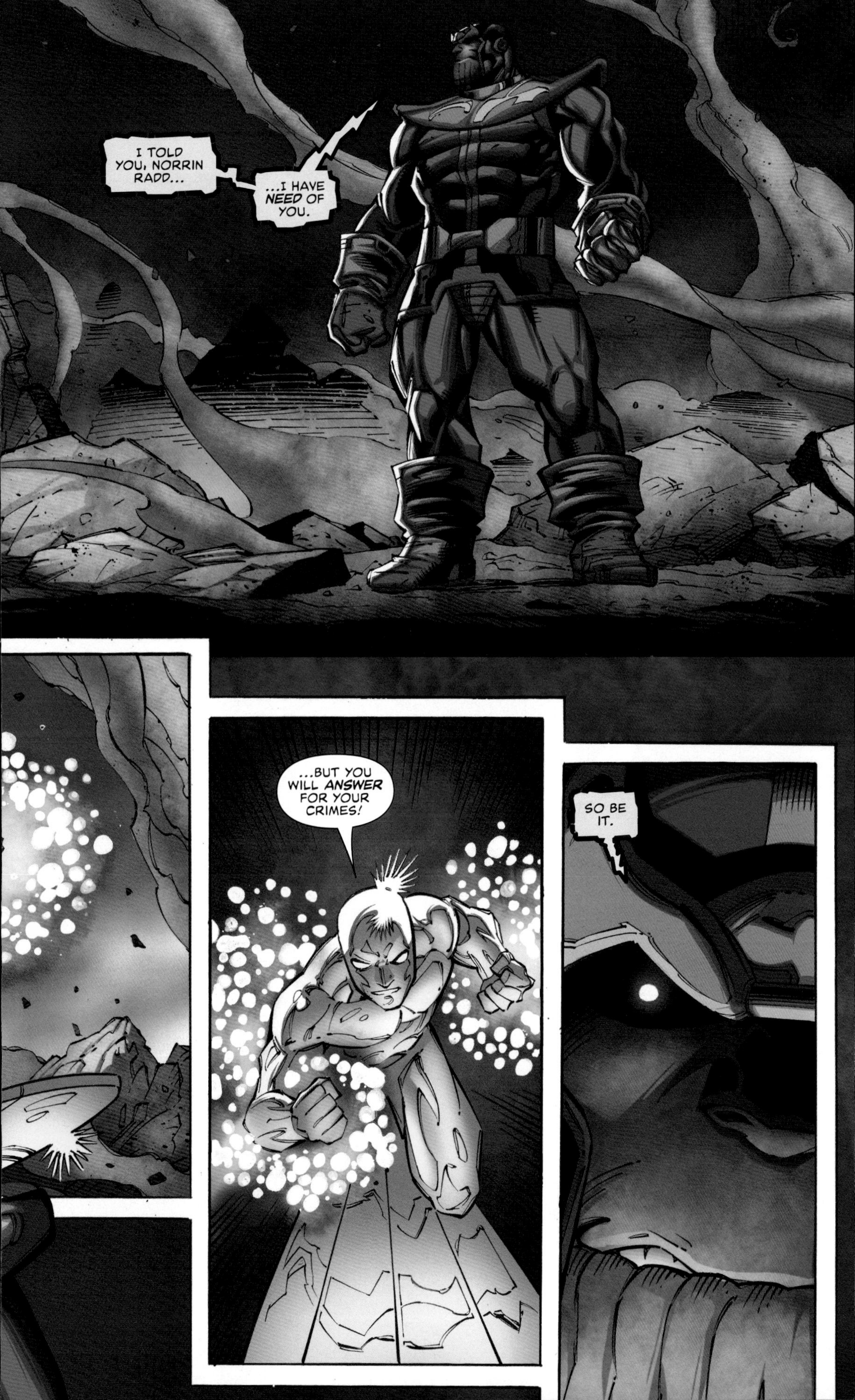
I TOLD YOU, NORRIN RADD...
...I HAVE NEED OF YOU.
...BUT YOU WILL ANSWER FOR YOUR CRIMES!
SO BE IT.

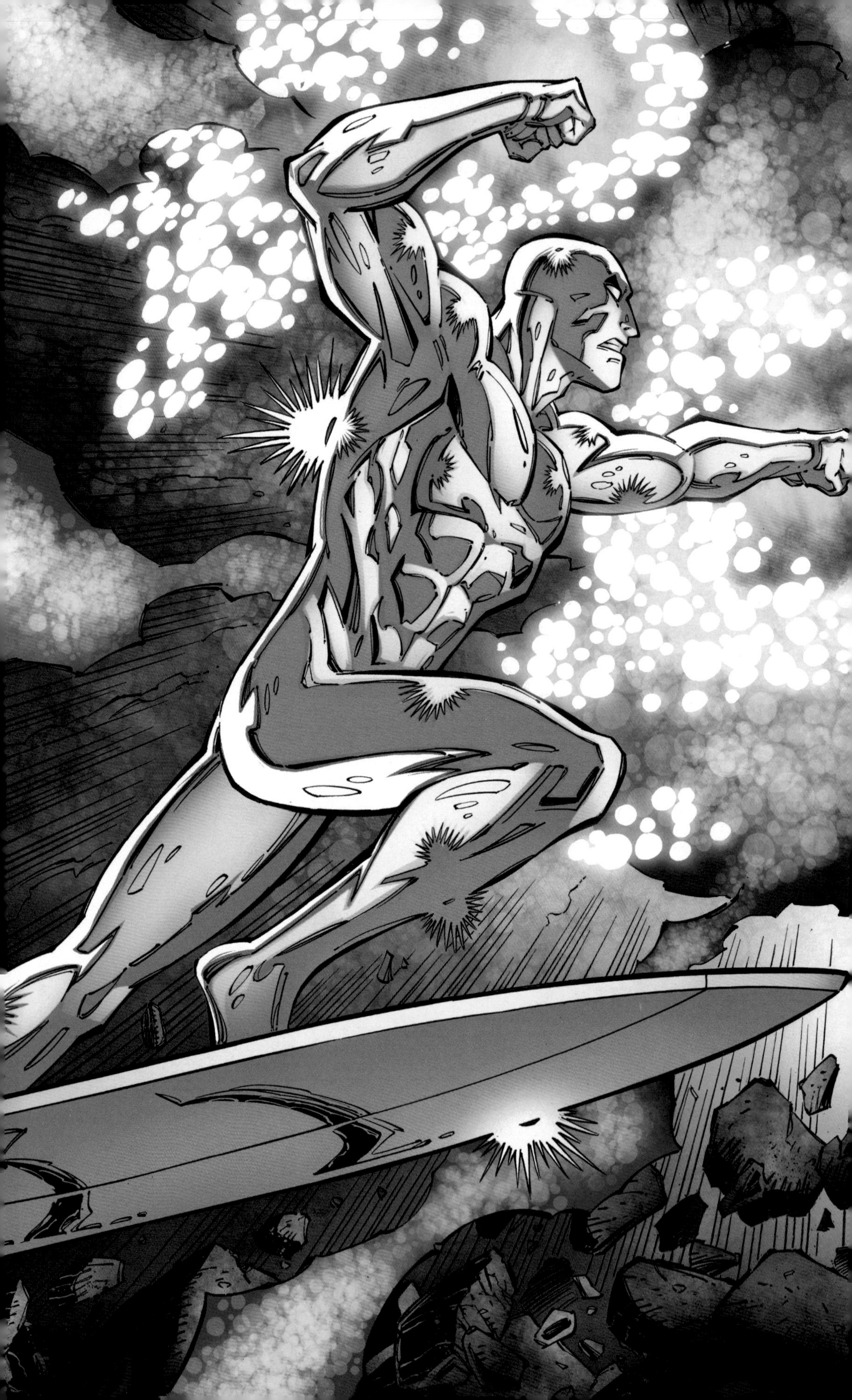

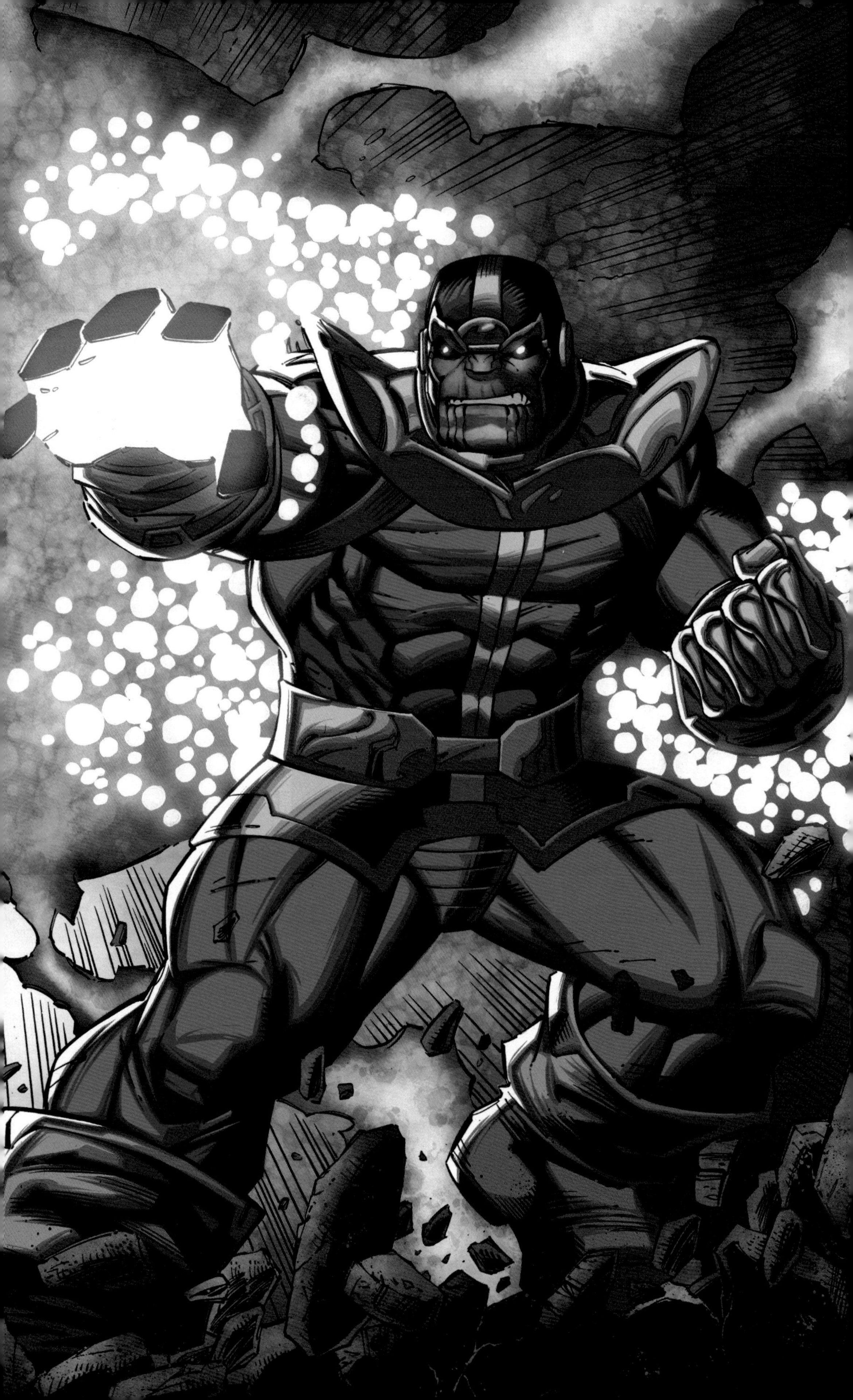

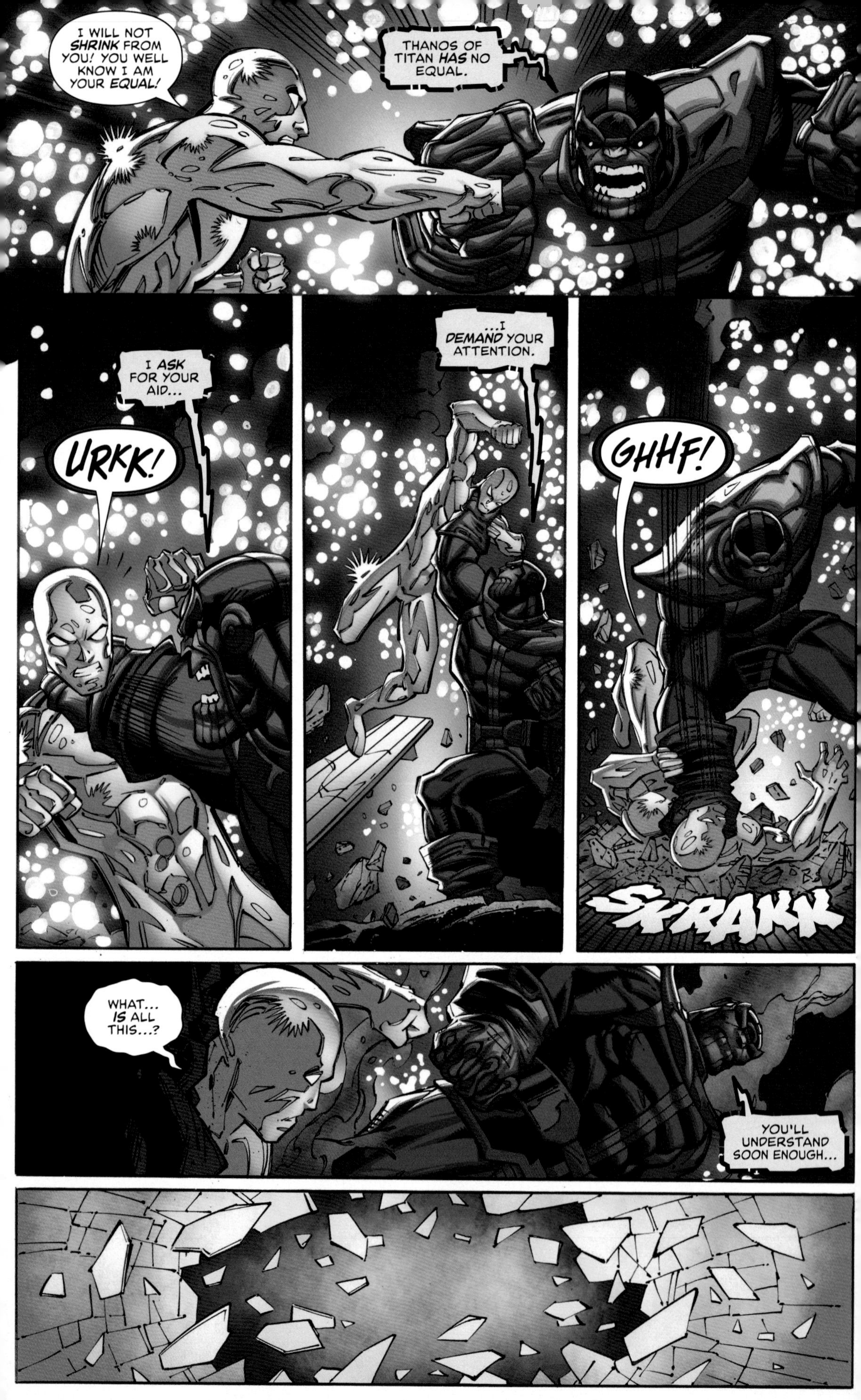

I WILL NOT SHRINK FROM YOU! YOU WELL KNOW I AM YOUR EQUAL!
THANOS OF TITAN HAS NO EQUAL.
I ASK FOR YOUR AID...
URKK!
...I DEMAND YOUR ATTENTION.
GHHF!
SKRAKK
WHAT... IS ALL THIS...?
YOU'LL UNDERSTAND SOON ENOUGH...

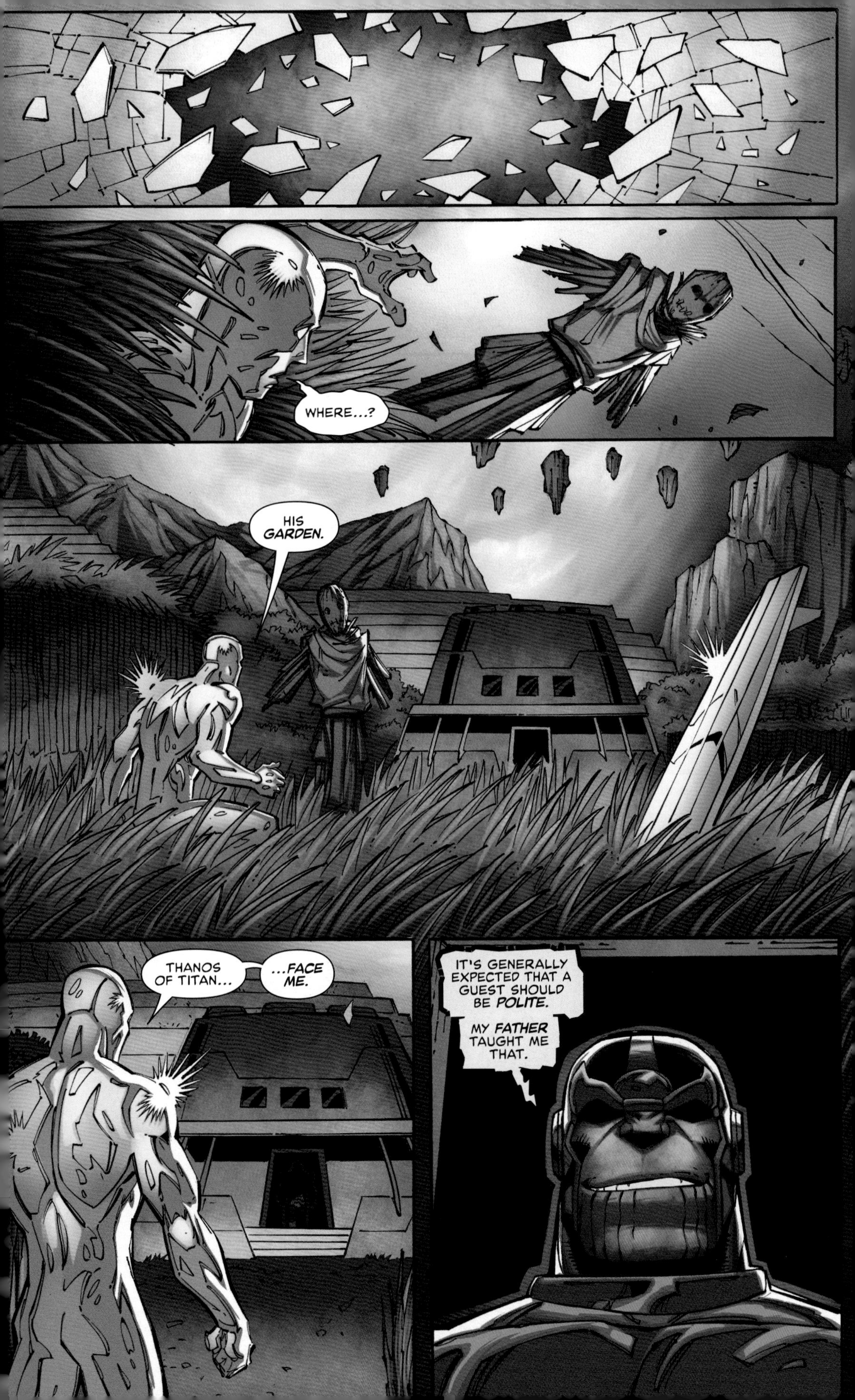
WHERE...?
HIS GARDEN.
THANOS OF TITAN...
...FACE ME.
IT'S GENERALLY EXPECTED THAT A GUEST SHOULD BE POLITE.
MY FATHER TAUGHT ME THAT.

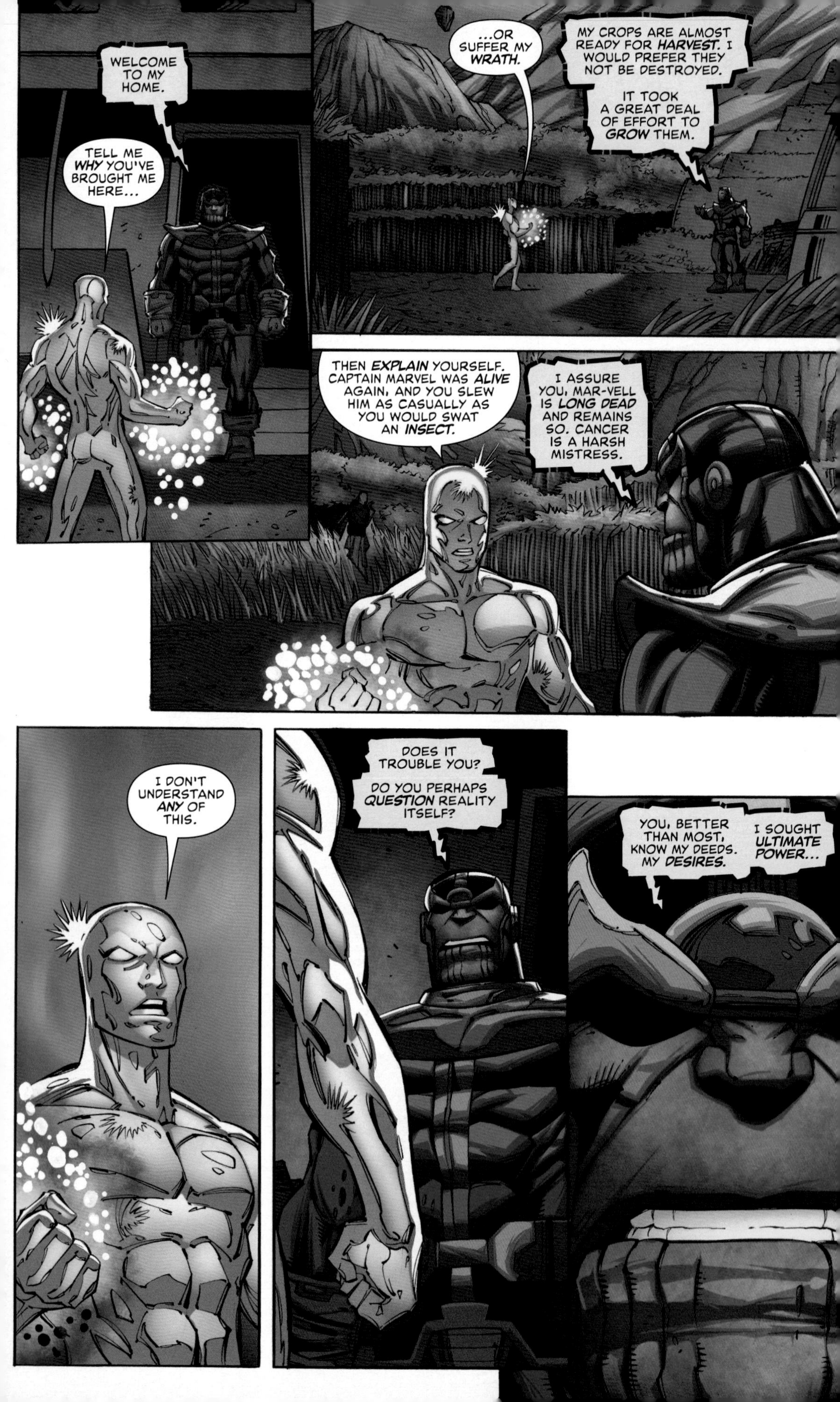
WELCOME TO MY HOME.
TELL ME WHY YOU'VE BROUGHT ME HERE...
...OR SUFFER MY WRATH.
MY CROPS ARE ALMOST READY FOR HARVEST. I WOULD PREFER THEY NOT BE DESTROYED.
IT TOOK A GREAT DEAL OF EFFORT TO GROW THEM.
THEN EXPLAIN YOURSELF. CAPTAIN MARVEL WAS ALIVE AGAIN, AND YOU SLEW HIM AS CASUALLY AS YOU WOULD SWAT AN INSECT.
I ASSURE YOU, MAR-VELL IS LONG DEAD AND REMAINS SO. CANCER IS A HARSH MISTRESS.
I DON'T UNDERSTAND ANY OF THIS.
DOES IT TROUBLE YOU?
DO YOU PERHAPS QUESTION REALITY ITSELF?
YOU, BETTER THAN MOST, KNOW MY DEEDS. MY DESIRES.
I SOUGHT ULTIMATE POWER...

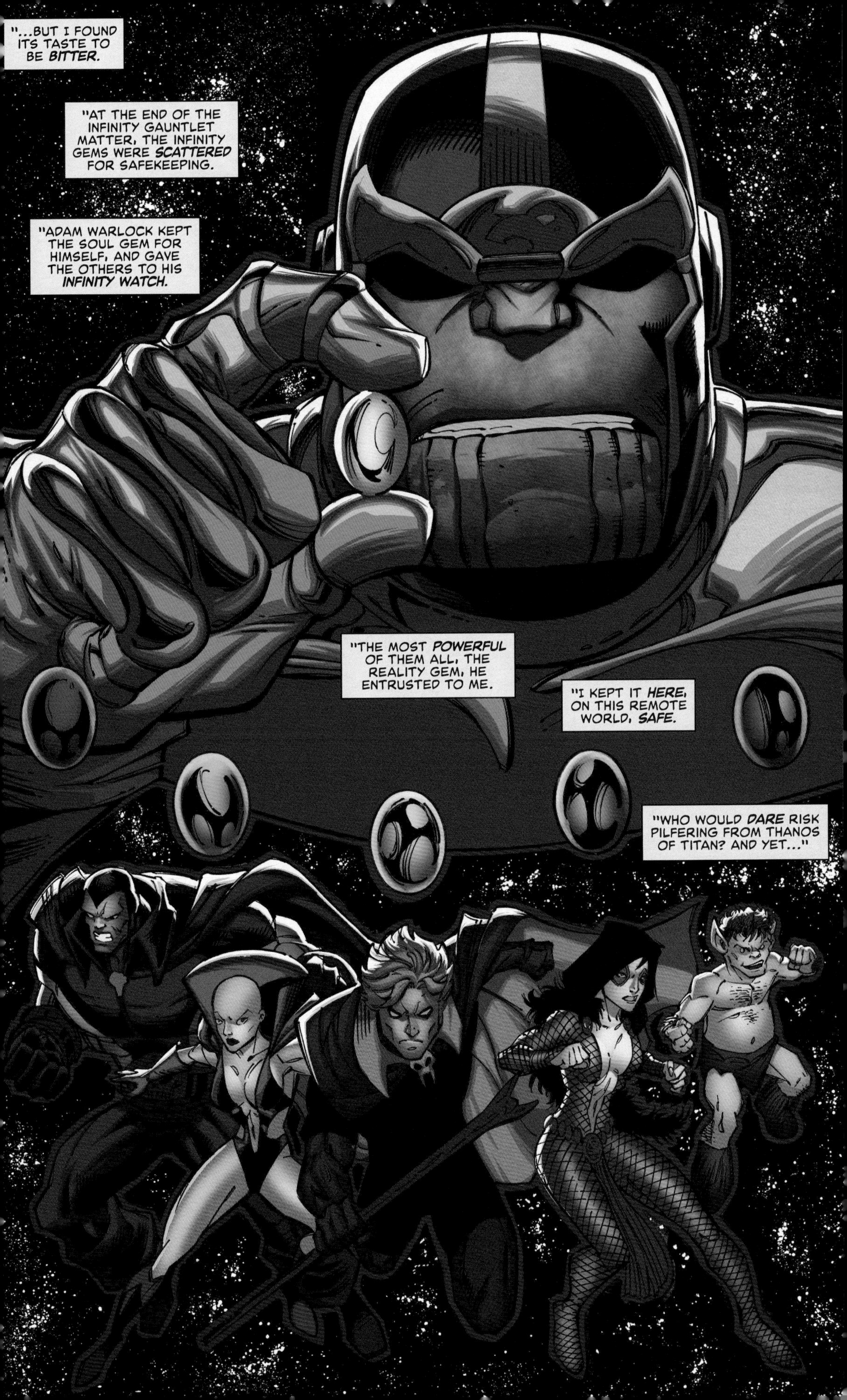
"...BUT I FOUND ITS TASTE TO BE *BITTER.*
"AT THE END OF THE INFINITY GAUNTLET MATTER, THE INFINITY GEMS WERE *SCATTERED* FOR SAFEKEEPING.
"ADAM WARLOCK KEPT THE SOUL GEM FOR HIMSELF, AND GAVE THE OTHERS TO HIS *INFINITY WATCH.*
"THE MOST *POWERFUL* OF THEM ALL, THE REALITY GEM, HE ENTRUSTED TO ME.
"I KEPT IT *HERE,* ON THIS REMOTE WORLD, *SAFE.*
"WHO WOULD *DARE* RISK PILFERING FROM THANOS OF TITAN? AND YET..."

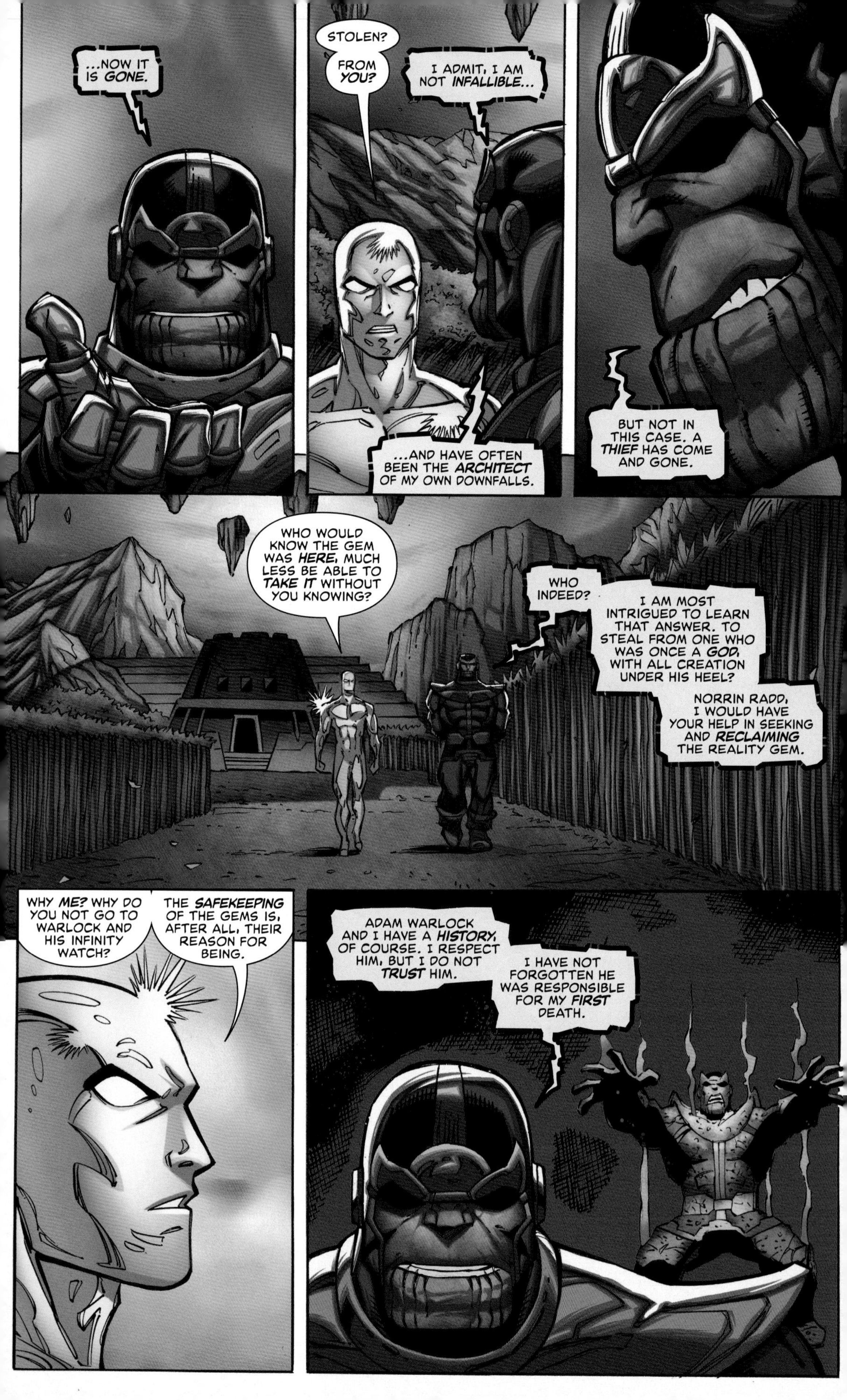
...NOW IT IS GONE.
STOLEN?
FROM YOU?
I ADMIT, I AM NOT INFALLIBLE...
...AND HAVE OFTEN BEEN THE ARCHITECT OF MY OWN DOWNFALLS.
BUT NOT IN THIS CASE. A THIEF HAS COME AND GONE.
WHO WOULD KNOW THE GEM WAS HERE, MUCH LESS BE ABLE TO TAKE IT WITHOUT YOU KNOWING?
WHO INDEED?
I AM MOST INTRIGUED TO LEARN THAT ANSWER. TO STEAL FROM ONE WHO WAS ONCE A GOD, WITH ALL CREATION UNDER HIS HEEL?
NORRIN RADD, I WOULD HAVE YOUR HELP IN SEEKING AND RECLAIMING THE REALITY GEM.
WHY ME? WHY DO YOU NOT GO TO WARLOCK AND HIS INFINITY WATCH?
THE SAFEKEEPING OF THE GEMS IS, AFTER ALL, THEIR REASON FOR BEING.
ADAM WARLOCK AND I HAVE A HISTORY, OF COURSE. I RESPECT HIM, BUT I DO NOT TRUST HIM.
I HAVE NOT FORGOTTEN HE WAS RESPONSIBLE FOR MY FIRST DEATH.

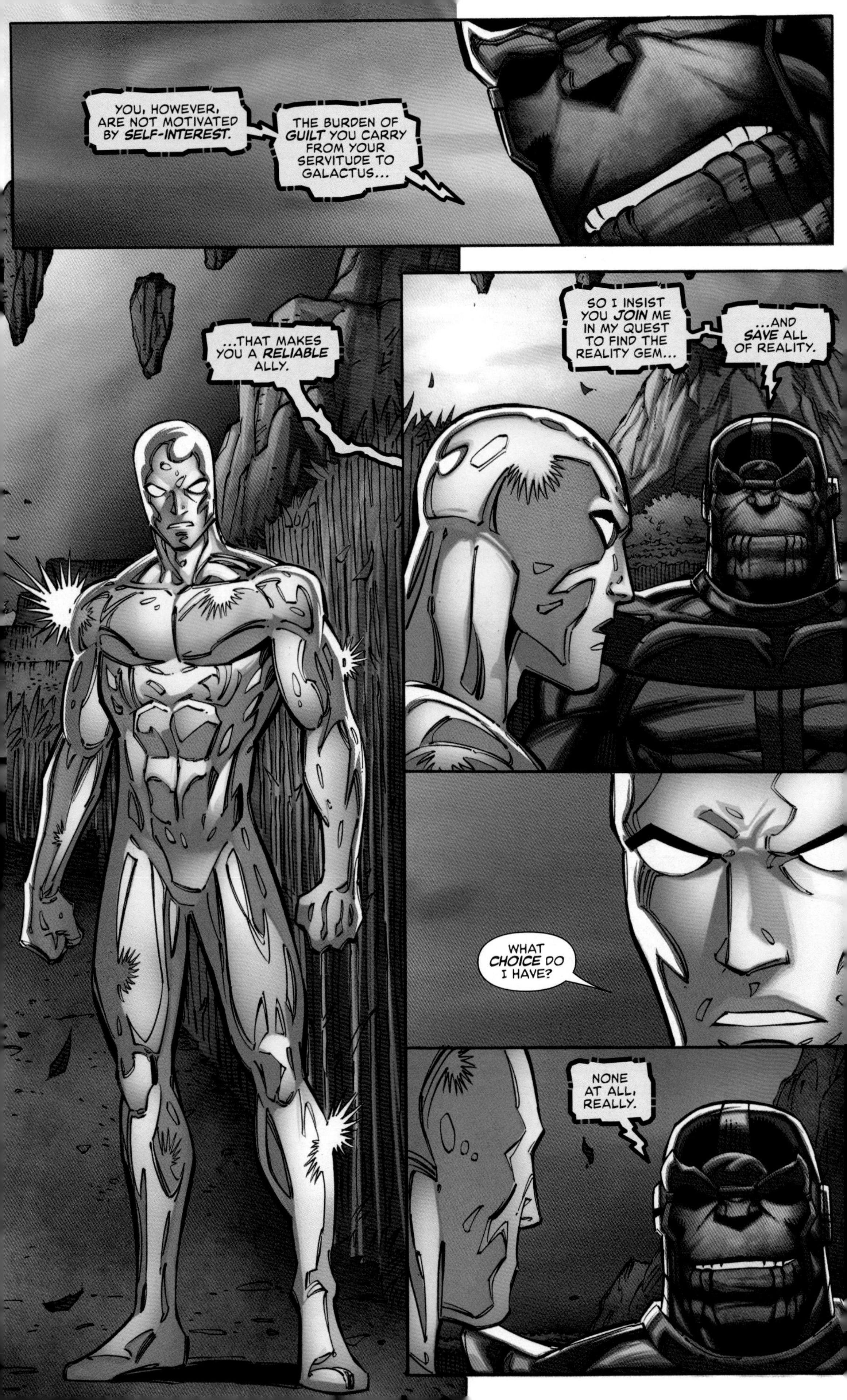
YOU, HOWEVER, ARE NOT MOTIVATED BY SELF-INTEREST.
THE BURDEN OF GUILT YOU CARRY FROM YOUR SERVITUDE TO GALACTUS...
...THAT MAKES YOU A RELIABLE ALLY.
SO I INSIST YOU JOIN ME IN MY QUEST TO FIND THE REALITY GEM...
...AND SAVE ALL OF REALITY.
WHAT CHOICE DO I HAVE?
NONE AT ALL, REALLY.

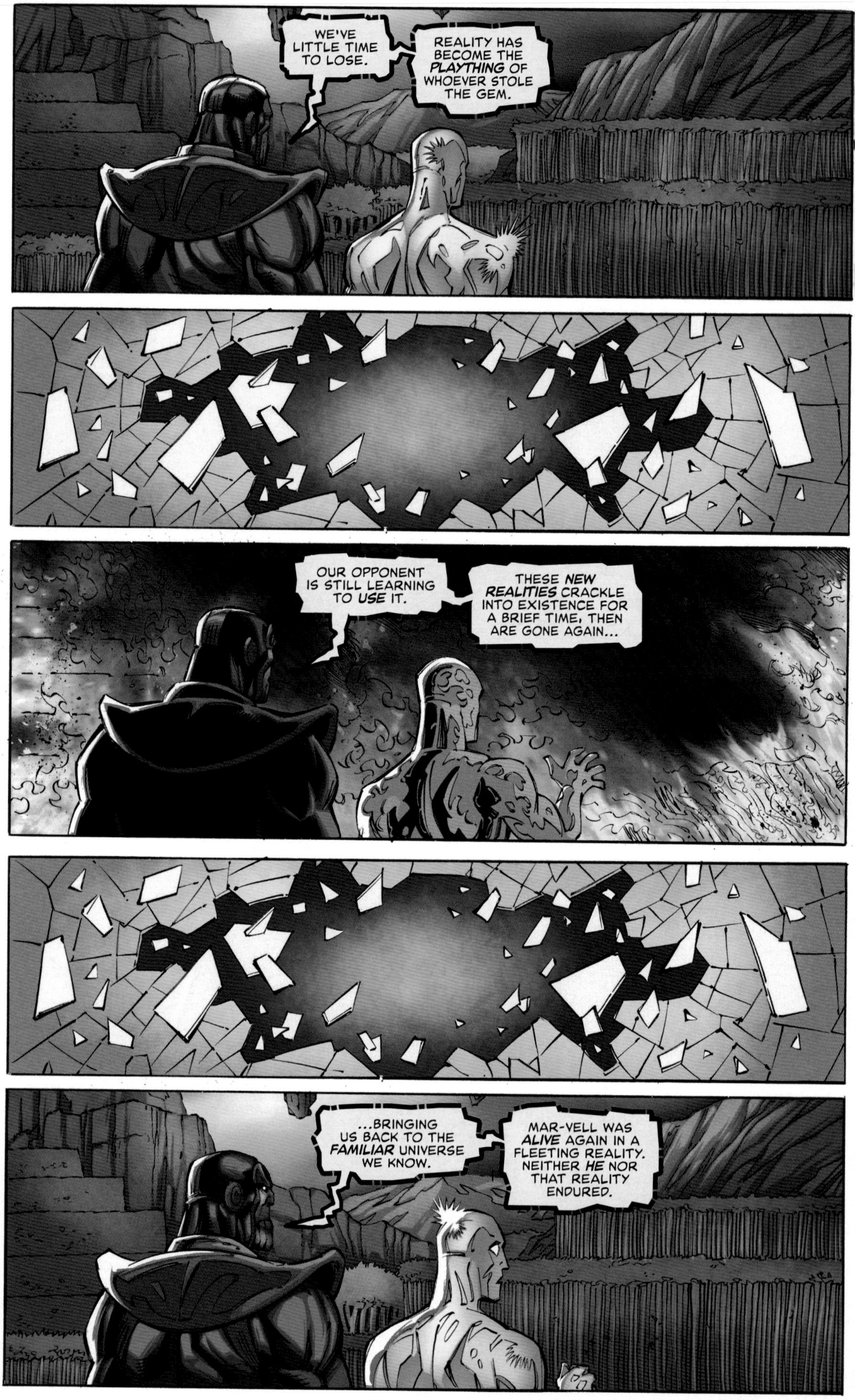
WE'VE LITTLE TIME TO LOSE.
REALITY HAS BECOME THE *PLAYTHING* OF WHOEVER STOLE THE GEM.
OUR OPPONENT IS STILL LEARNING TO *USE* IT.
THESE *NEW REALITIES* CRACKLE INTO EXISTENCE FOR A BRIEF TIME, THEN ARE GONE AGAIN...
...BRINGING US BACK TO THE *FAMILIAR* UNIVERSE WE KNOW.
MAR-VELL WAS *ALIVE* AGAIN IN A FLEETING REALITY. NEITHER *HE* NOR THAT REALITY ENDURED.

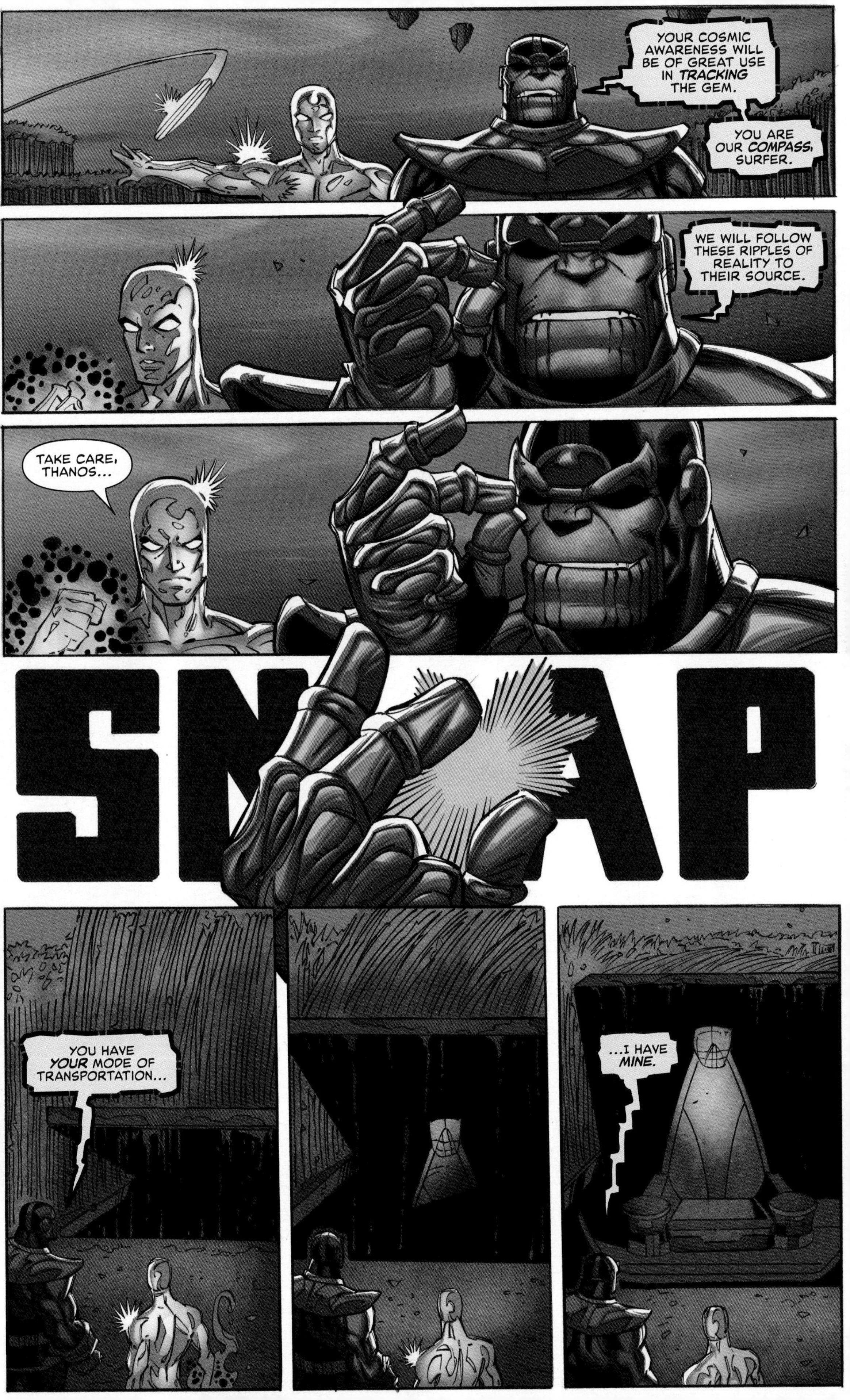
YOUR COSMIC AWARENESS WILL BE OF GREAT USE IN TRACKING THE GEM.
YOU ARE OUR COMPASS, SURFER.
WE WILL FOLLOW THESE RIPPLES OF REALITY TO THEIR SOURCE.
TAKE CARE, THANOS...
SNAP
YOU HAVE YOUR MODE OF TRANSPORTATION...
...I HAVE MINE.

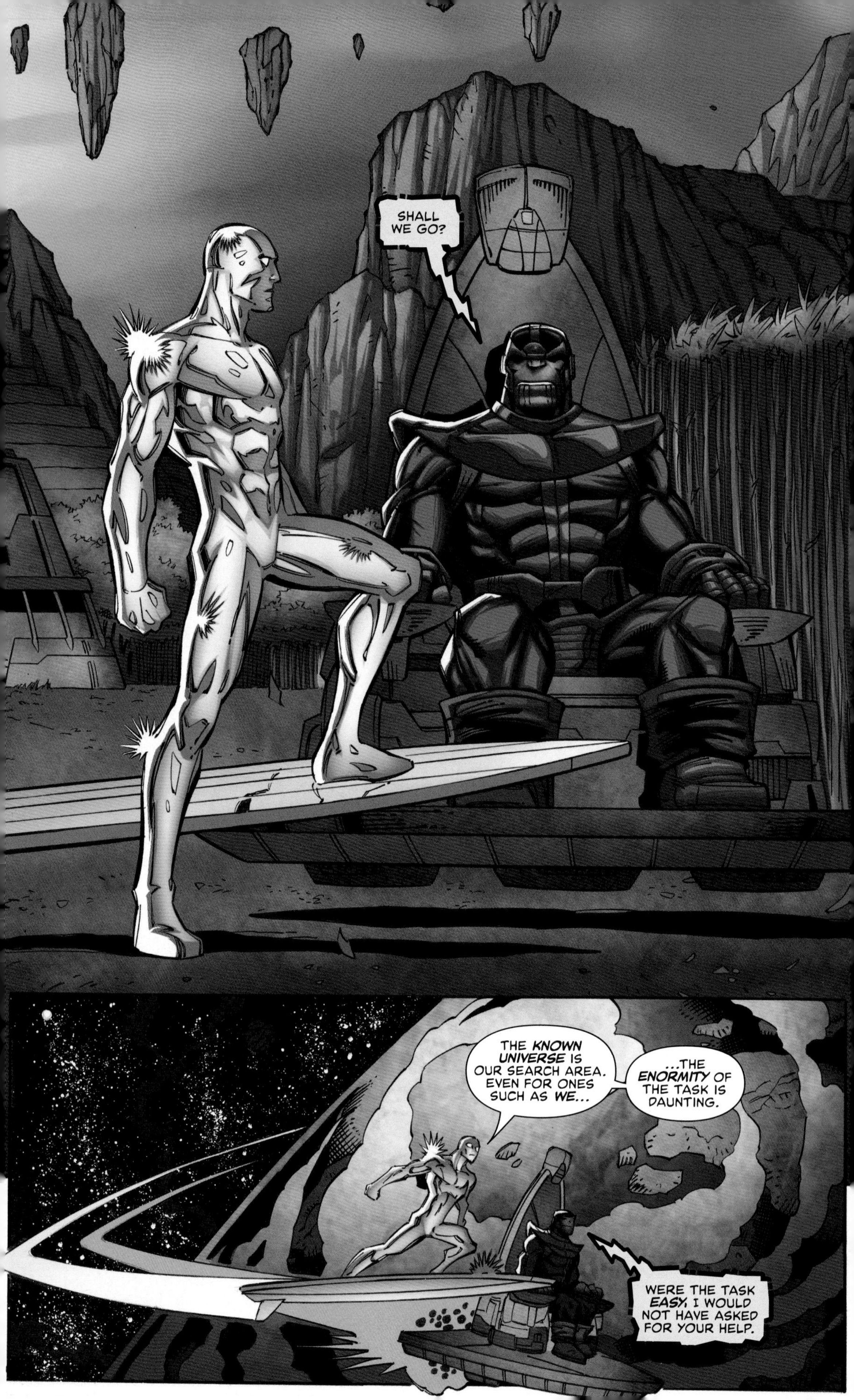
SHALL WE GO?
THE *KNOWN UNIVERSE* IS OUR SEARCH AREA. EVEN FOR ONES SUCH AS *WE*...
...THE *ENORMITY* OF THE TASK IS DAUNTING.
WERE THE TASK *EASY*, I WOULD NOT HAVE ASKED FOR YOUR HELP.

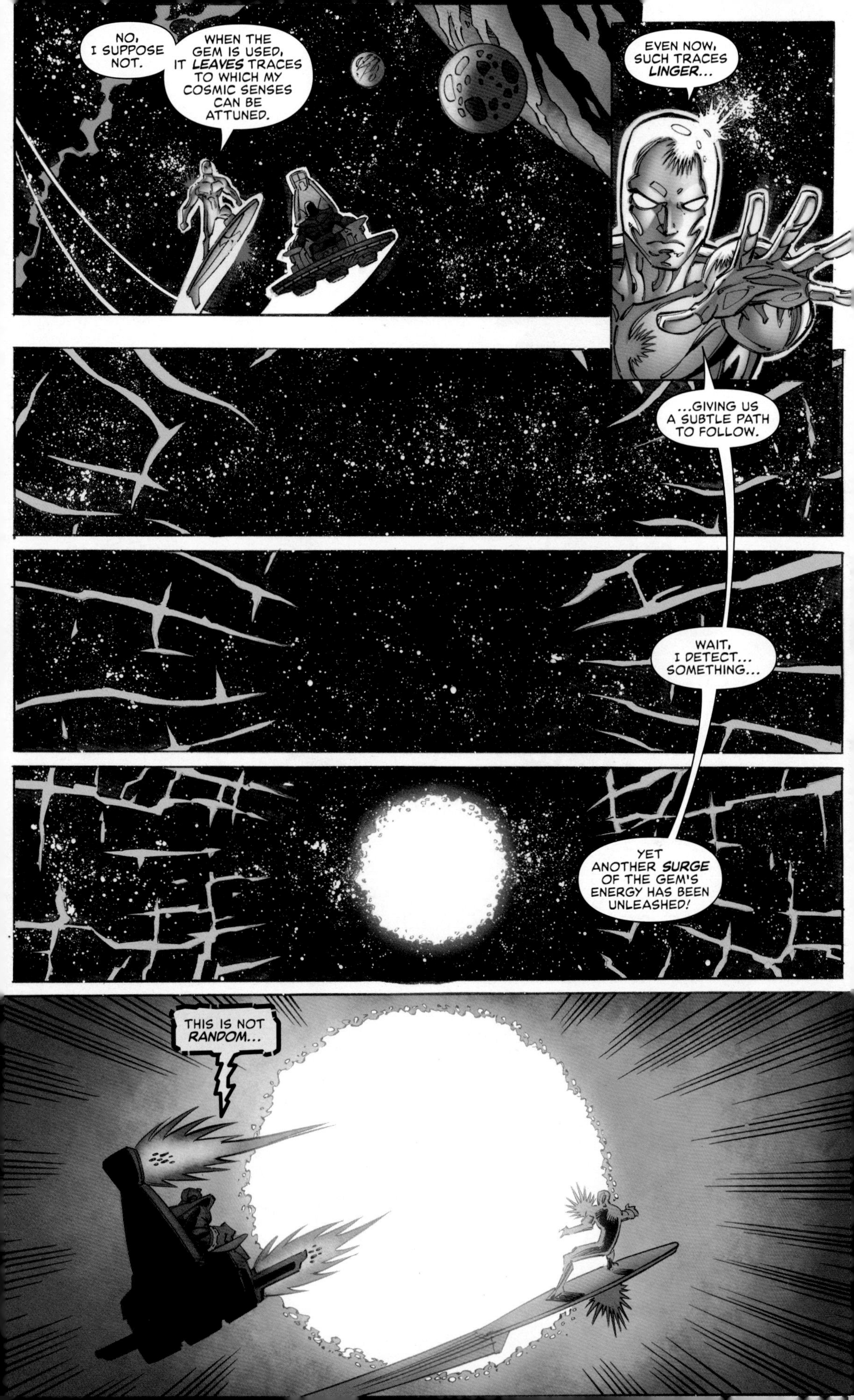
NO, I SUPPOSE NOT.
WHEN THE GEM IS USED, IT LEAVES TRACES TO WHICH MY COSMIC SENSES CAN BE ATTUNED.
EVEN NOW, SUCH TRACES LINGER...
...GIVING US A SUBTLE PATH TO FOLLOW.
WAIT, I DETECT... SOMETHING...
YET ANOTHER SURGE OF THE GEM'S ENERGY HAS BEEN UNLEASHED!
THIS IS NOT RANDOM...

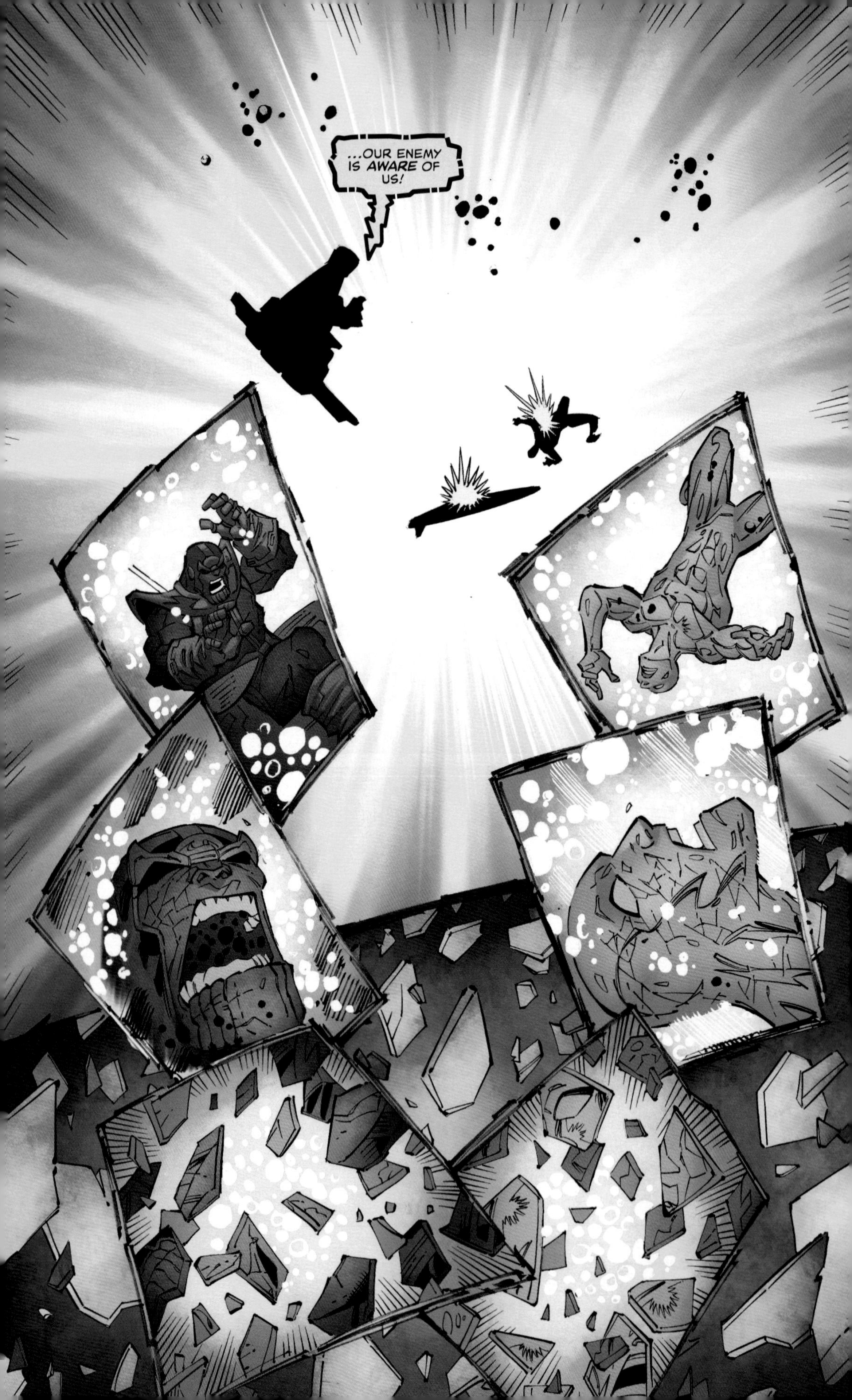
...OUR ENEMY IS AWARE OF US!

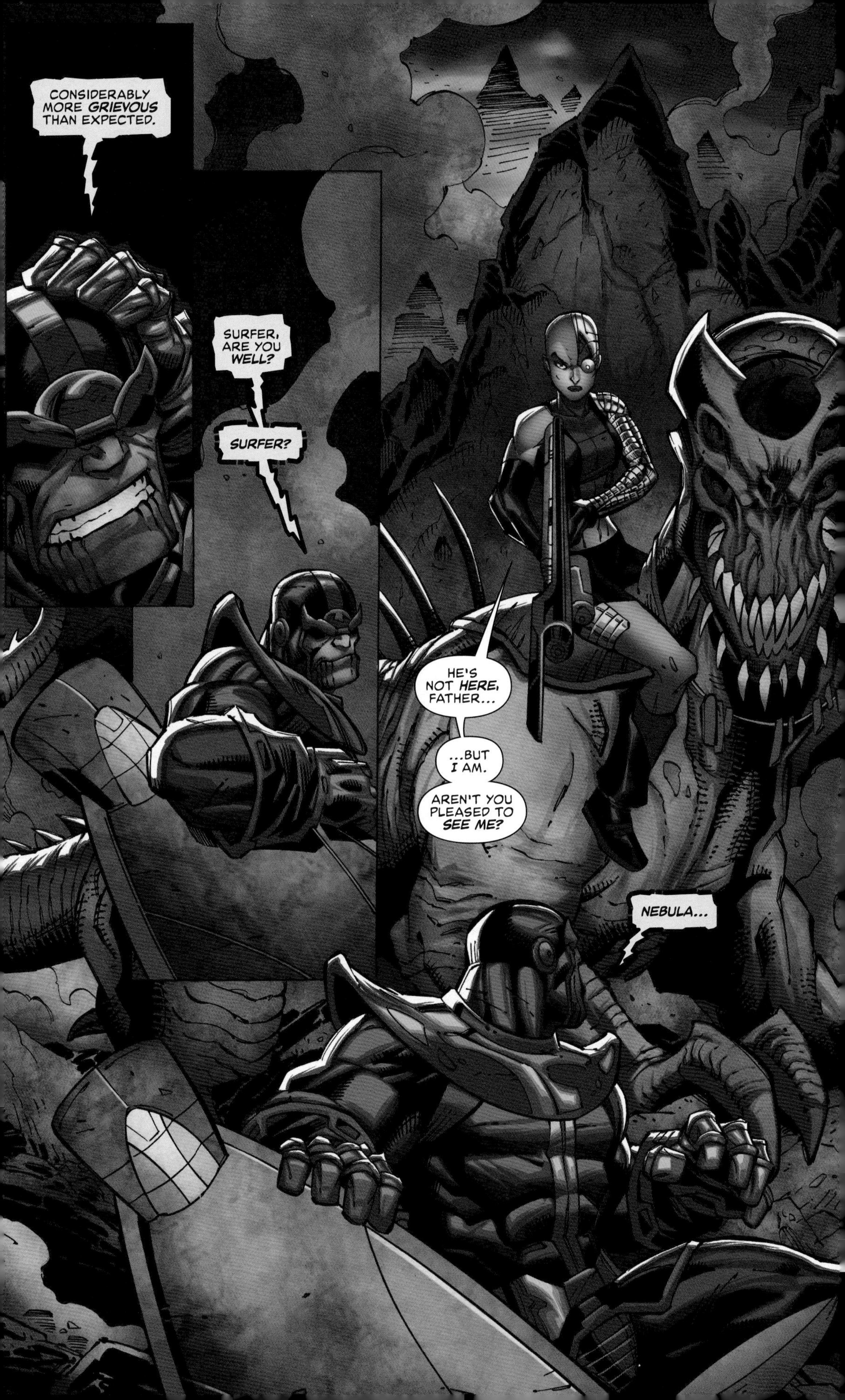
CONSIDERABLY MORE GRIEVOUS THAN EXPECTED.
SURFER, ARE YOU WELL?
SURFER?
HE'S NOT HERE, FATHER...
...BUT I AM.
AREN'T YOU PLEASED TO SEE ME?
NEBULA...

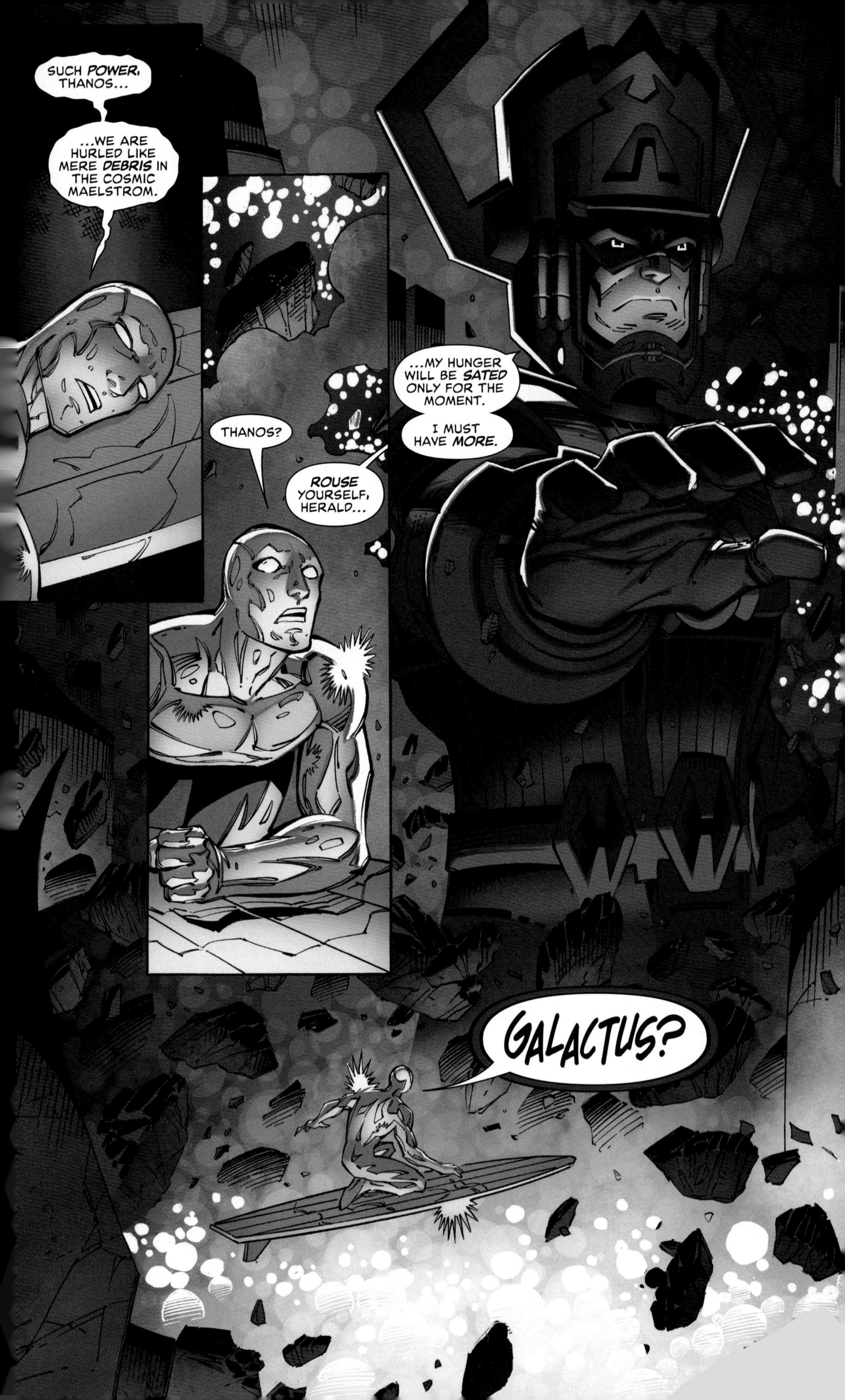
SUCH POWER, THANOS...
...WE ARE HURLED LIKE MERE DEBRIS IN THE COSMIC MAELSTROM.
THANOS?
ROUSE YOURSELF, HERALD...
...MY HUNGER WILL BE SATED ONLY FOR THE MOMENT.
I MUST HAVE MORE.
GALACTUS?

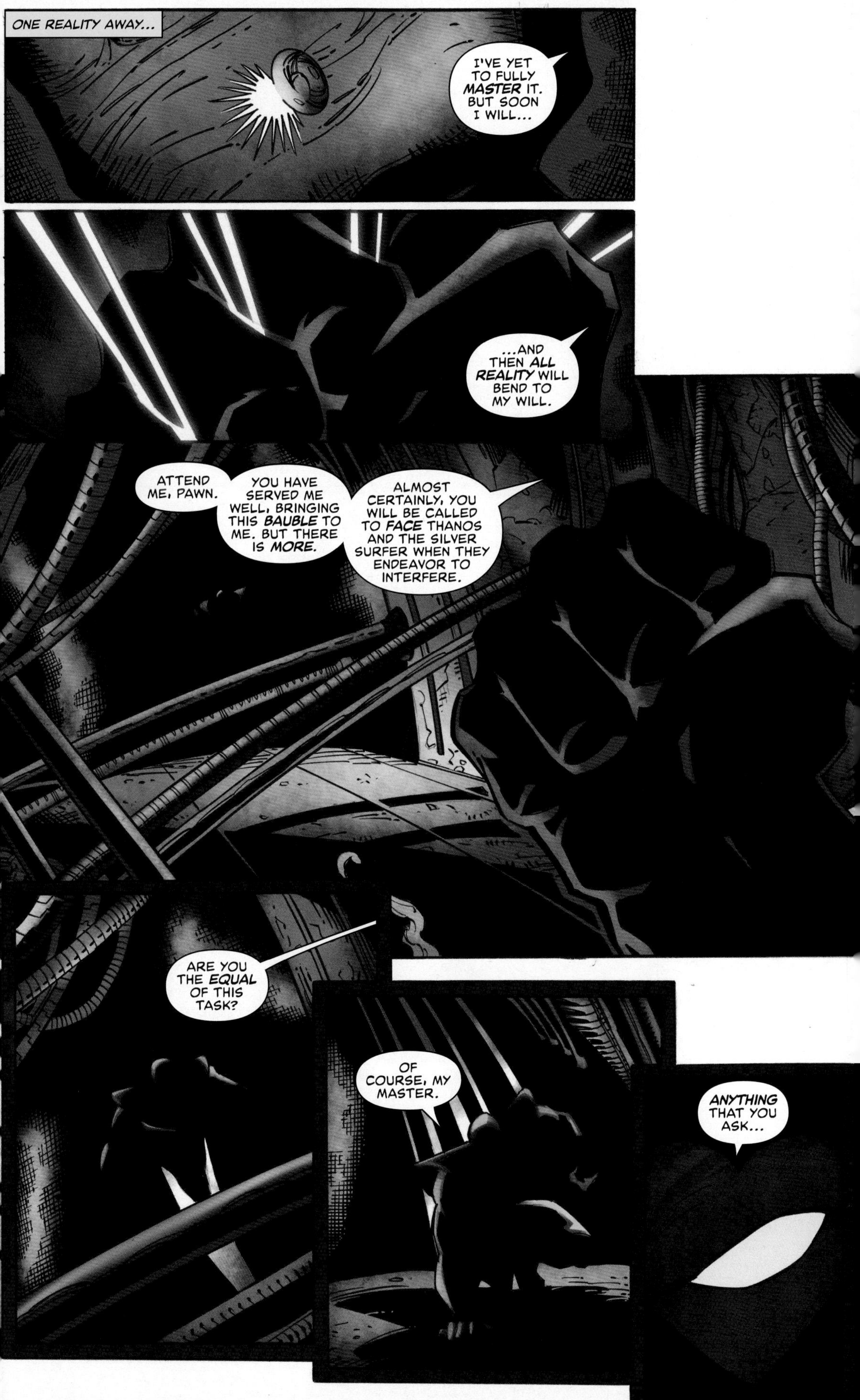
ONE REALITY AWAY...
I'VE YET TO FULLY MASTER IT. BUT SOON I WILL...
...AND THEN ALL REALITY WILL BEND TO MY WILL.
ATTEND ME, PAWN.
YOU HAVE SERVED ME WELL, BRINGING THIS BAUBLE TO ME. BUT THERE IS MORE.
ALMOST CERTAINLY, YOU WILL BE CALLED TO FACE THANOS AND THE SILVER SURFER WHEN THEY ENDEAVOR TO INTERFERE.
ARE YOU THE EQUAL OF THIS TASK?
OF COURSE, MY MASTER.
ANYTHING THAT YOU ASK...

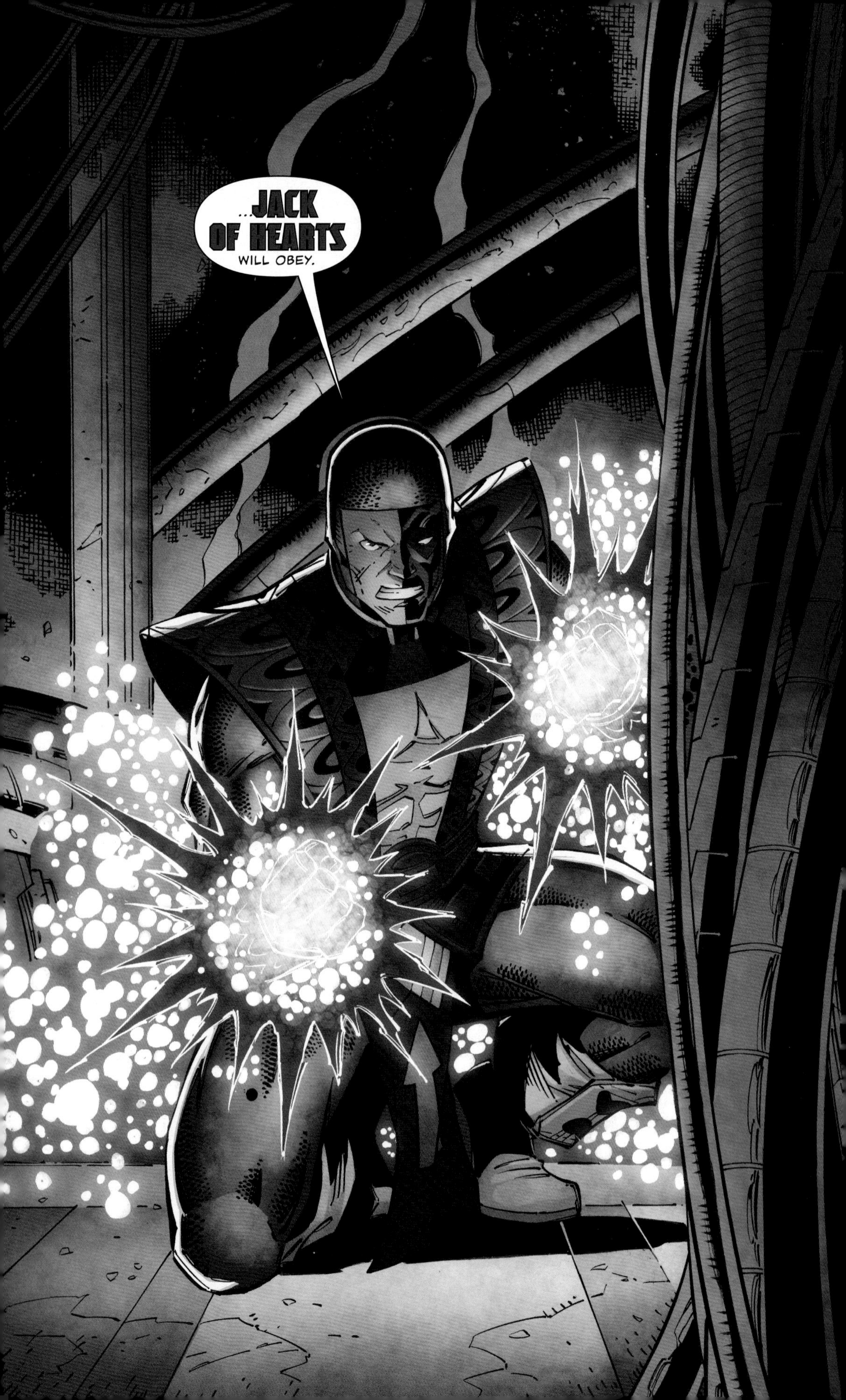
...JACK OF HEARTS WILL OBEY.

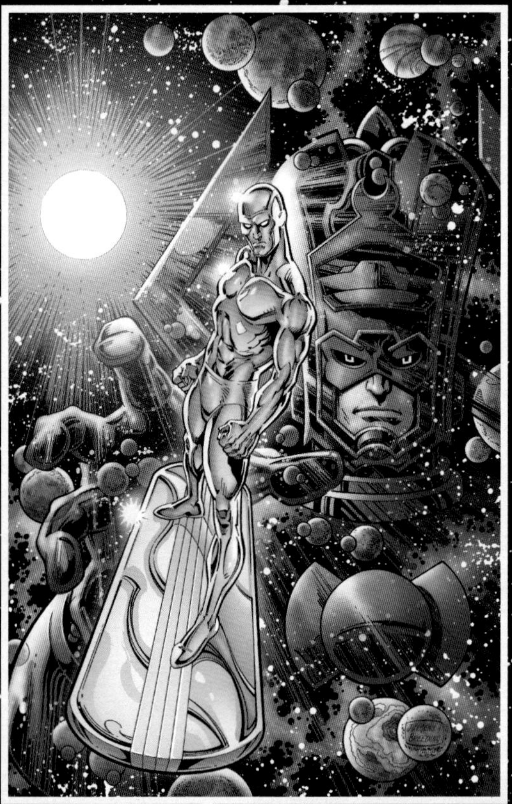

#1 VARIANT BY
DAN JURGENS, BRETT BREEDING & EDGAR DELGADO

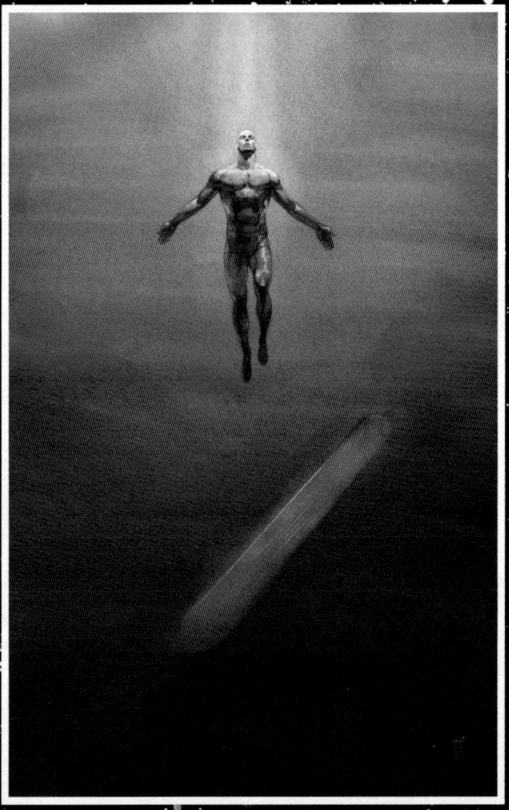

#1 VARIANT BY
ALEX MALEEV

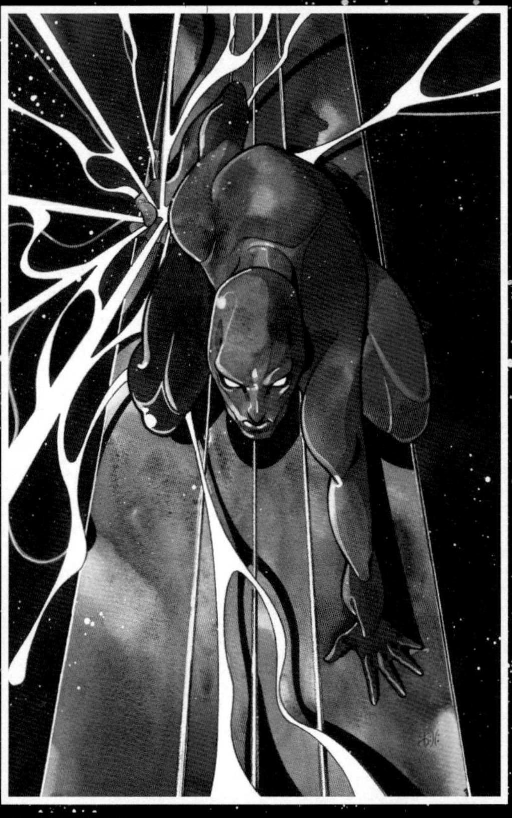

#1 VARIANT BY
PEACH MOMOKO

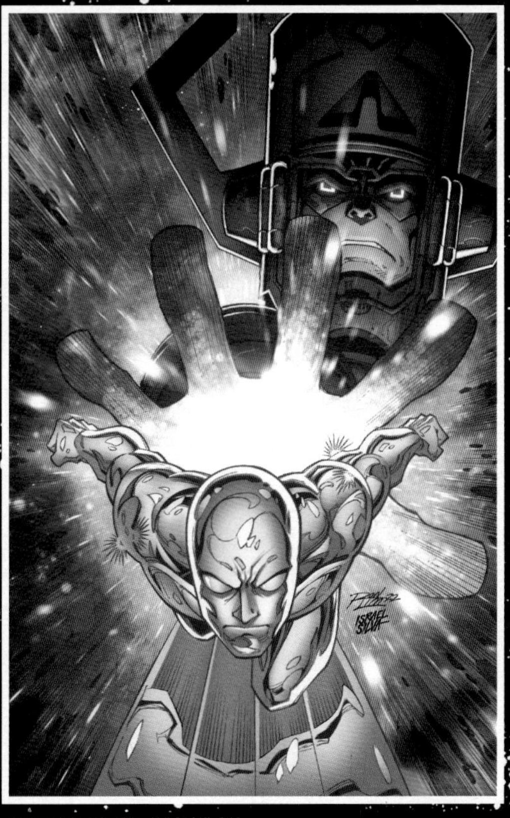

#1 2ND PRINTING VARIANT BY
RON LIM & ISRAEL SILVA

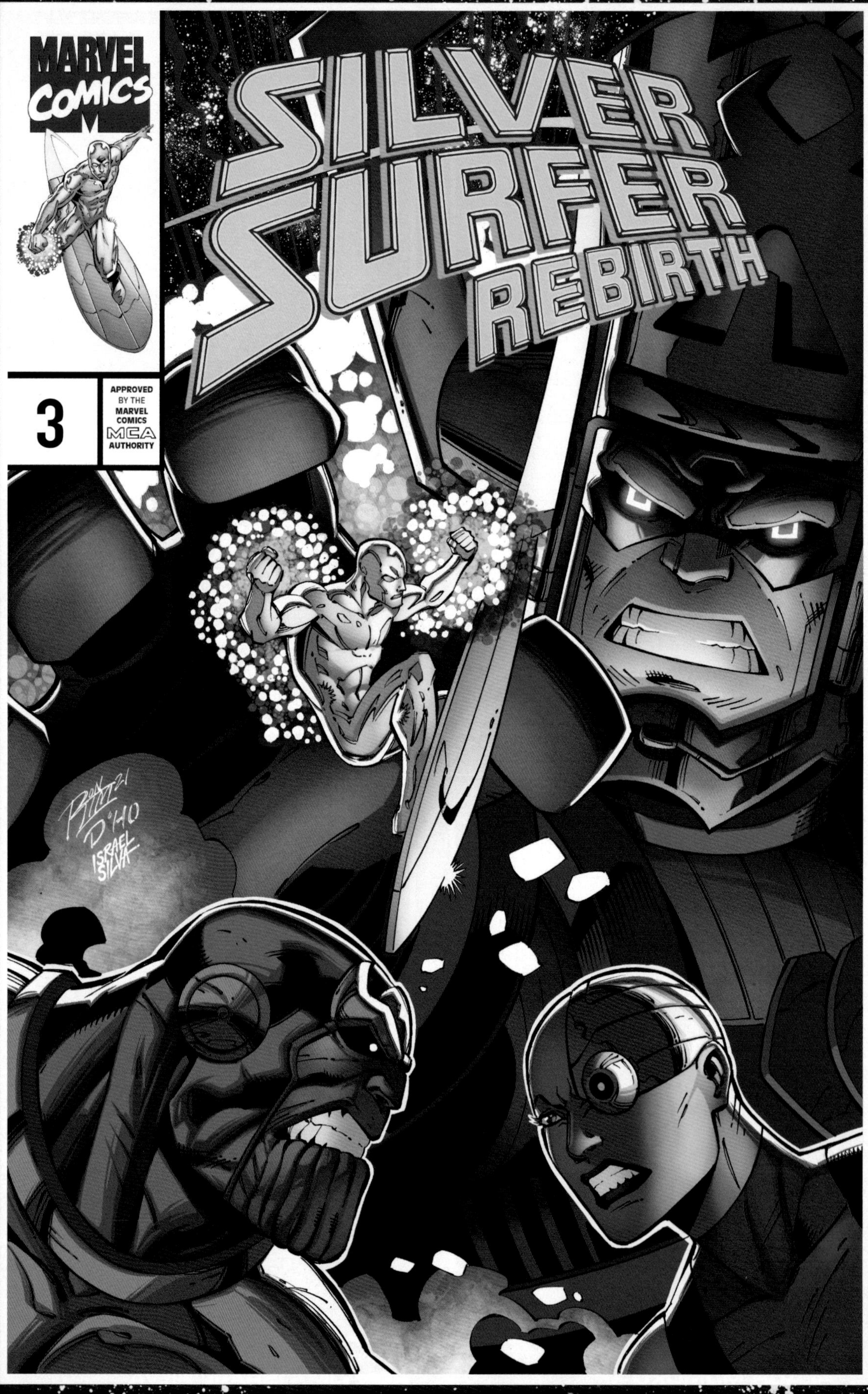
MARVEL COMICS
SILVER SURFER REBIRTH
3
APPROVED BY THE MARVEL COMICS MCA AUTHORITY
ISRAEL SILVA

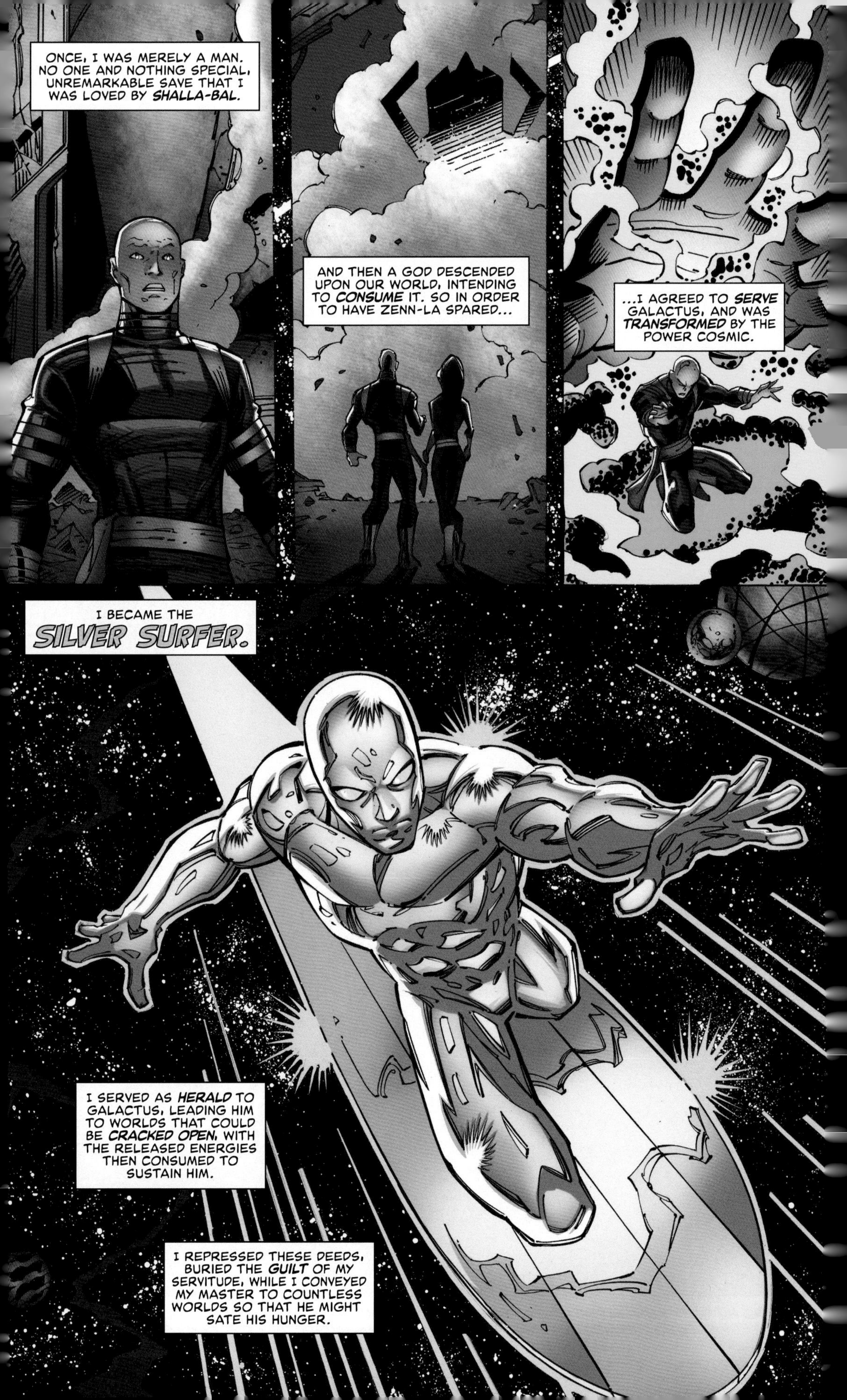
ONCE, I WAS MERELY A MAN. NO ONE AND NOTHING SPECIAL, UNREMARKABLE SAVE THAT I WAS LOVED BY SHALLA-BAL.
AND THEN A GOD DESCENDED UPON OUR WORLD, INTENDING TO CONSUME IT. SO IN ORDER TO HAVE ZENN-LA SPARED...
...I AGREED TO SERVE GALACTUS, AND WAS TRANSFORMED BY THE POWER COSMIC.
I BECAME THE SILVER SURFER.
I SERVED AS HERALD TO GALACTUS, LEADING HIM TO WORLDS THAT COULD BE CRACKED OPEN, WITH THE RELEASED ENERGIES THEN CONSUMED TO SUSTAIN HIM.
I REPRESSED THESE DEEDS, BURIED THE GUILT OF MY SERVITUDE, WHILE I CONVEYED MY MASTER TO COUNTLESS WORLDS SO THAT HE MIGHT SATE HIS HUNGER.

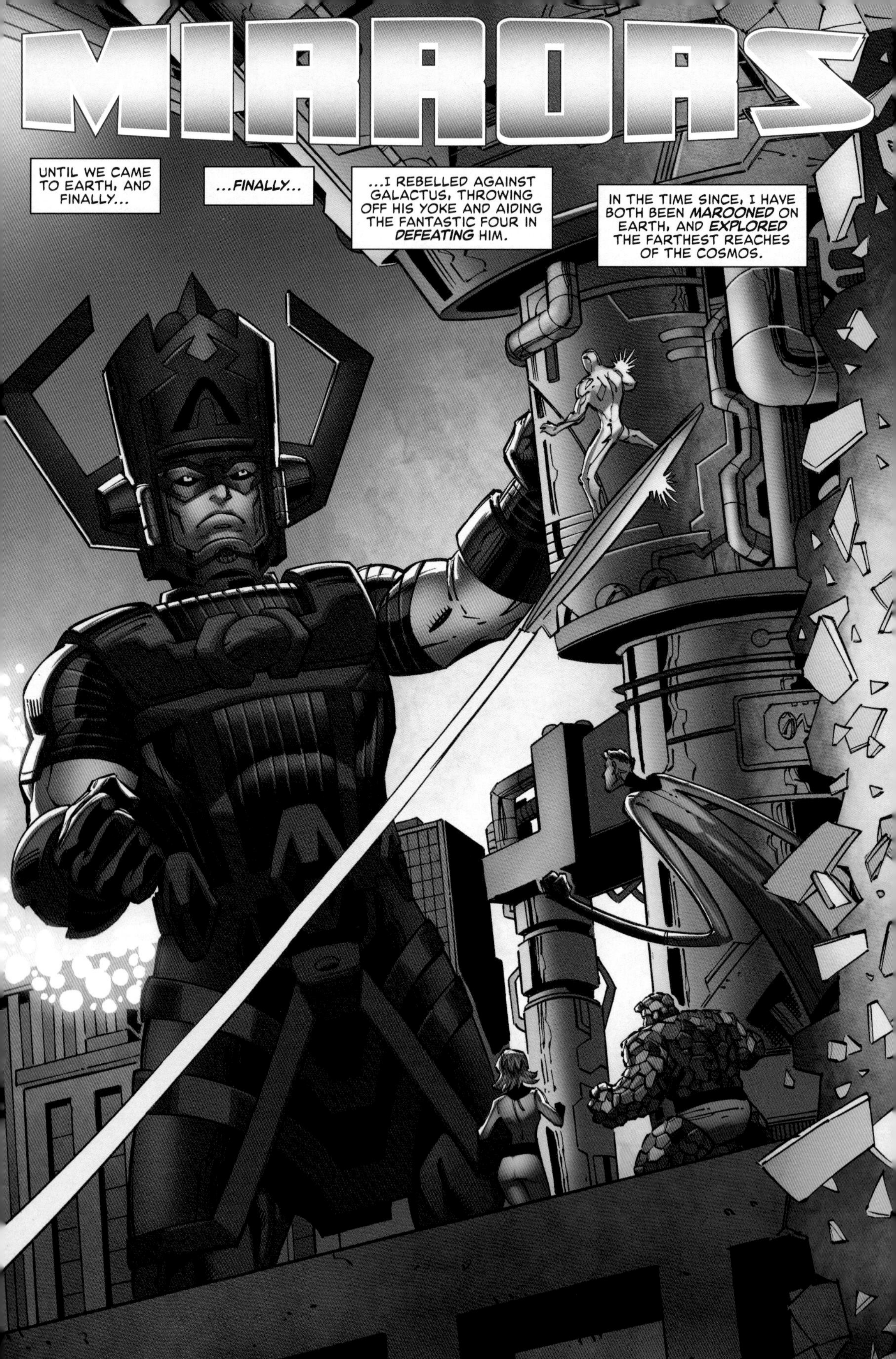
MIRRORS
UNTIL WE CAME TO EARTH, AND FINALLY...
...FINALLY...
...I REBELLED AGAINST GALACTUS, THROWING OFF HIS YOKE AND AIDING THE FANTASTIC FOUR IN DEFEATING HIM.
IN THE TIME SINCE, I HAVE BOTH BEEN MAROONED ON EARTH, AND EXPLORED THE FARTHEST REACHES OF THE COSMOS.

RON MARZ WRITER • **RON LIM** PENCILER • **DON HO** INKER • **ISRAEL SILVA** COLORIST • **VC's JOE SABINO** LETTERER
KAT GREGOROWICZ ASSISTANT EDITOR • **DARREN SHAN** EDITOR • **C.B. CEBULSKI** CHIEF
SILVER SURFER CREATED BY **STAN LEE** & **JACK KIRBY**

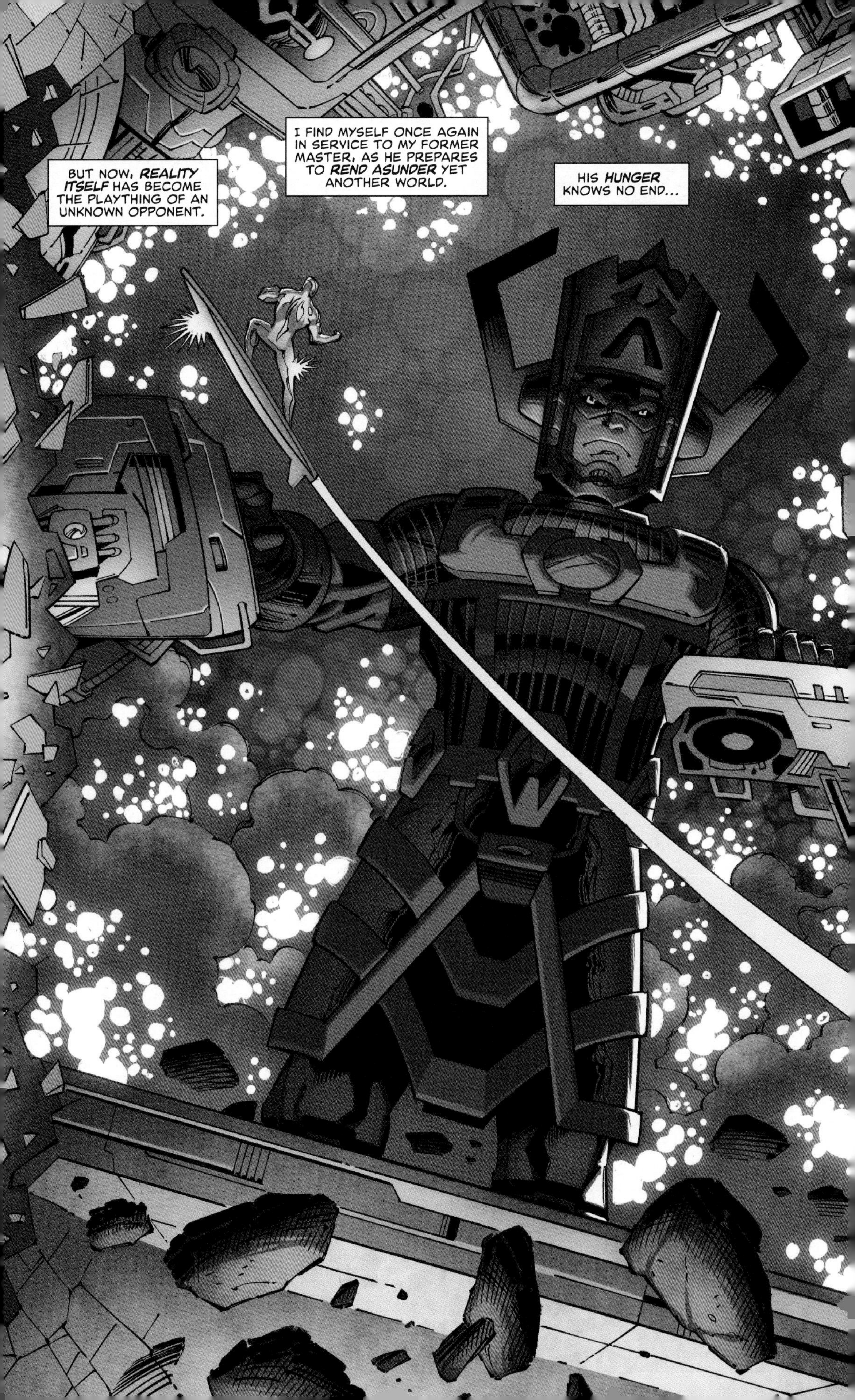
BUT NOW, REALITY ITSELF HAS BECOME THE PLAYTHING OF AN UNKNOWN OPPONENT.
I FIND MYSELF ONCE AGAIN IN SERVICE TO MY FORMER MASTER, AS HE PREPARES TO REND ASUNDER YET ANOTHER WORLD.
HIS HUNGER KNOWS NO END...

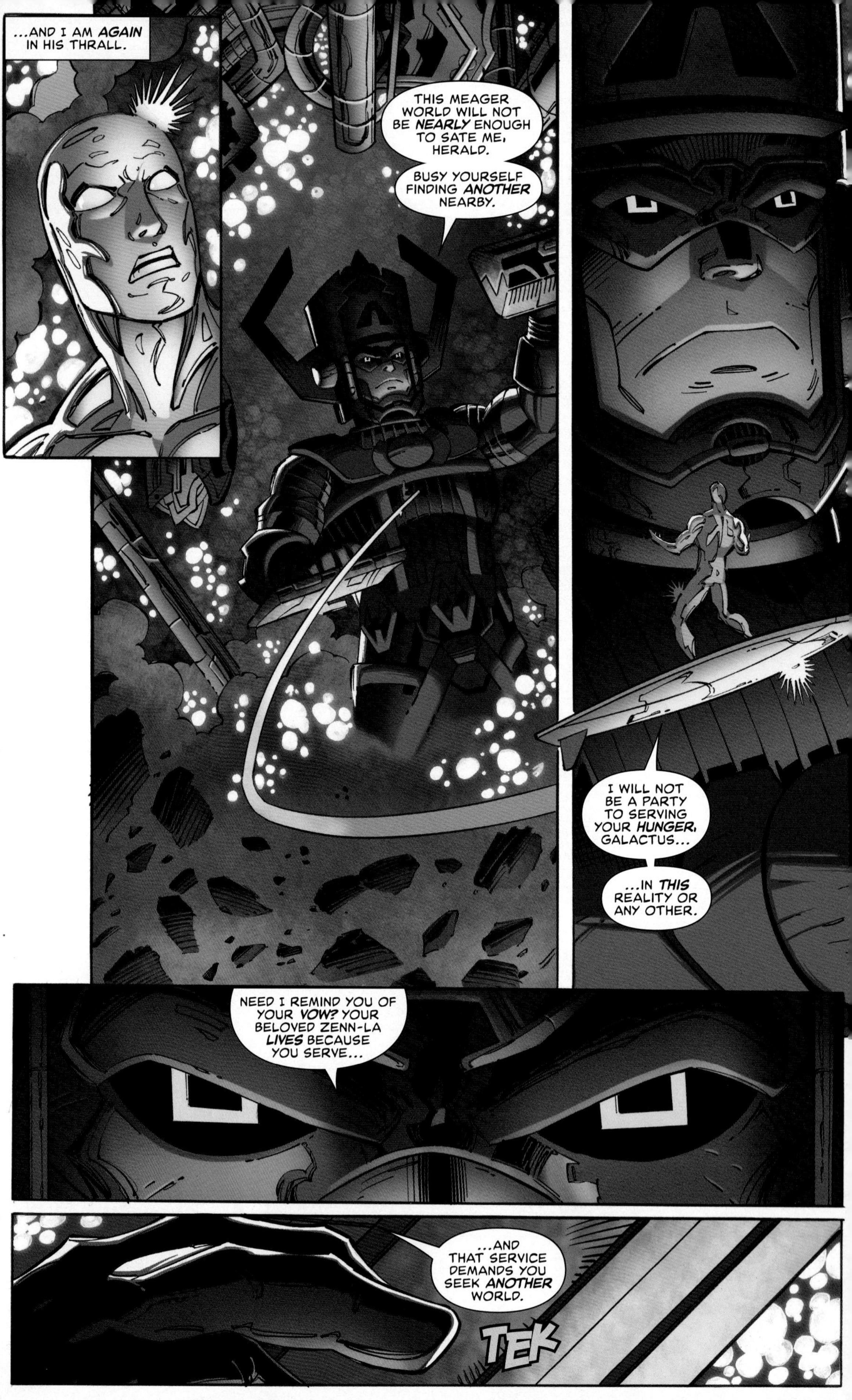
...AND I AM AGAIN IN HIS THRALL.
THIS MEAGER WORLD WILL NOT BE NEARLY ENOUGH TO SATE ME, HERALD.
BUSY YOURSELF FINDING ANOTHER NEARBY.
I WILL NOT BE A PARTY TO SERVING YOUR HUNGER, GALACTUS...
...IN THIS REALITY OR ANY OTHER.
NEED I REMIND YOU OF YOUR VOW? YOUR BELOVED ZENN-LA LIVES BECAUSE YOU SERVE...
...AND THAT SERVICE DEMANDS YOU SEEK ANOTHER WORLD.
TEK

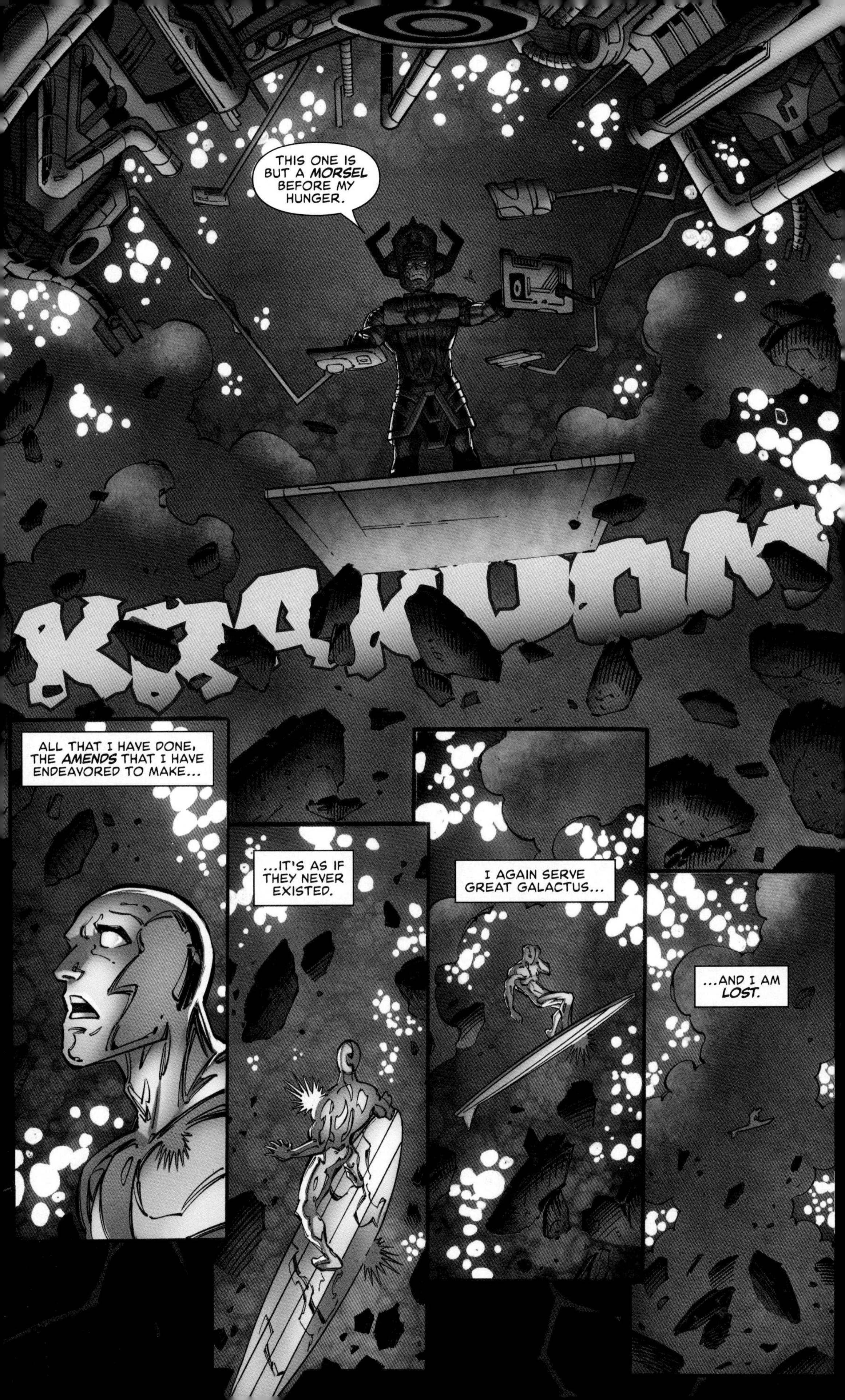
THIS ONE IS BUT A MORSEL BEFORE MY HUNGER.
ALL THAT I HAVE DONE, THE AMENDS THAT I HAVE ENDEAVORED TO MAKE...
...IT'S AS IF THEY NEVER EXISTED.
I AGAIN SERVE GREAT GALACTUS...
...AND I AM LOST.

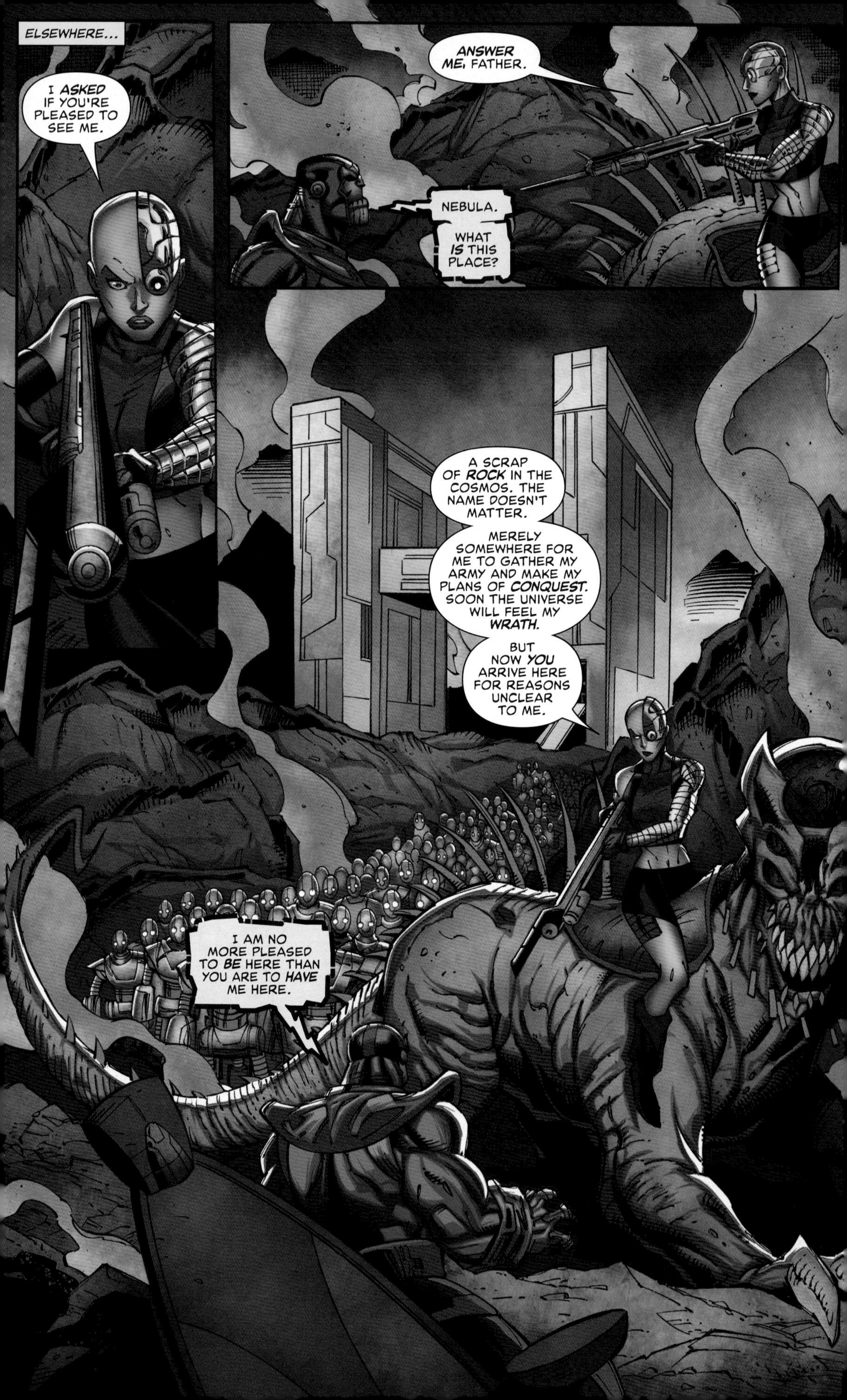
ELSEWHERE...
I ASKED IF YOU'RE PLEASED TO SEE ME.
ANSWER ME, FATHER.
NEBULA.
WHAT IS THIS PLACE?
A SCRAP OF ROCK IN THE COSMOS. THE NAME DOESN'T MATTER.
MERELY SOMEWHERE FOR ME TO GATHER MY ARMY AND MAKE MY PLANS OF CONQUEST. SOON THE UNIVERSE WILL FEEL MY WRATH.
BUT NOW YOU ARRIVE HERE FOR REASONS UNCLEAR TO ME.
I AM NO MORE PLEASED TO BE HERE THAN YOU ARE TO HAVE ME HERE.

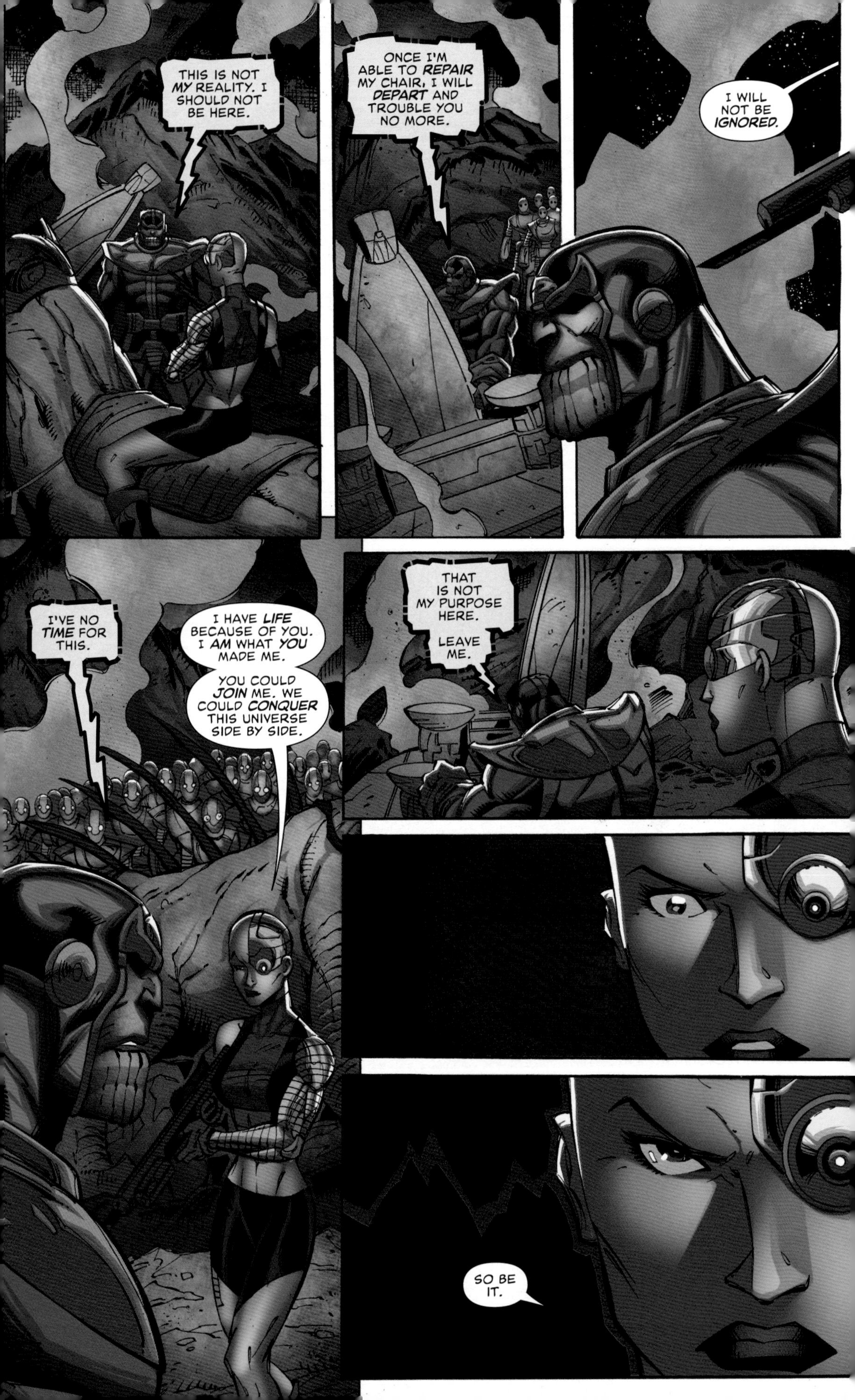
THIS IS NOT MY REALITY. I SHOULD NOT BE HERE.
ONCE I'M ABLE TO REPAIR MY CHAIR, I WILL DEPART AND TROUBLE YOU NO MORE.
I WILL NOT BE IGNORED.
I'VE NO TIME FOR THIS.
I HAVE LIFE BECAUSE OF YOU. I AM WHAT YOU MADE ME.
YOU COULD JOIN ME. WE COULD CONQUER THIS UNIVERSE SIDE BY SIDE.
THAT IS NOT MY PURPOSE HERE.
LEAVE ME.
SO BE IT.

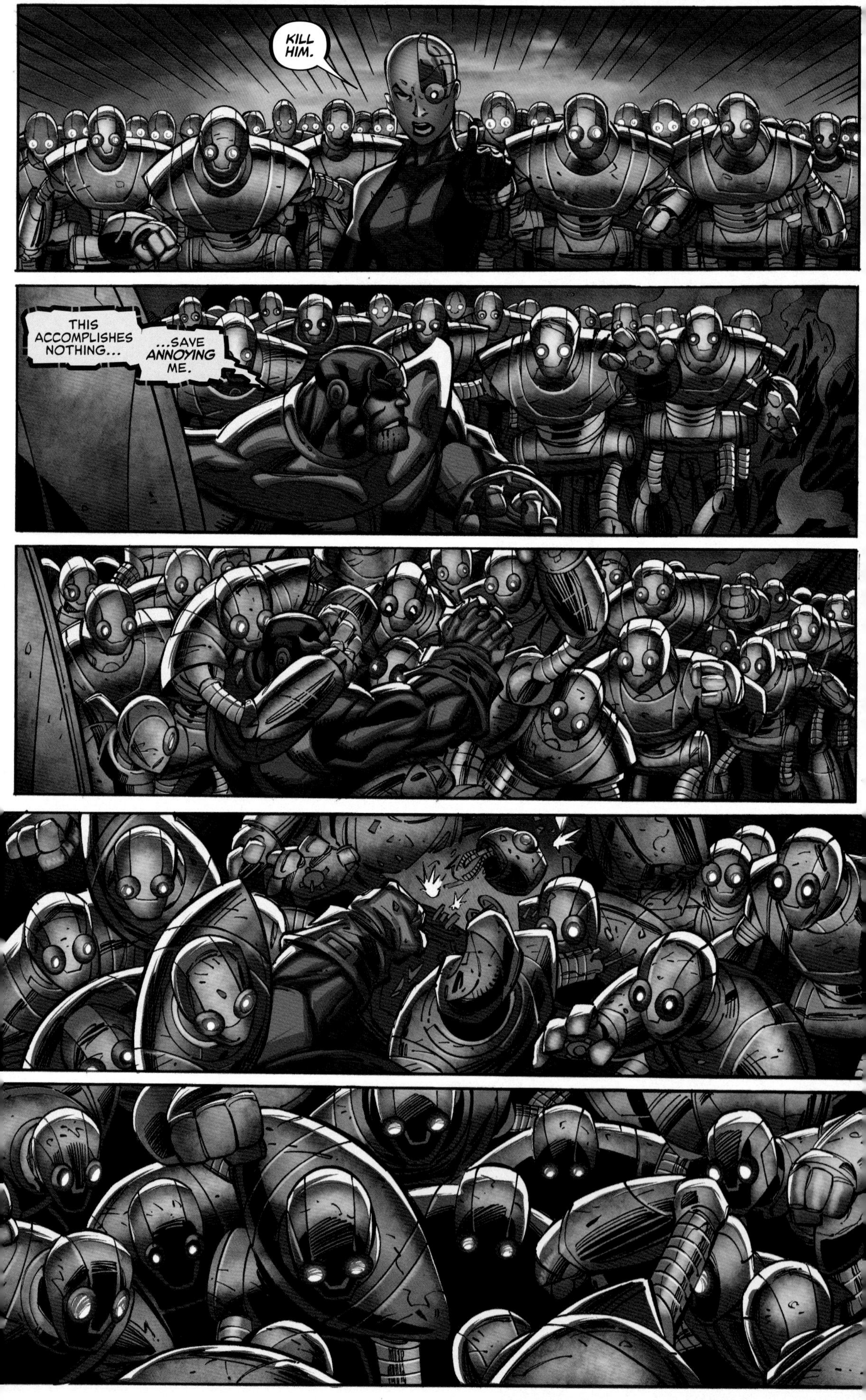

KILL HIM.
THIS ACCOMPLISHES NOTHING...
...SAVE ANNOYING ME.

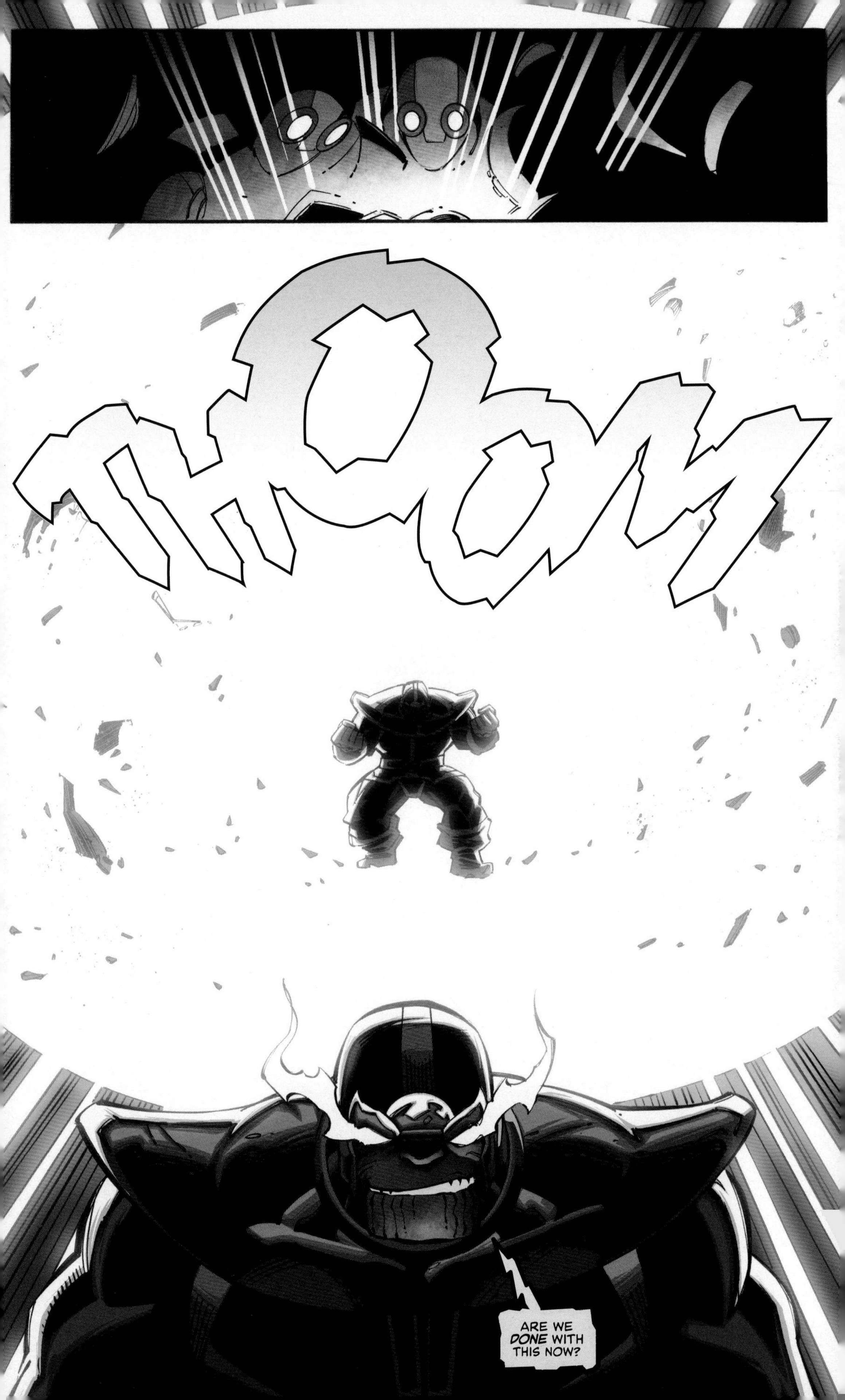
THOOM
ARE WE DONE WITH THIS NOW?

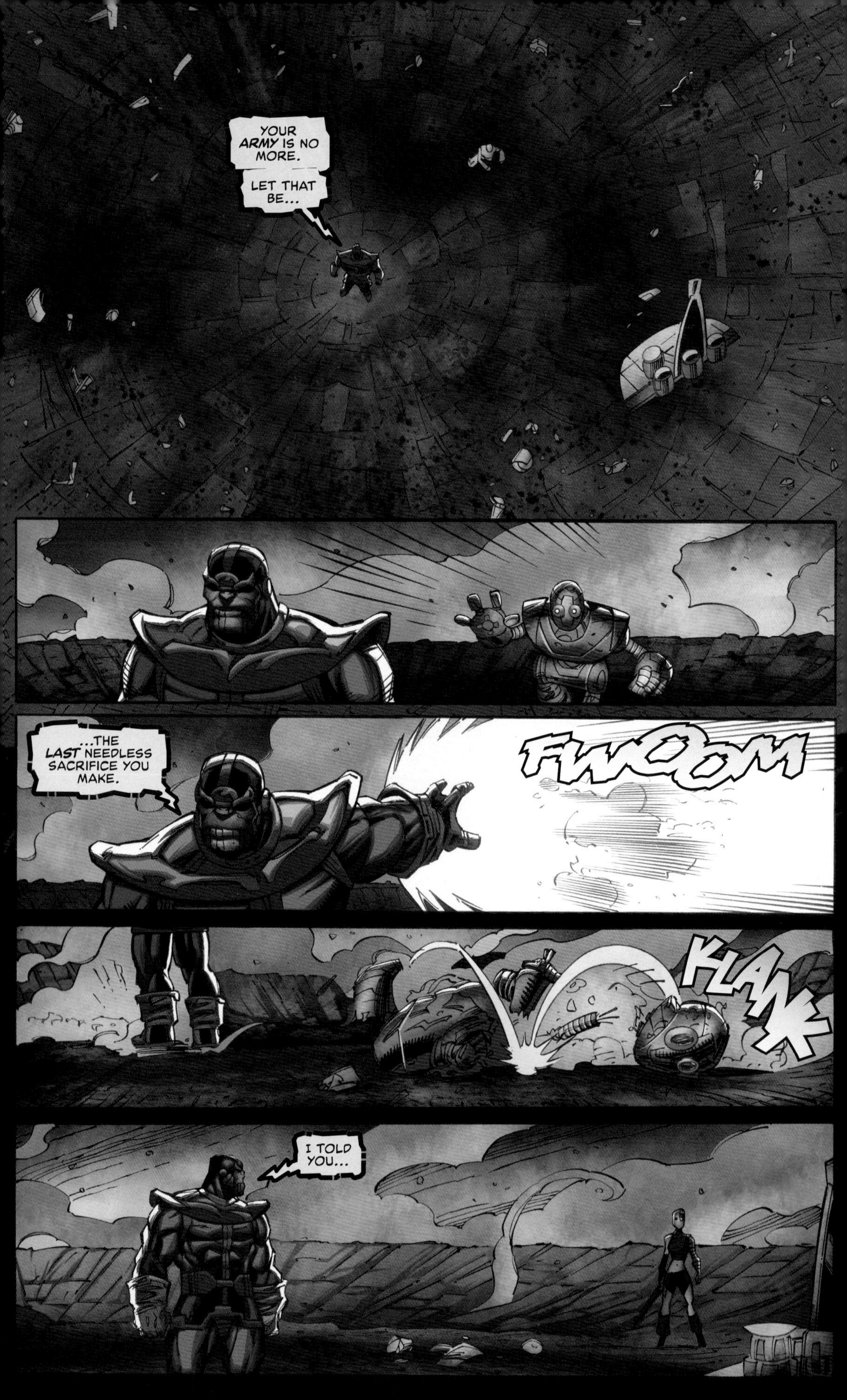
YOUR ARMY IS NO MORE.
LET THAT BE...
...THE LAST NEEDLESS SACRIFICE YOU MAKE.
FWOOM
KLANK
I TOLD YOU...

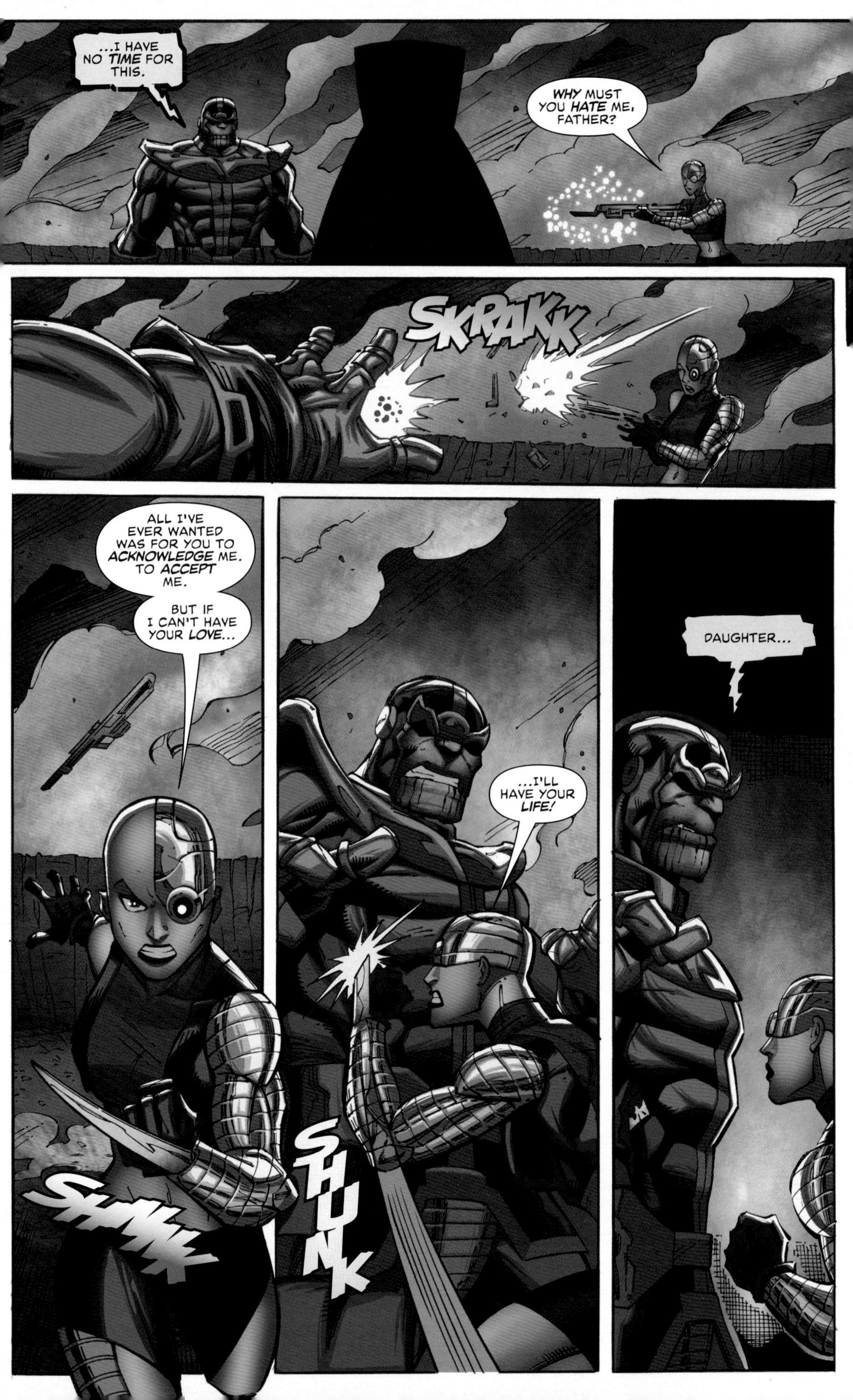
...I HAVE NO *TIME* FOR THIS.
WHY MUST YOU *HATE* ME, FATHER?
SKRAKK
ALL I'VE EVER WANTED WAS FOR YOU TO *ACKNOWLEDGE* ME. TO *ACCEPT* ME.
BUT IF I CAN'T HAVE YOUR *LOVE*...
SHHK
...I'LL HAVE YOUR *LIFE!*
SHUNK
DAUGHTER...

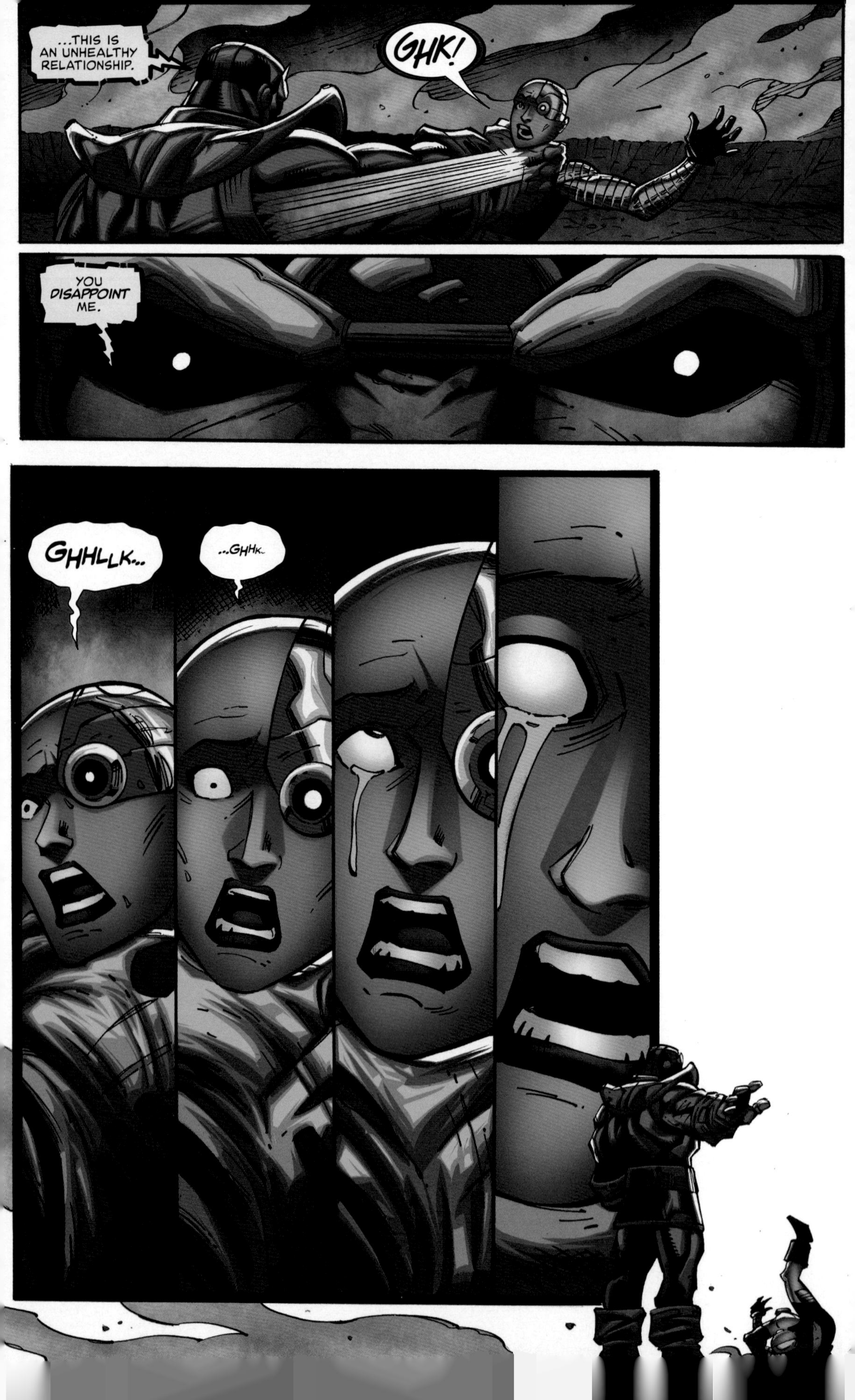
...THIS IS AN UNHEALTHY RELATIONSHIP.
GHK!
YOU DISAPPOINT ME.
GHHLLK...
...GHHK...

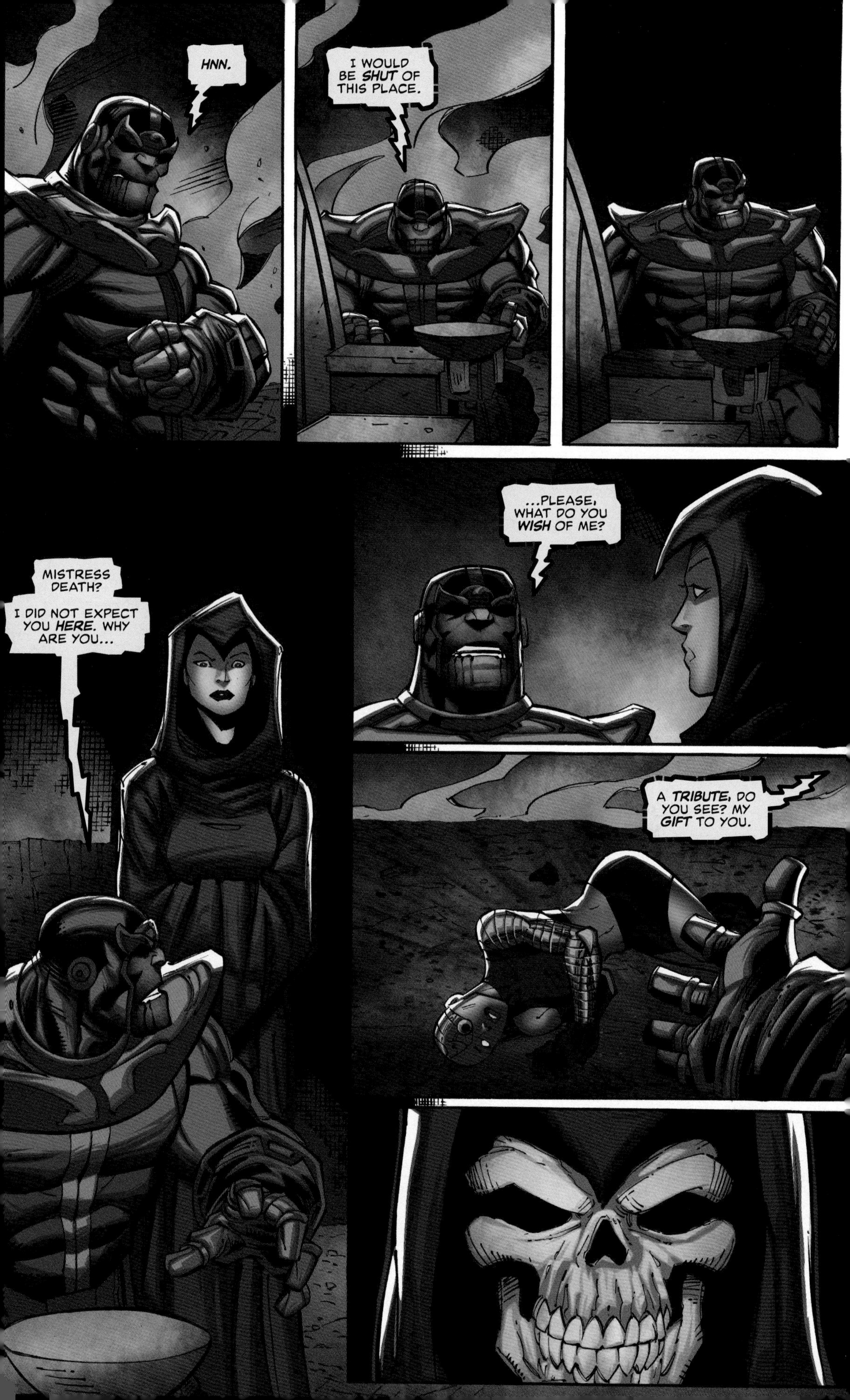
HNN.
I WOULD BE SHUT OF THIS PLACE.
MISTRESS DEATH?
I DID NOT EXPECT YOU HERE. WHY ARE YOU...
...PLEASE, WHAT DO YOU WISH OF ME?
A TRIBUTE, DO YOU SEE? MY GIFT TO YOU.

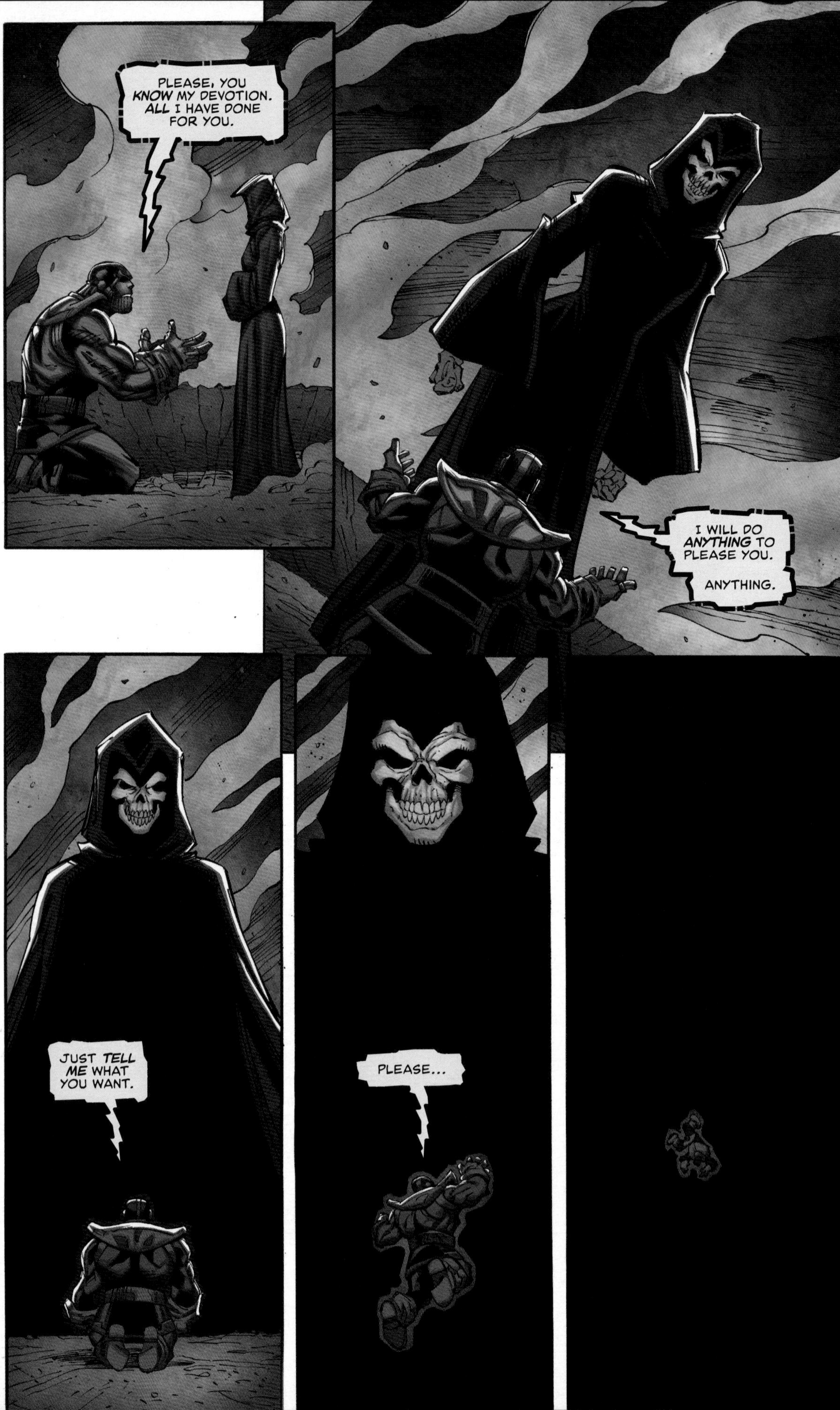
PLEASE, YOU KNOW MY DEVOTION. ALL I HAVE DONE FOR YOU.
I WILL DO ANYTHING TO PLEASE YOU.
ANYTHING.
JUST TELL ME WHAT YOU WANT.
PLEASE...

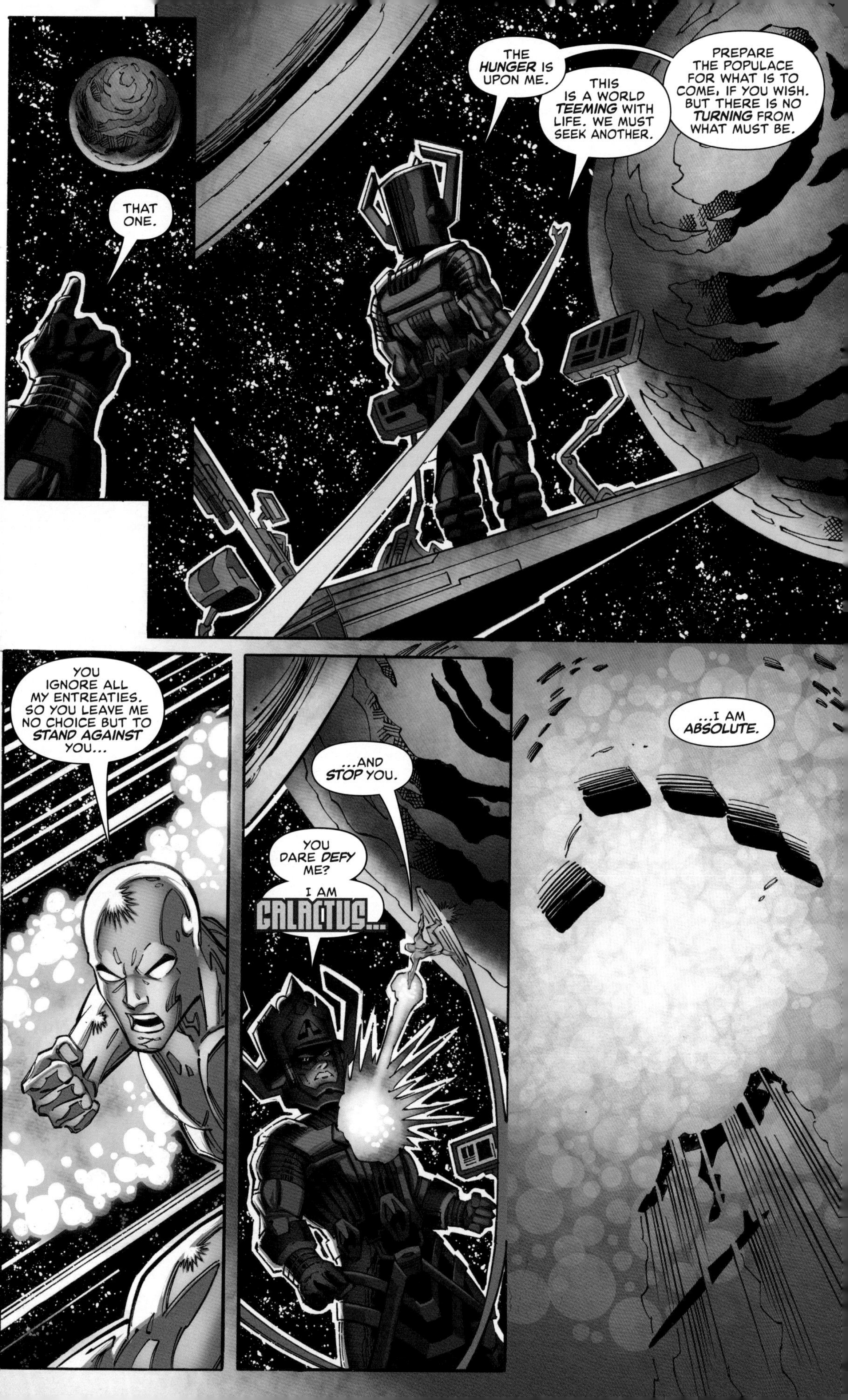
THAT ONE.
THE HUNGER IS UPON ME.
THIS IS A WORLD TEEMING WITH LIFE. WE MUST SEEK ANOTHER.
PREPARE THE POPULACE FOR WHAT IS TO COME, IF YOU WISH. BUT THERE IS NO TURNING FROM WHAT MUST BE.
YOU IGNORE ALL MY ENTREATIES. SO YOU LEAVE ME NO CHOICE BUT TO STAND AGAINST YOU...
...AND STOP YOU.
YOU DARE DEFY ME?
I AM GALACTUS...
...I AM ABSOLUTE.

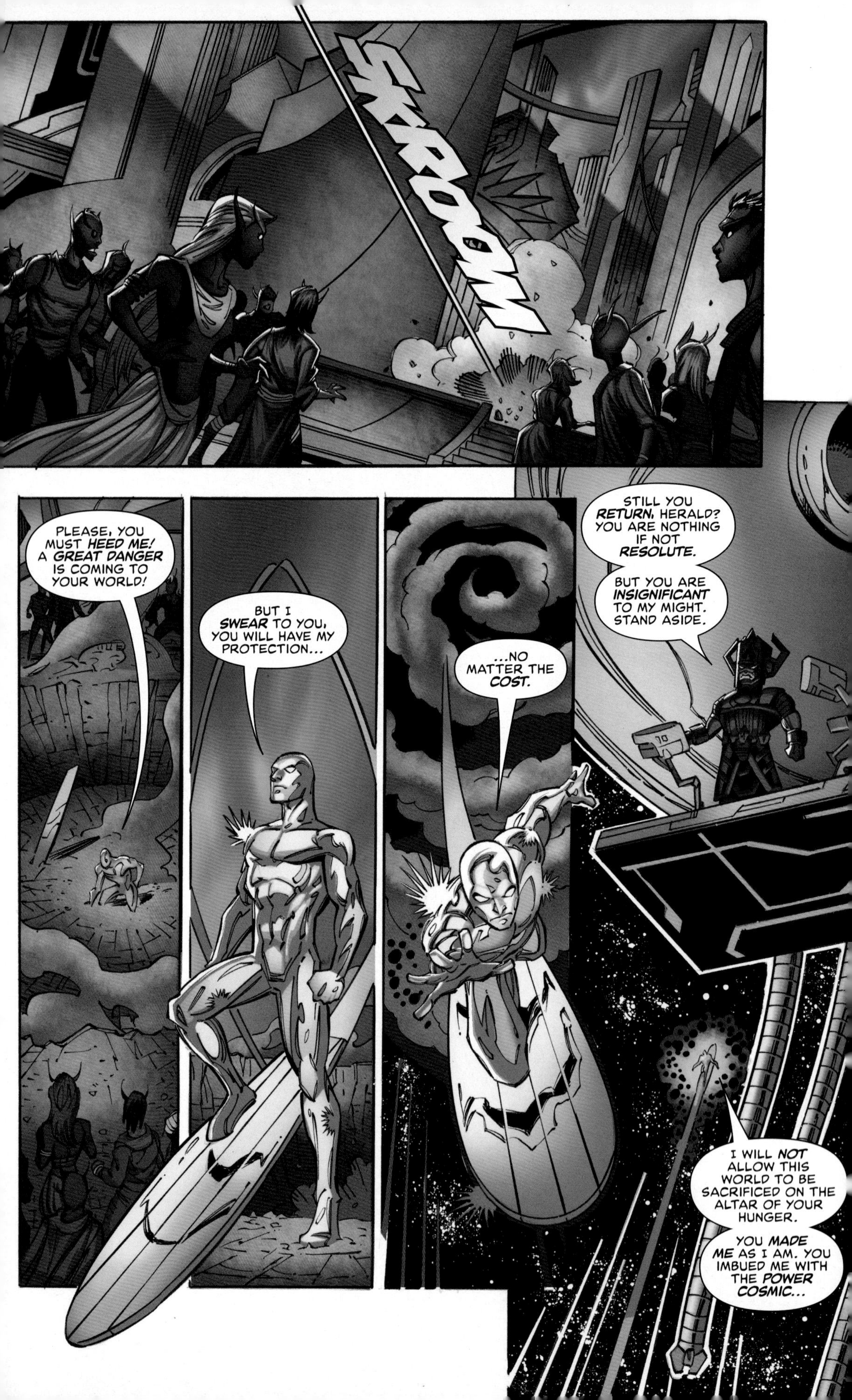
SKROOM!
PLEASE, YOU MUST HEED ME! A GREAT DANGER IS COMING TO YOUR WORLD!
BUT I SWEAR TO YOU, YOU WILL HAVE MY PROTECTION...
...NO MATTER THE COST.
STILL YOU RETURN, HERALD? YOU ARE NOTHING IF NOT RESOLUTE.
BUT YOU ARE INSIGNIFICANT TO MY MIGHT. STAND ASIDE.
I WILL NOT ALLOW THIS WORLD TO BE SACRIFICED ON THE ALTAR OF YOUR HUNGER.
YOU MADE ME AS I AM. YOU IMBUED ME WITH THE POWER COSMIC...

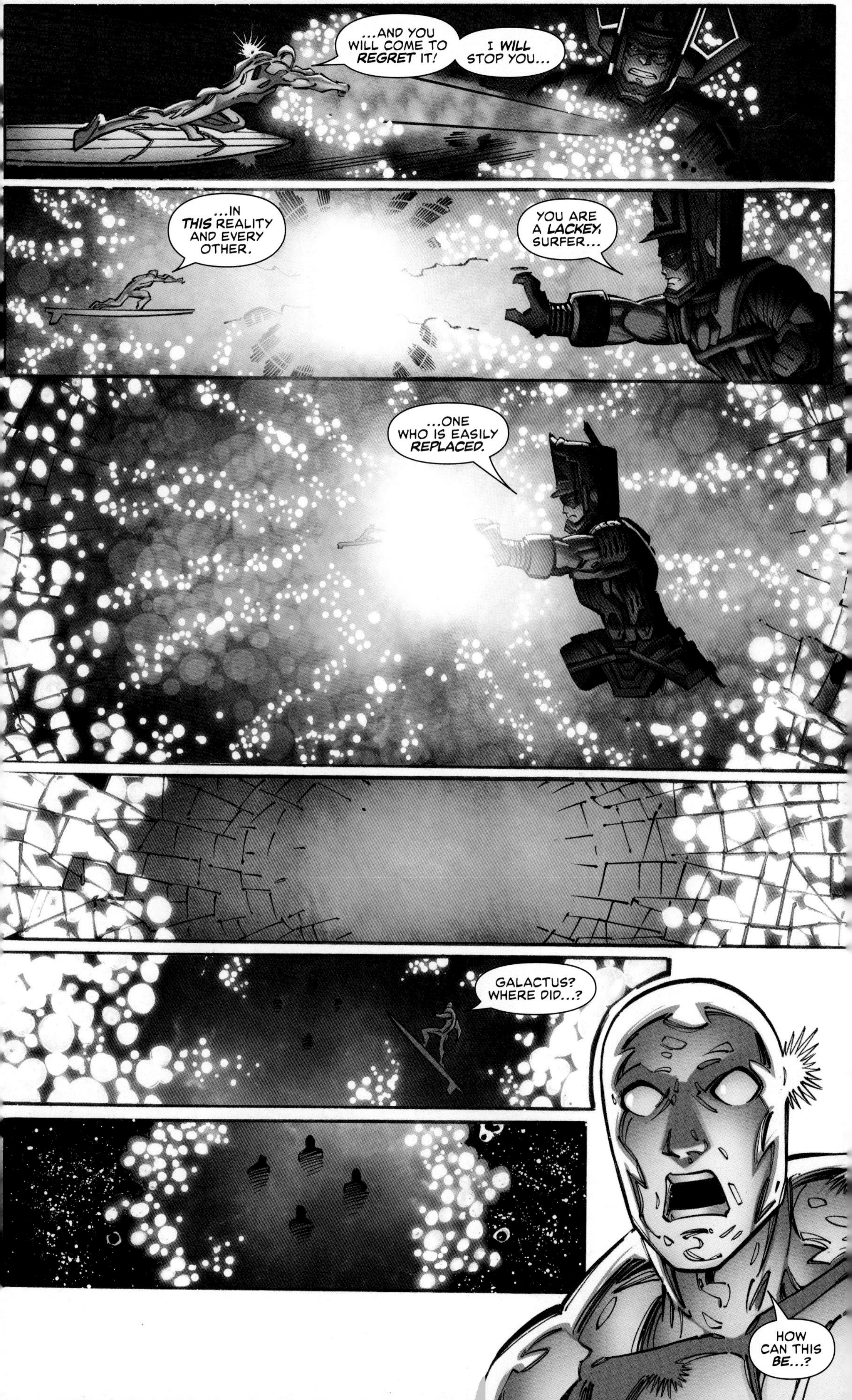
...AND YOU WILL COME TO REGRET IT!
I WILL STOP YOU...
...IN THIS REALITY AND EVERY OTHER.
YOU ARE A LACKEY, SURFER...
...ONE WHO IS EASILY REPLACED.
GALACTUS? WHERE DID...?
HOW CAN THIS BE...?

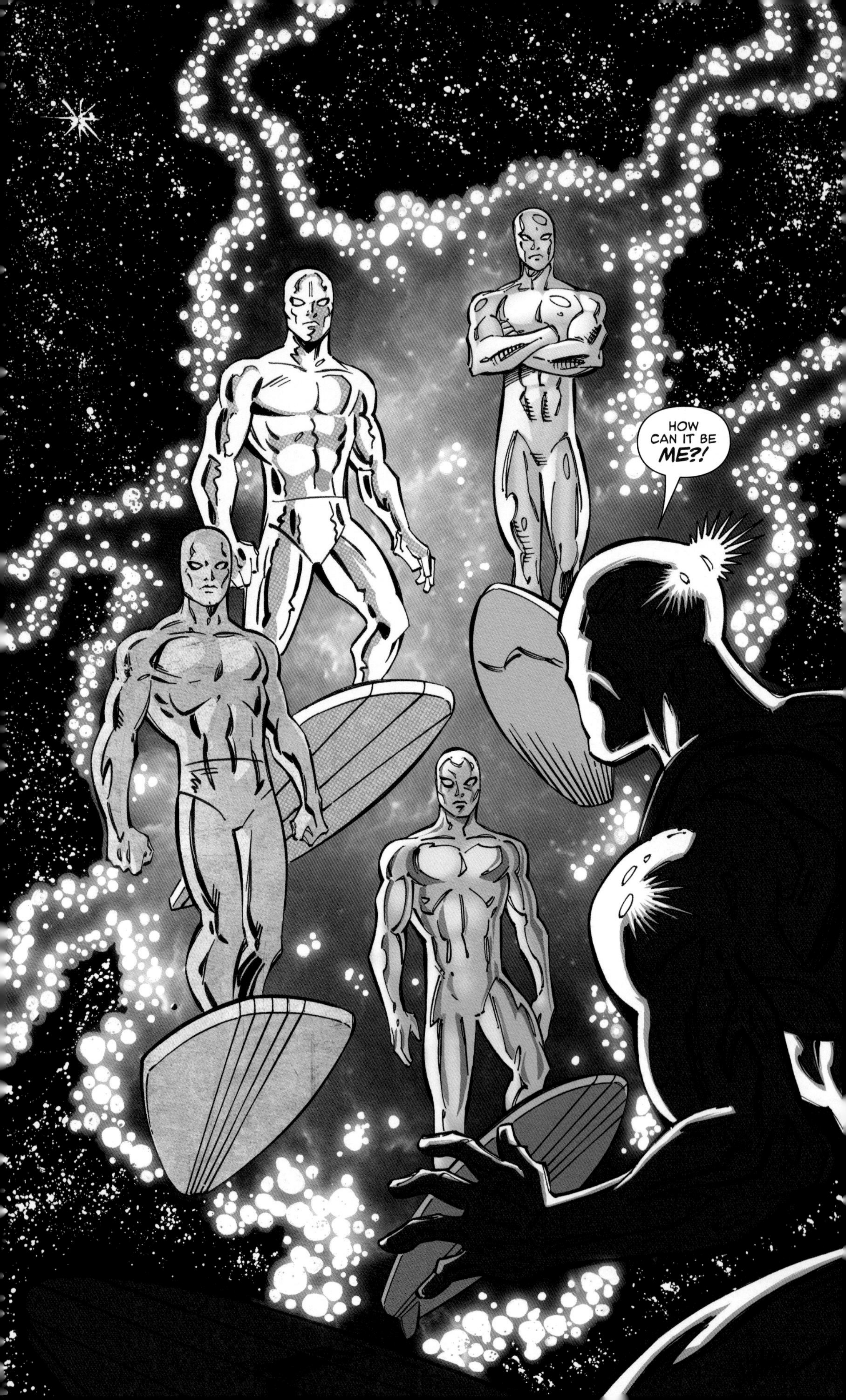
HOW CAN IT BE ME?!

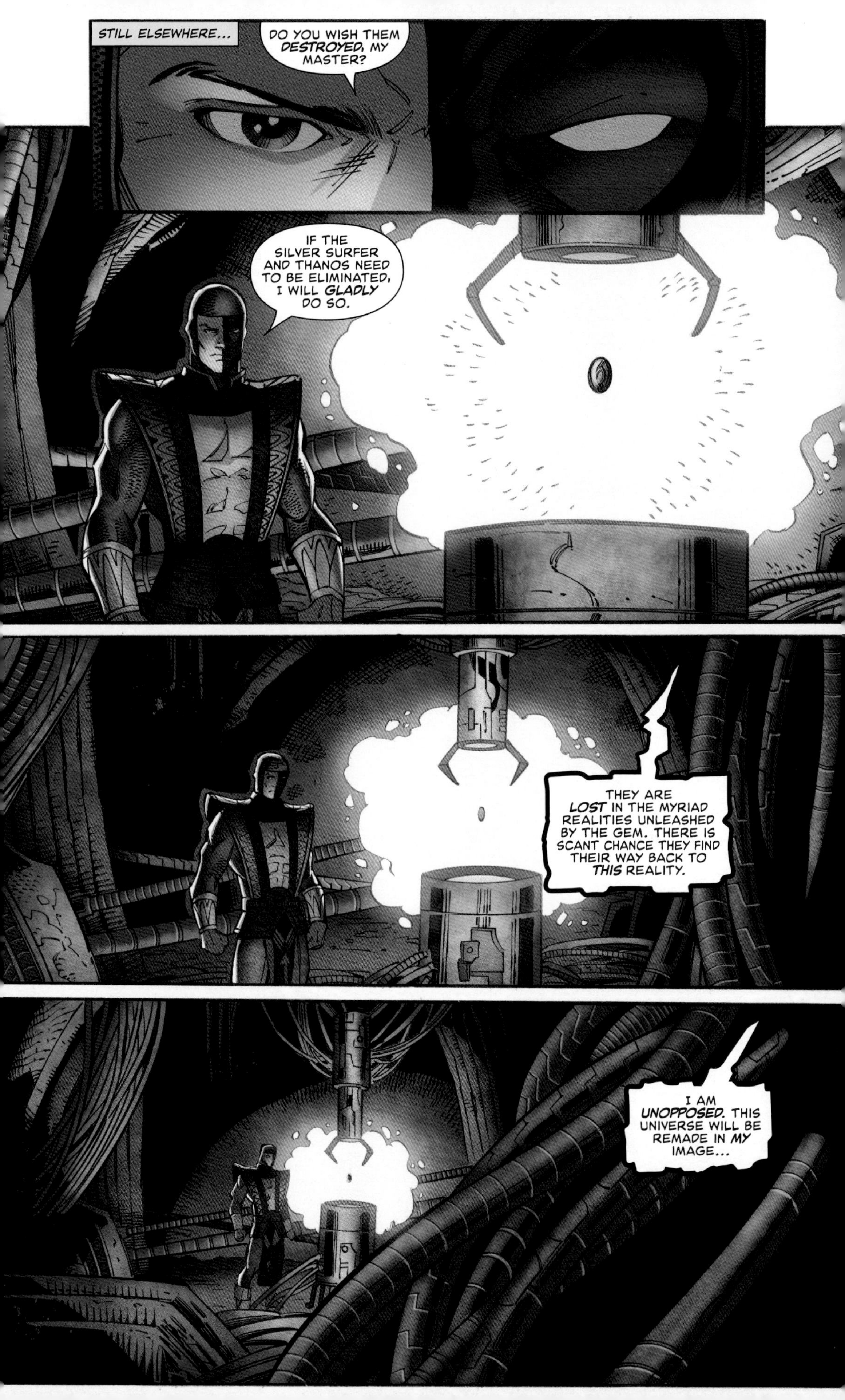
STILL ELSEWHERE...
DO YOU WISH THEM DESTROYED, MY MASTER?
IF THE SILVER SURFER AND THANOS NEED TO BE ELIMINATED, I WILL GLADLY DO SO.
THEY ARE LOST IN THE MYRIAD REALITIES UNLEASHED BY THE GEM. THERE IS SCANT CHANCE THEY FIND THEIR WAY BACK TO THIS REALITY.
I AM UNOPPOSED. THIS UNIVERSE WILL BE REMADE IN MY IMAGE...

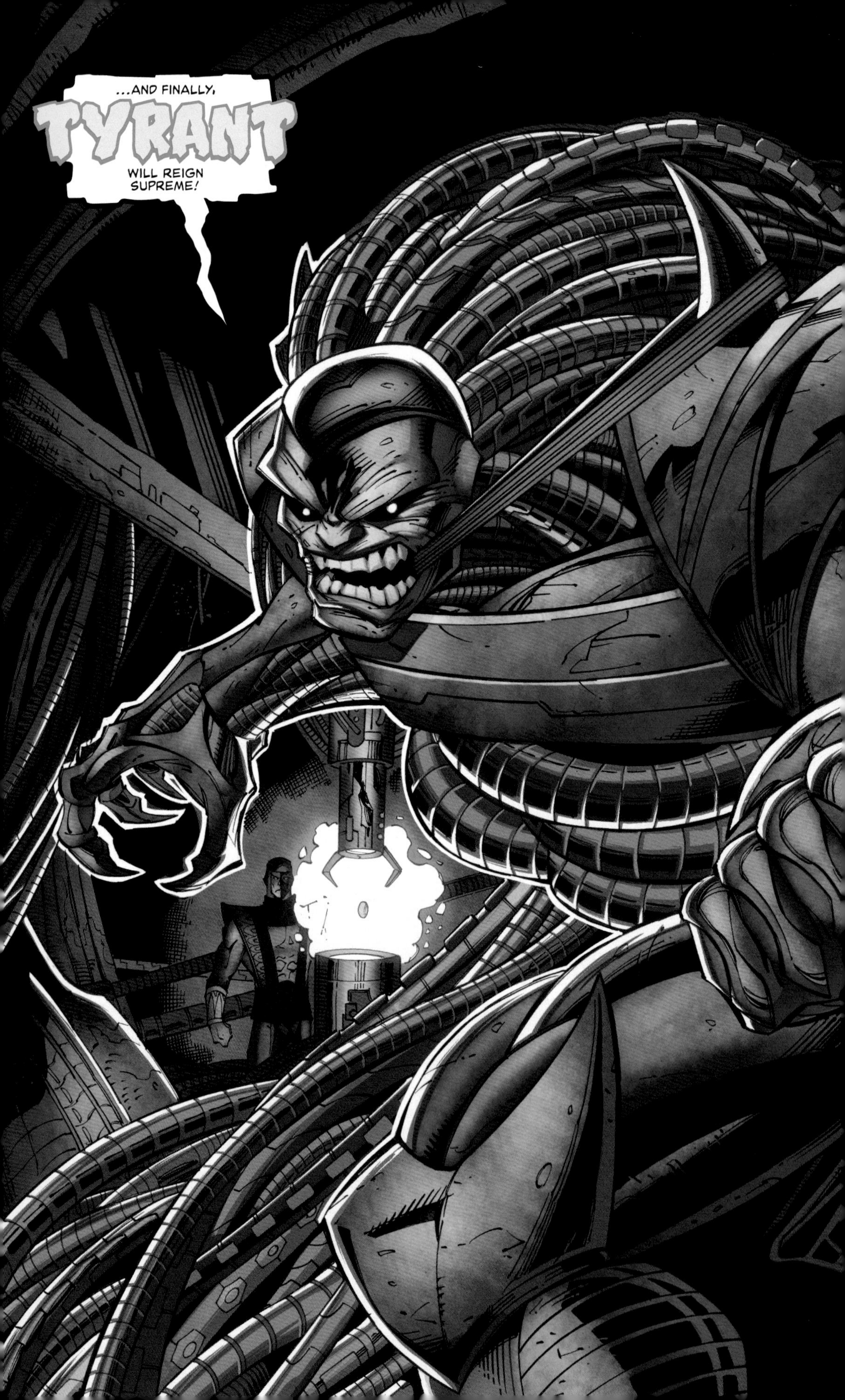
...AND FINALLY, TYRANT WILL REIGN SUPREME!

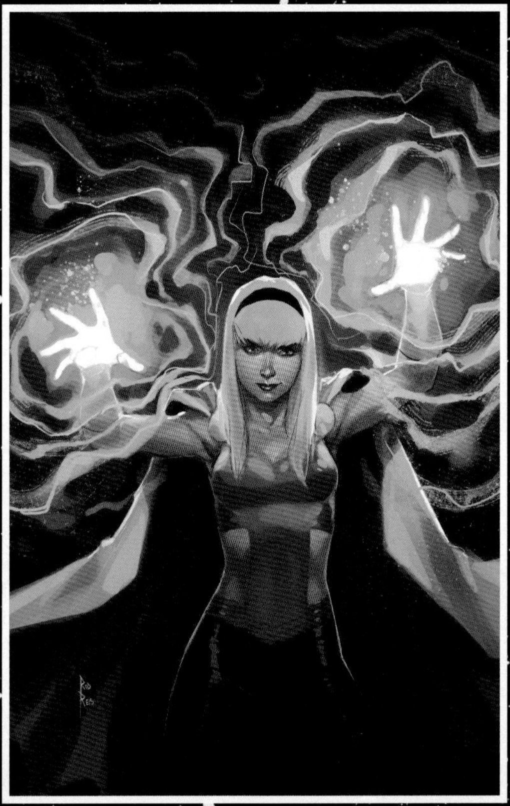

#2 X-GWEN VARIANT BY
ROD REIS

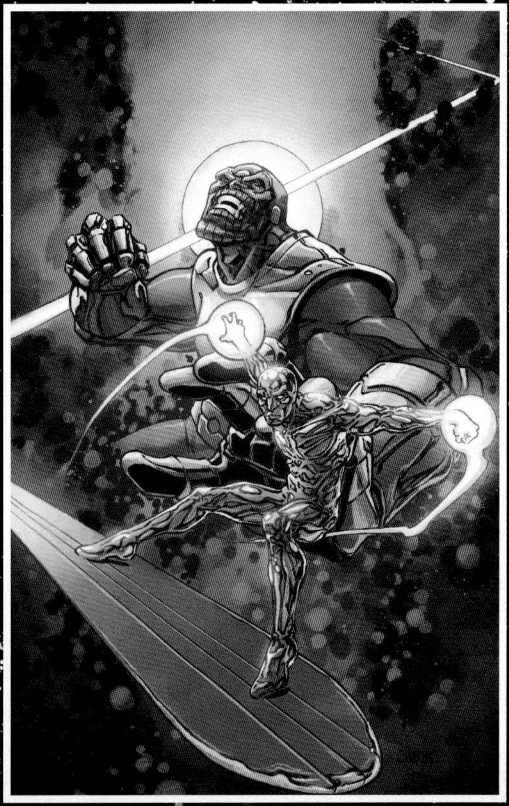

#2 VARIANT BY
KYLE CHARLES
& RACHELLE ROSENBERG

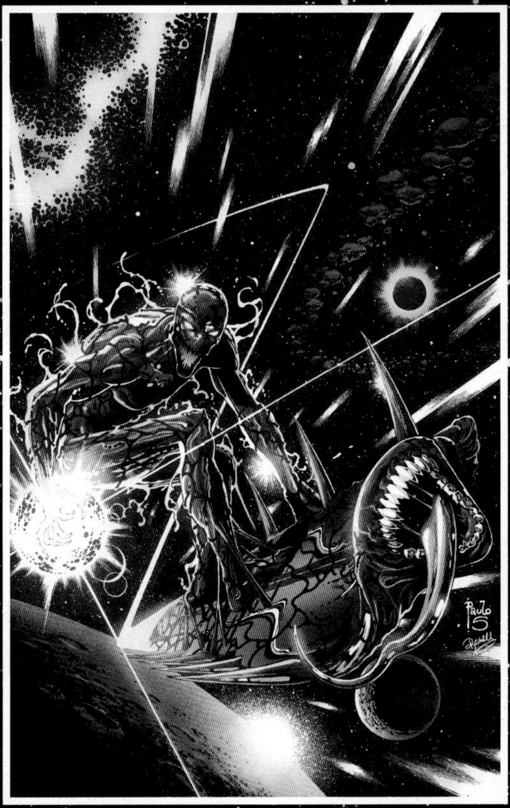

#3 CARNAGE FOREVER VARIANT BY
PAULO SIQUEIRA
& RACHELLE ROSENBERG

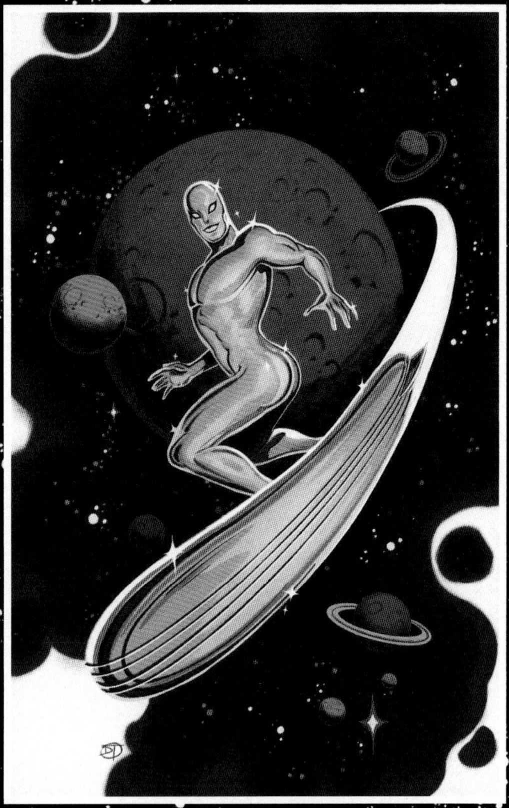

#3 VARIANT BY
DAVID TALASKI

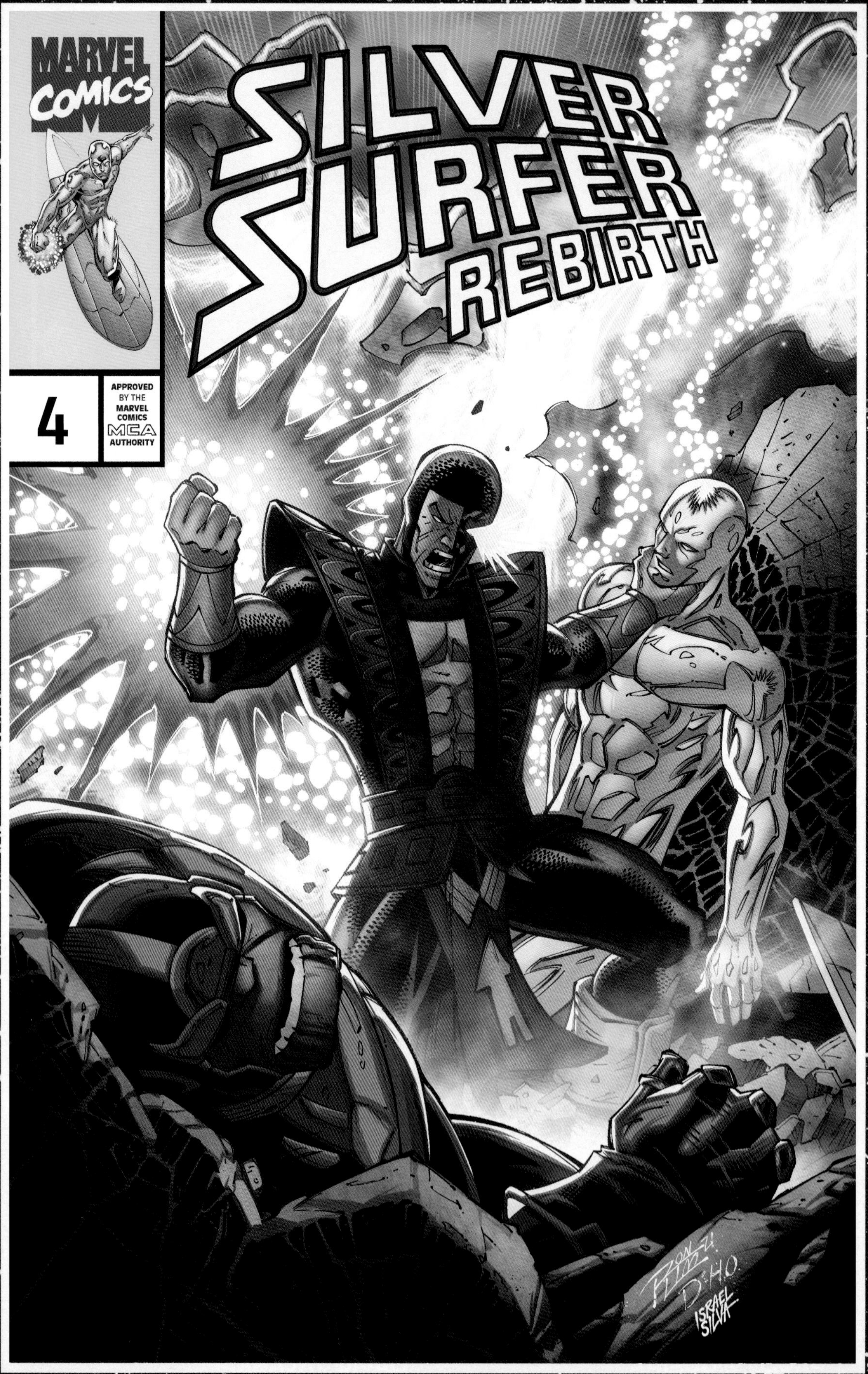
MARVEL COMICS
SILVER SURFER REBIRTH
4
APPROVED BY THE MARVEL COMICS MCA AUTHORITY
ISRAEL SILVA

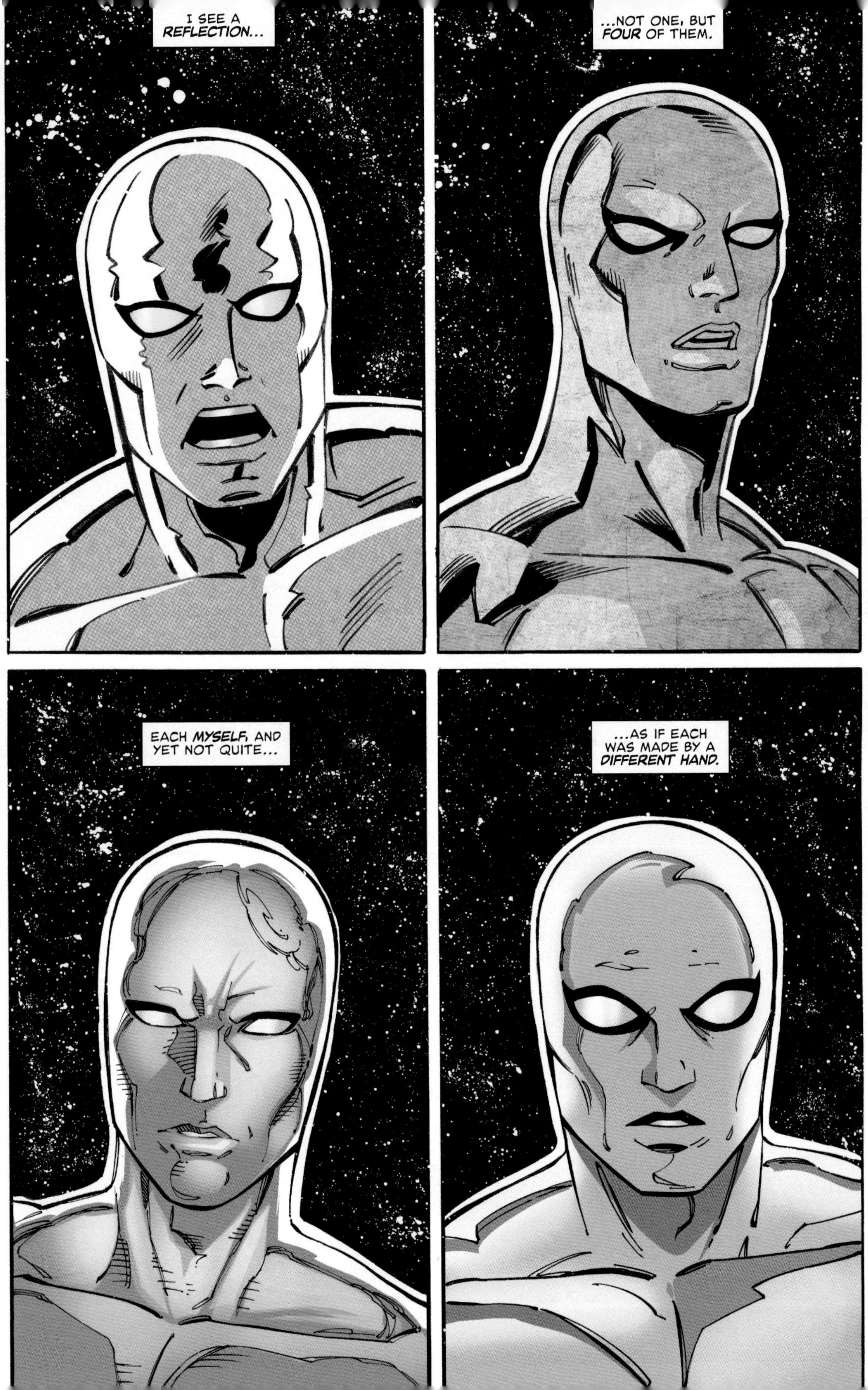
I SEE A REFLECTION...
...NOT ONE, BUT FOUR OF THEM.
EACH MYSELF, AND YET NOT QUITE...
...AS IF EACH WAS MADE BY A DIFFERENT HAND.

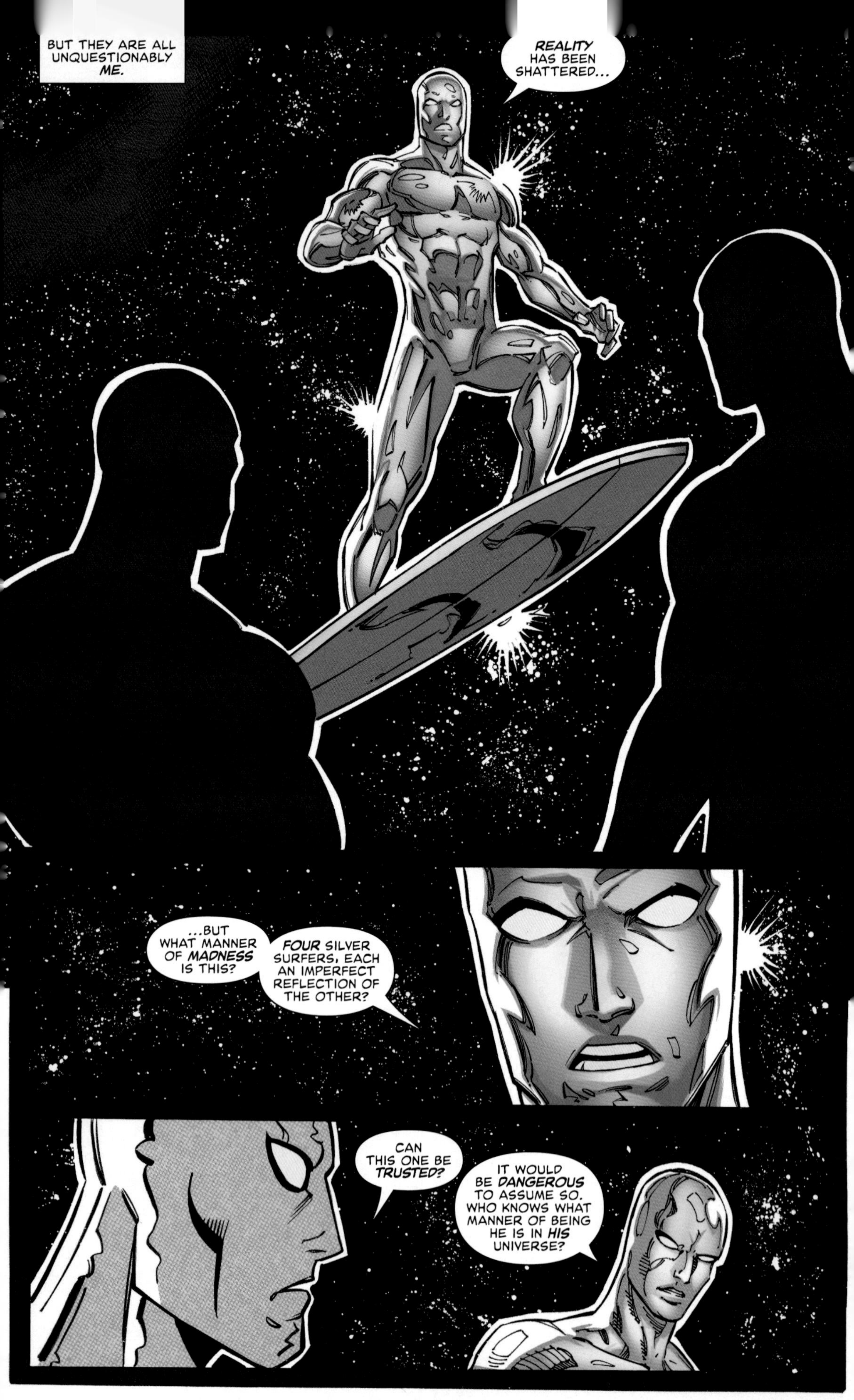
BUT THEY ARE ALL UNQUESTIONABLY ME.
REALITY HAS BEEN SHATTERED...
...BUT WHAT MANNER OF MADNESS IS THIS?
FOUR SILVER SURFERS, EACH AN IMPERFECT REFLECTION OF THE OTHER?
CAN THIS ONE BE TRUSTED?
IT WOULD BE DANGEROUS TO ASSUME SO. WHO KNOWS WHAT MANNER OF BEING HE IS IN HIS UNIVERSE?

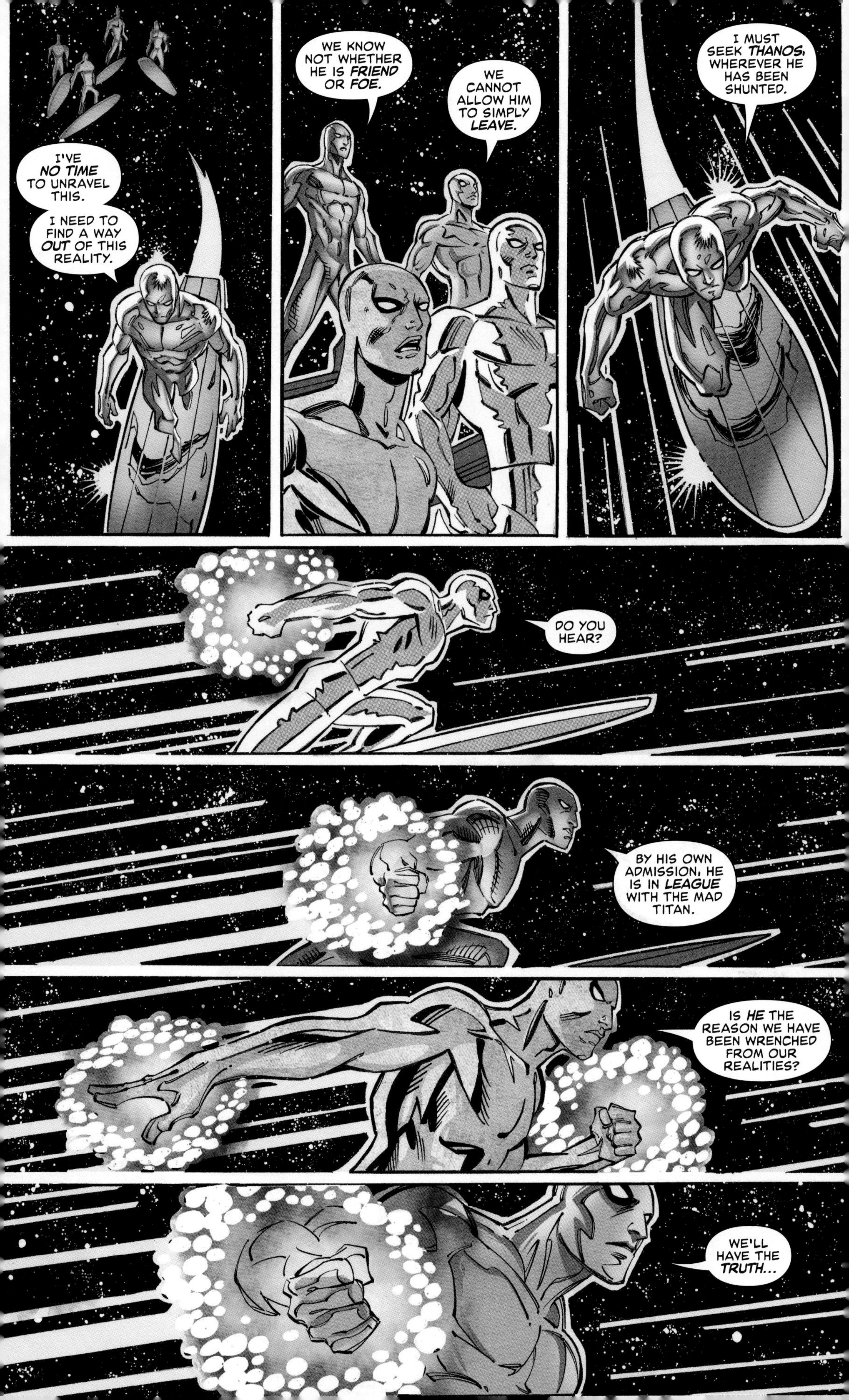
I'VE NO TIME TO UNRAVEL THIS.
I NEED TO FIND A WAY OUT OF THIS REALITY.
WE KNOW NOT WHETHER HE IS FRIEND OR FOE.
WE CANNOT ALLOW HIM TO SIMPLY LEAVE.
I MUST SEEK THANOS, WHEREVER HE HAS BEEN SHUNTED.
DO YOU HEAR?
BY HIS OWN ADMISSION, HE IS IN LEAGUE WITH THE MAD TITAN.
IS HE THE REASON WE HAVE BEEN WRENCHED FROM OUR REALITIES?
WE'LL HAVE THE TRUTH...

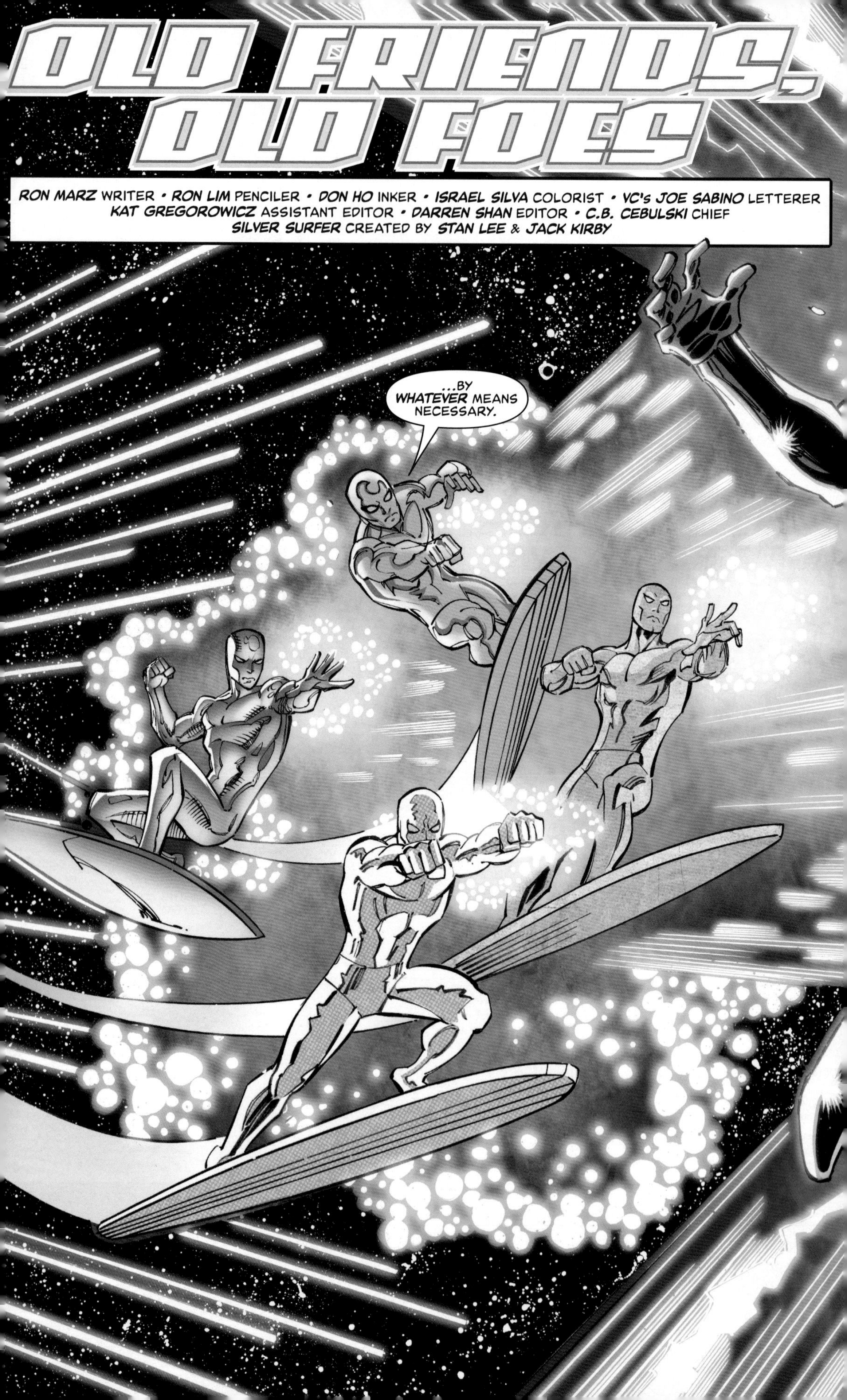
OLD FRIENDS, OLD FOES
RON MARZ WRITER • RON LIM PENCILER • DON HO INKER • ISRAEL SILVA COLORIST • VC's JOE SABINO LETTERER
KAT GREGOROWICZ ASSISTANT EDITOR • DARREN SHAN EDITOR • C.B. CEBULSKI CHIEF
SILVER SURFER CREATED BY STAN LEE & JACK KIRBY
...BY WHATEVER MEANS NECESSARY.

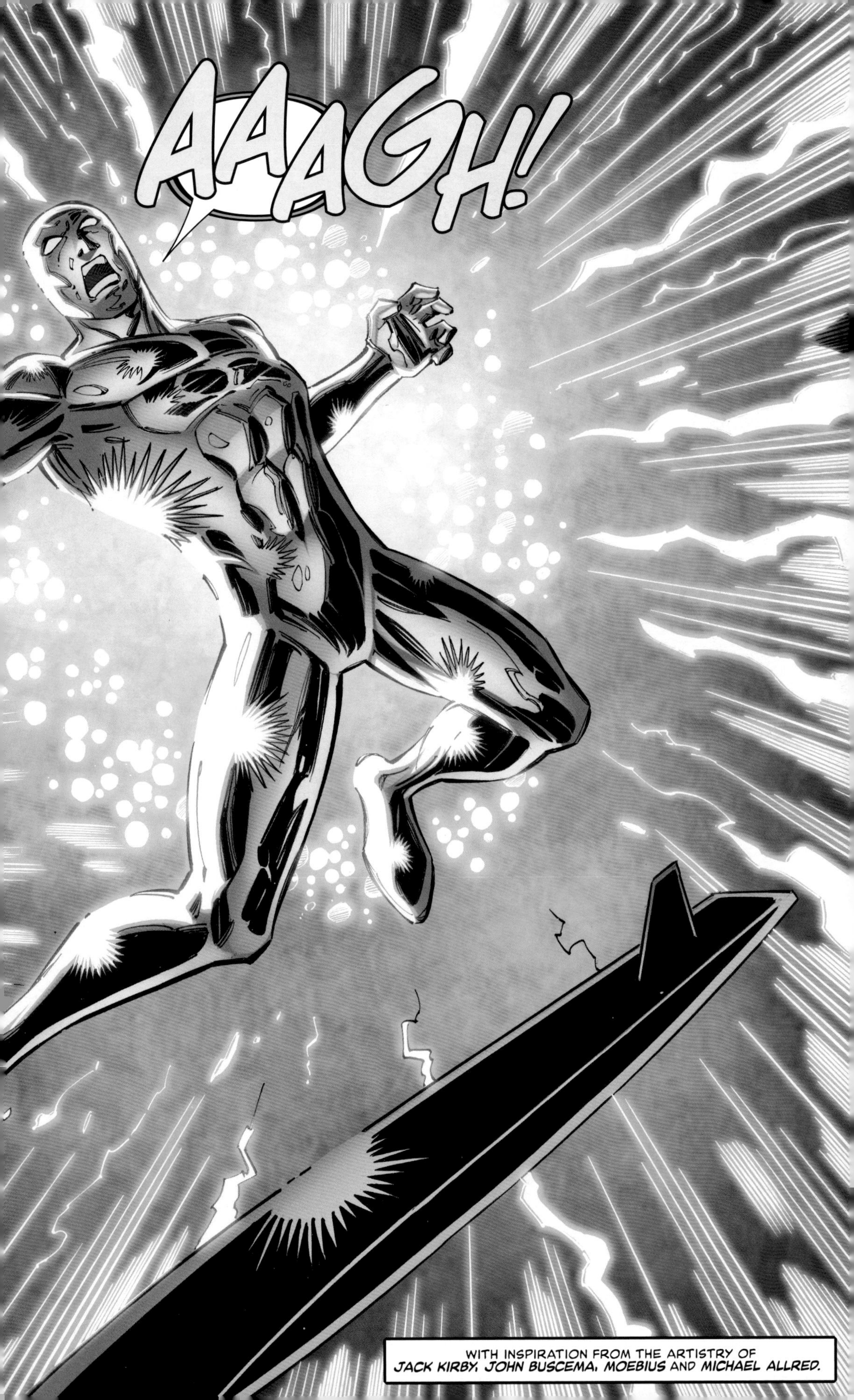
AAAGH!
WITH INSPIRATION FROM THE ARTISTRY OF
JACK KIRBY, JOHN BUSCEMA, MOEBIUS AND MICHAEL ALLRED.

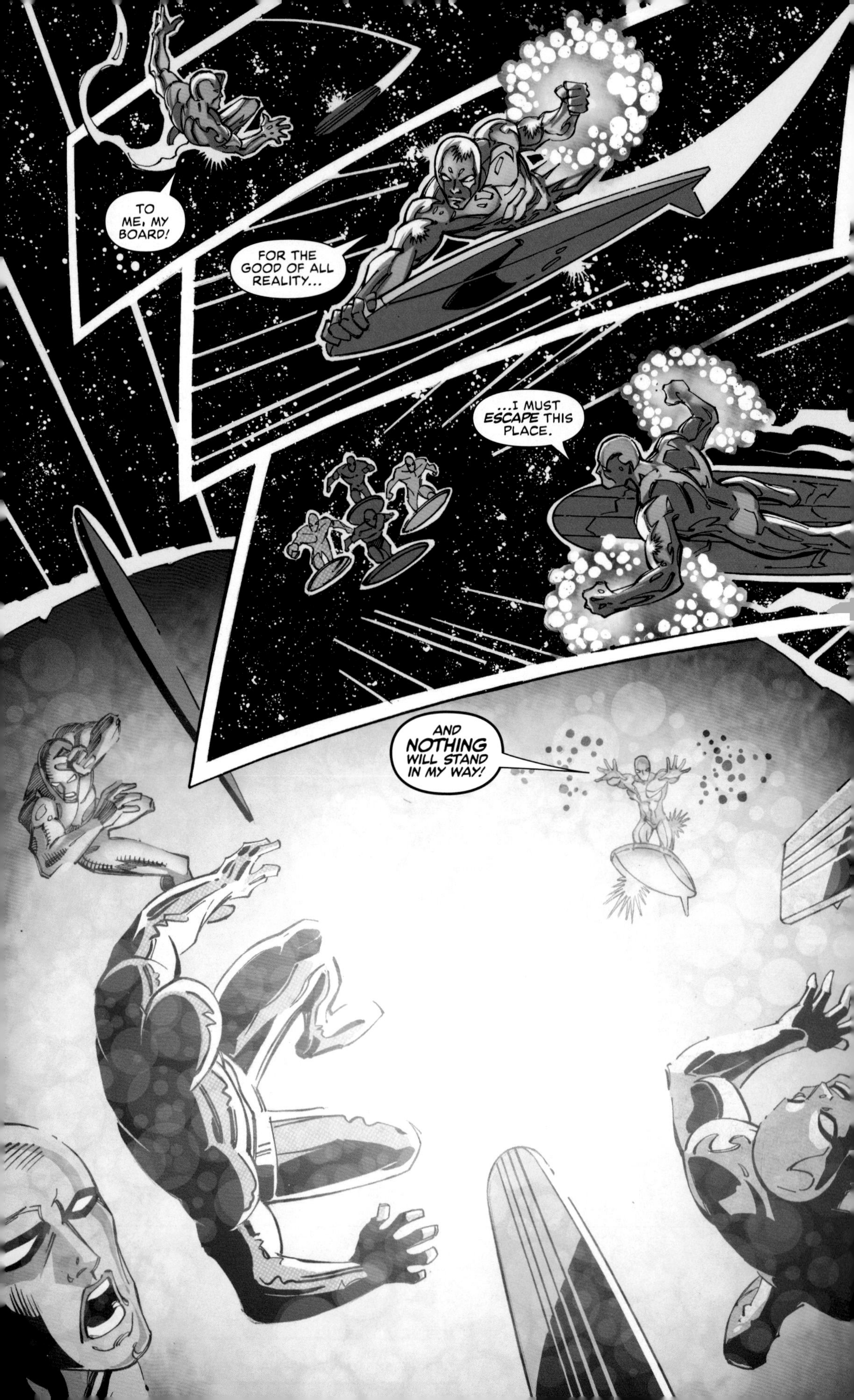
TO ME, MY BOARD!
FOR THE GOOD OF ALL REALITY...
...I MUST ESCAPE THIS PLACE.
AND NOTHING WILL STAND IN MY WAY!

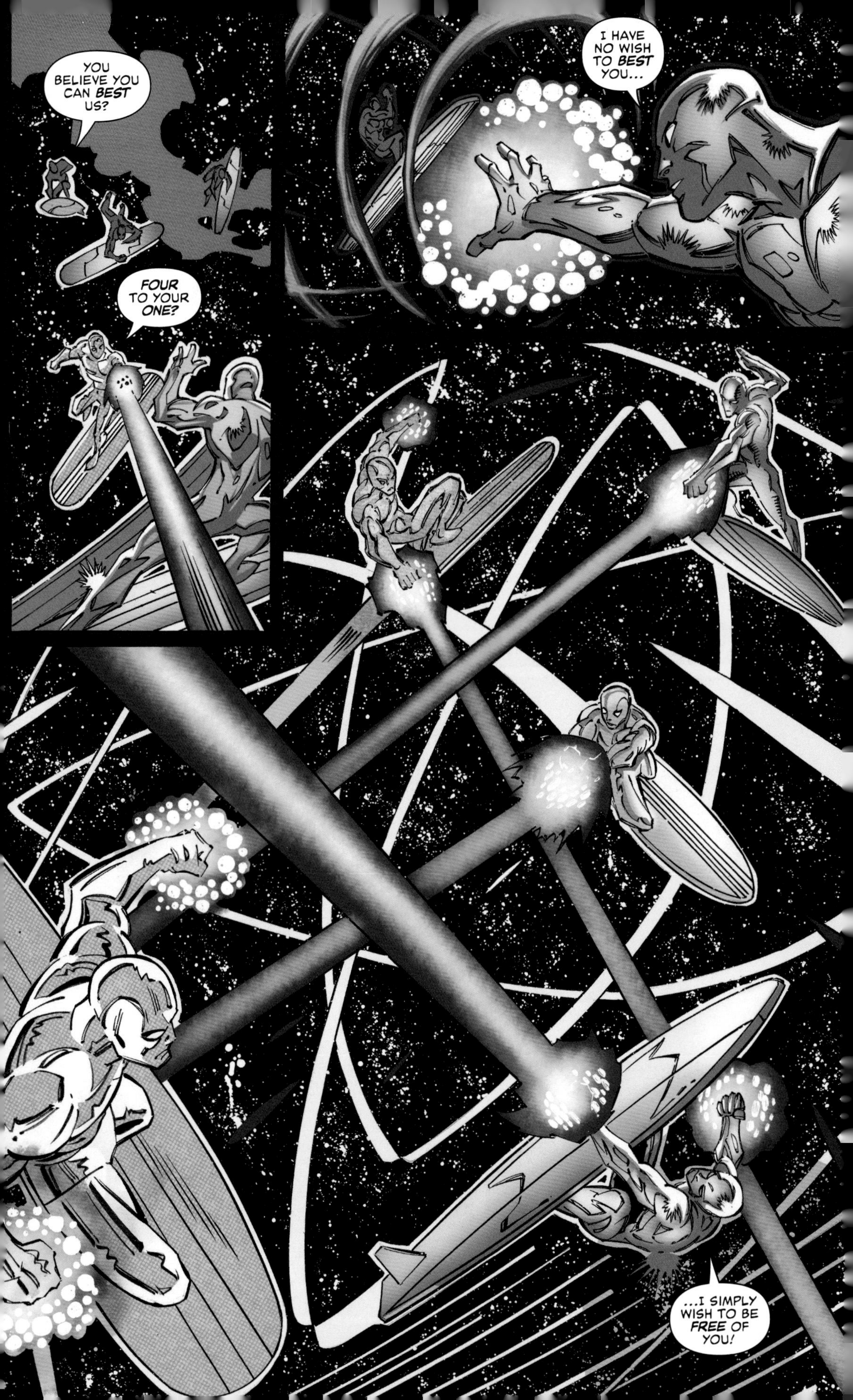
YOU BELIEVE YOU CAN *BEST* US?
I HAVE NO WISH TO *BEST* YOU...
FOUR TO YOUR *ONE?*
...I SIMPLY WISH TO BE *FREE* OF YOU!

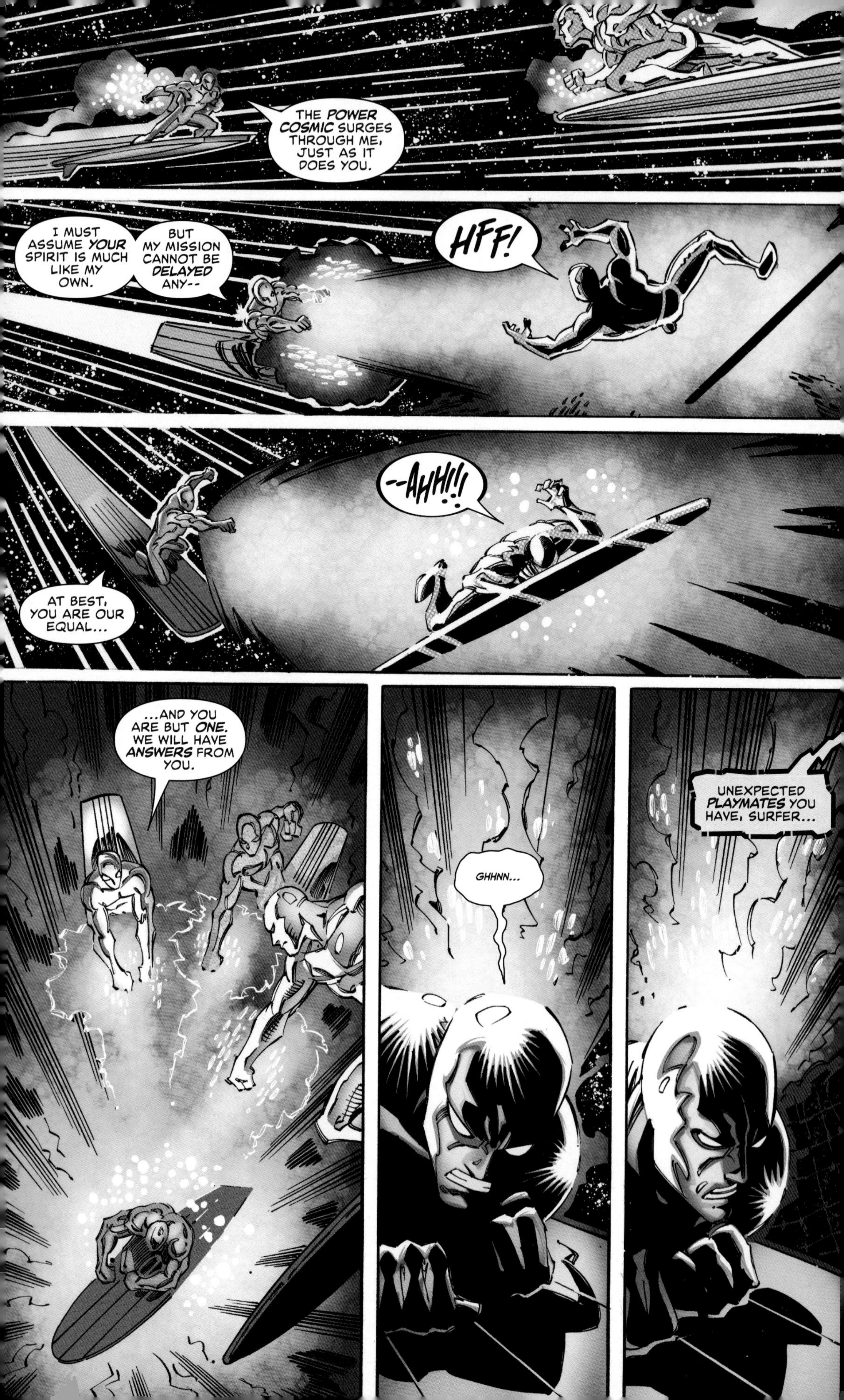
THE POWER COSMIC SURGES THROUGH ME, JUST AS IT DOES YOU.
I MUST ASSUME YOUR SPIRIT IS MUCH LIKE MY OWN.
BUT MY MISSION CANNOT BE DELAYED ANY--
HFF!
--AHH!!!
AT BEST, YOU ARE OUR EQUAL...
...AND YOU ARE BUT ONE. WE WILL HAVE ANSWERS FROM YOU.
GHHNN...
UNEXPECTED PLAYMATES YOU HAVE, SURFER...

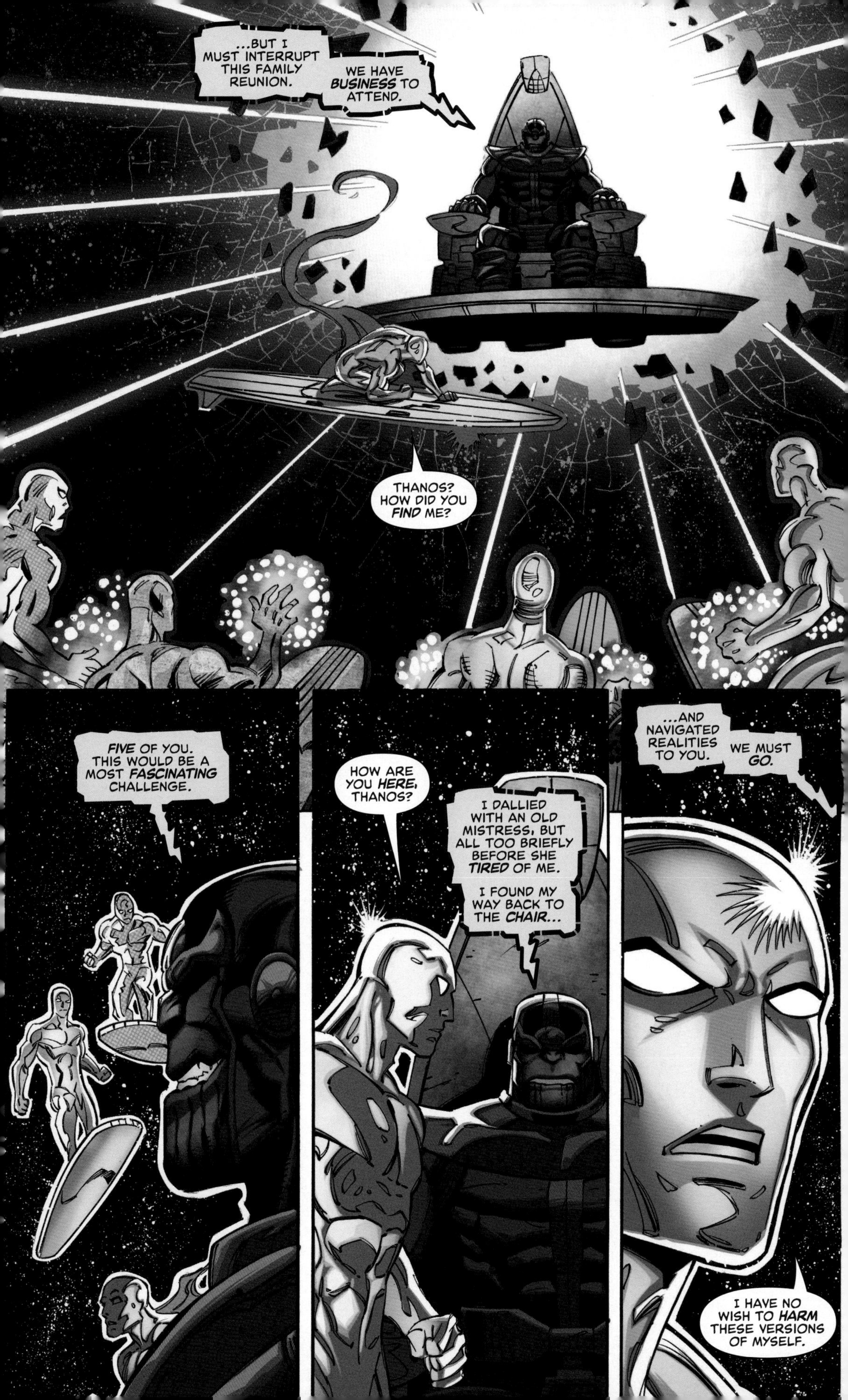
...BUT I MUST INTERRUPT THIS FAMILY REUNION.
WE HAVE BUSINESS TO ATTEND.
THANOS? HOW DID YOU FIND ME?
FIVE OF YOU. THIS WOULD BE A MOST FASCINATING CHALLENGE.
HOW ARE YOU HERE, THANOS?
I DALLIED WITH AN OLD MISTRESS, BUT ALL TOO BRIEFLY BEFORE SHE TIRED OF ME.
I FOUND MY WAY BACK TO THE CHAIR...
...AND NAVIGATED REALITIES TO YOU.
WE MUST GO.
I HAVE NO WISH TO HARM THESE VERSIONS OF MYSELF.

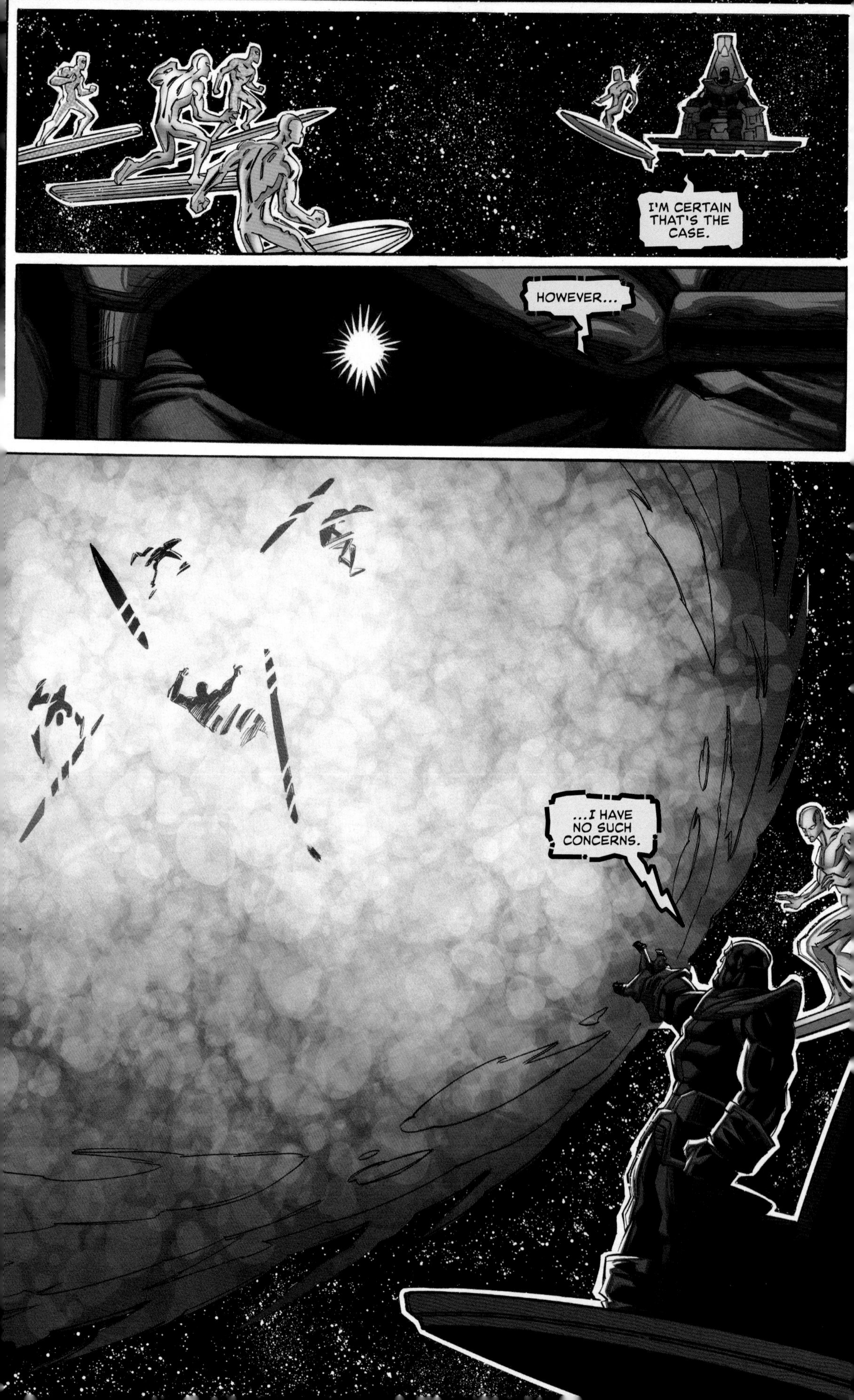
I'M CERTAIN THAT'S THE CASE.
HOWEVER...
...I HAVE NO SUCH CONCERNS.

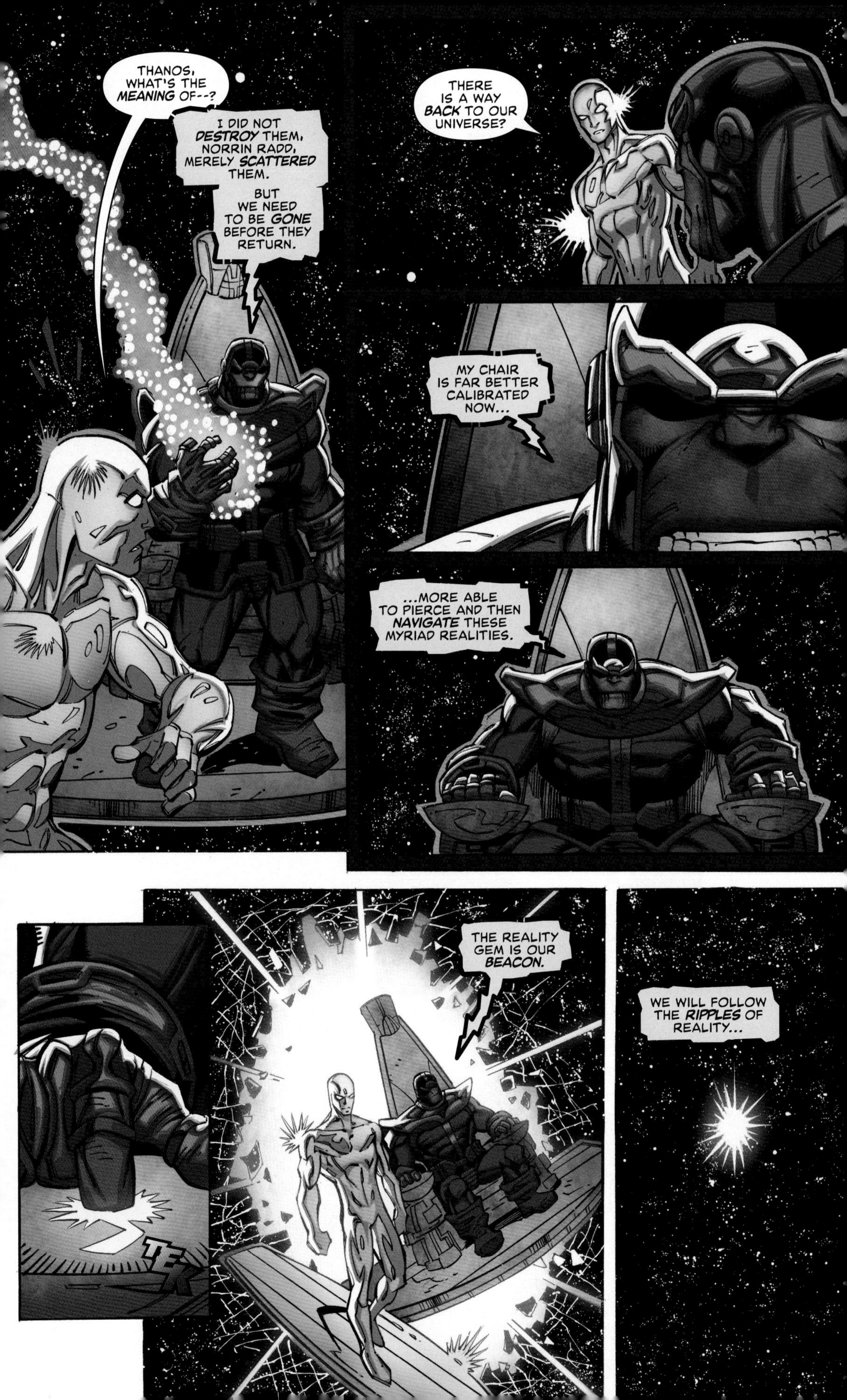
THANOS, WHAT'S THE MEANING OF--?
I DID NOT DESTROY THEM, NORRIN RADD, MERELY SCATTERED THEM.
BUT WE NEED TO BE GONE BEFORE THEY RETURN.
THERE IS A WAY BACK TO OUR UNIVERSE?
MY CHAIR IS FAR BETTER CALIBRATED NOW...
...MORE ABLE TO PIERCE AND THEN NAVIGATE THESE MYRIAD REALITIES.
TEK
THE REALITY GEM IS OUR BEACON.
WE WILL FOLLOW THE RIPPLES OF REALITY...

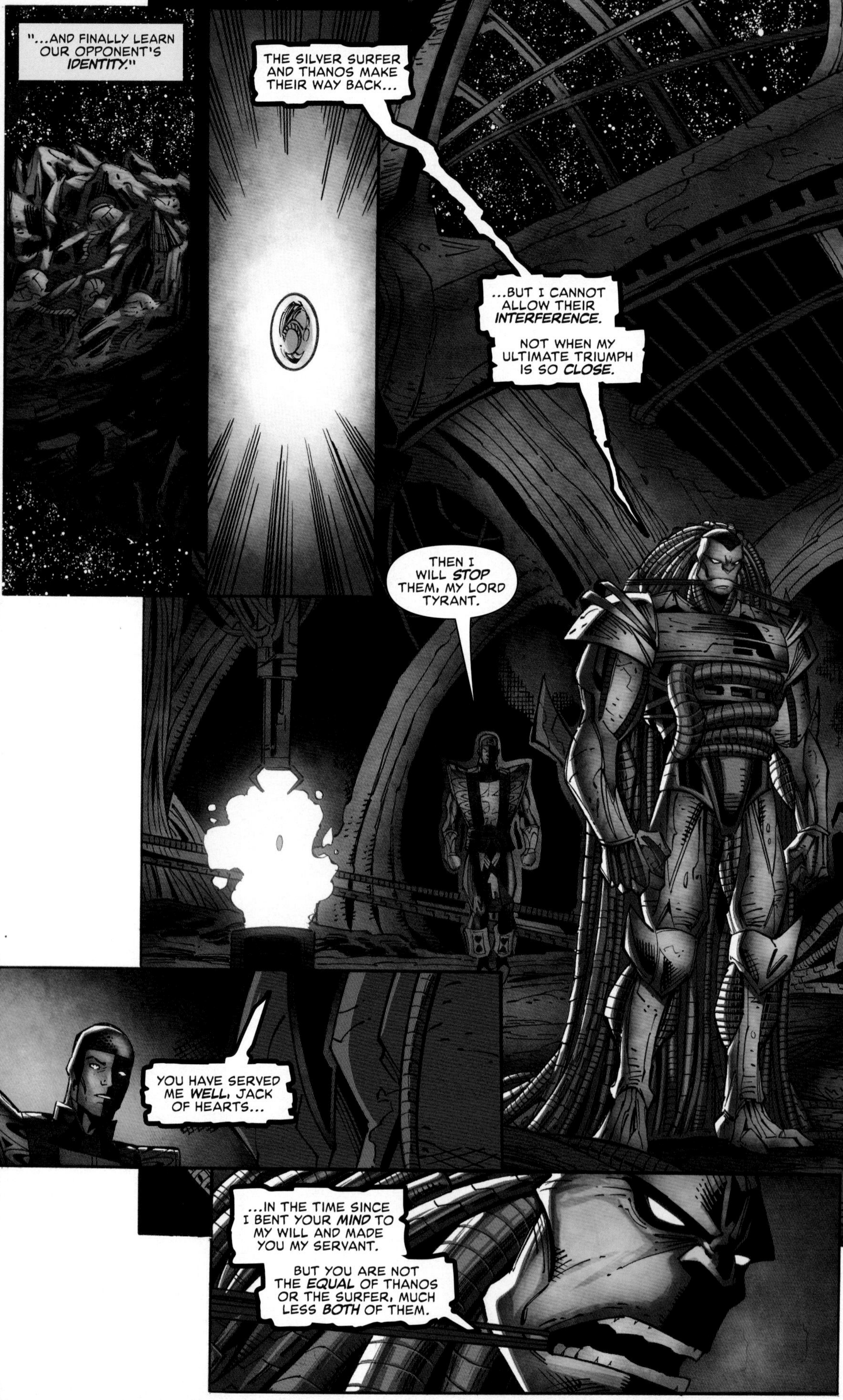
"...AND FINALLY LEARN OUR OPPONENT'S IDENTITY."
THE SILVER SURFER AND THANOS MAKE THEIR WAY BACK...
...BUT I CANNOT ALLOW THEIR INTERFERENCE.
NOT WHEN MY ULTIMATE TRIUMPH IS SO CLOSE.
THEN I WILL STOP THEM, MY LORD TYRANT.
YOU HAVE SERVED ME WELL, JACK OF HEARTS...
...IN THE TIME SINCE I BENT YOUR MIND TO MY WILL AND MADE YOU MY SERVANT.
BUT YOU ARE NOT THE EQUAL OF THANOS OR THE SURFER, MUCH LESS BOTH OF THEM.

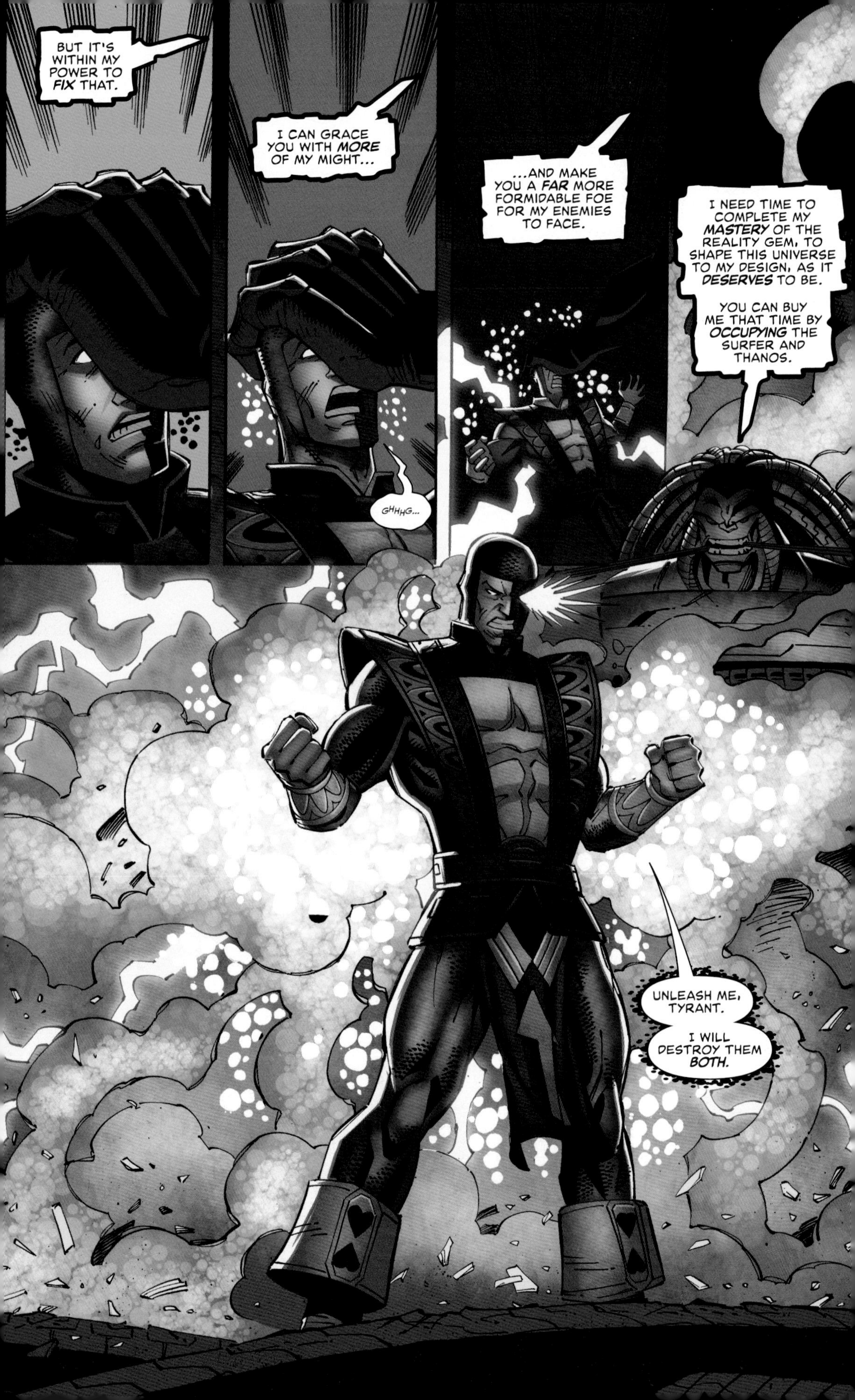
BUT IT'S WITHIN MY POWER TO FIX THAT.
I CAN GRACE YOU WITH MORE OF MY MIGHT...
GHHHG...
...AND MAKE YOU A FAR MORE FORMIDABLE FOE FOR MY ENEMIES TO FACE.
I NEED TIME TO COMPLETE MY MASTERY OF THE REALITY GEM, TO SHAPE THIS UNIVERSE TO MY DESIGN, AS IT DESERVES TO BE.
YOU CAN BUY ME THAT TIME BY OCCUPYING THE SURFER AND THANOS.
UNLEASH ME, TYRANT.
I WILL DESTROY THEM BOTH.

THE EMANATIONS OF THE REALITY GEM ARE *STRONG*.

WE SHOULD BE *CLOSE* TO OUR QUARRY.

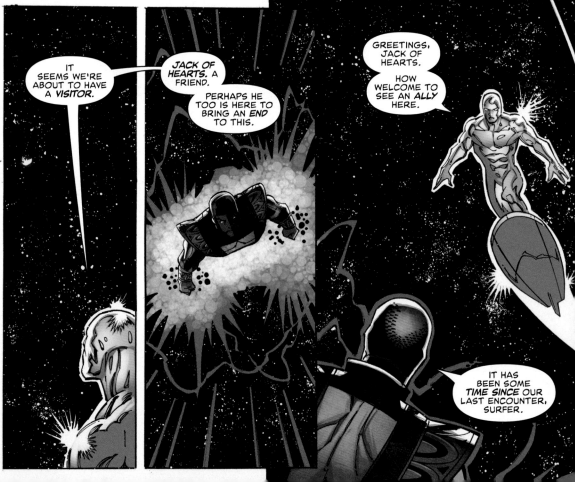

IT SEEMS WE'RE ABOUT TO HAVE A *VISITOR*.

JACK OF HEARTS. A FRIEND.

PERHAPS HE TOO IS HERE TO BRING AN *END* TO THIS.

GREETINGS, JACK OF HEARTS.

HOW WELCOME TO SEE AN *ALLY* HERE.

IT HAS BEEN SOME *TIME SINCE* OUR LAST ENCOUNTER, SURFER.

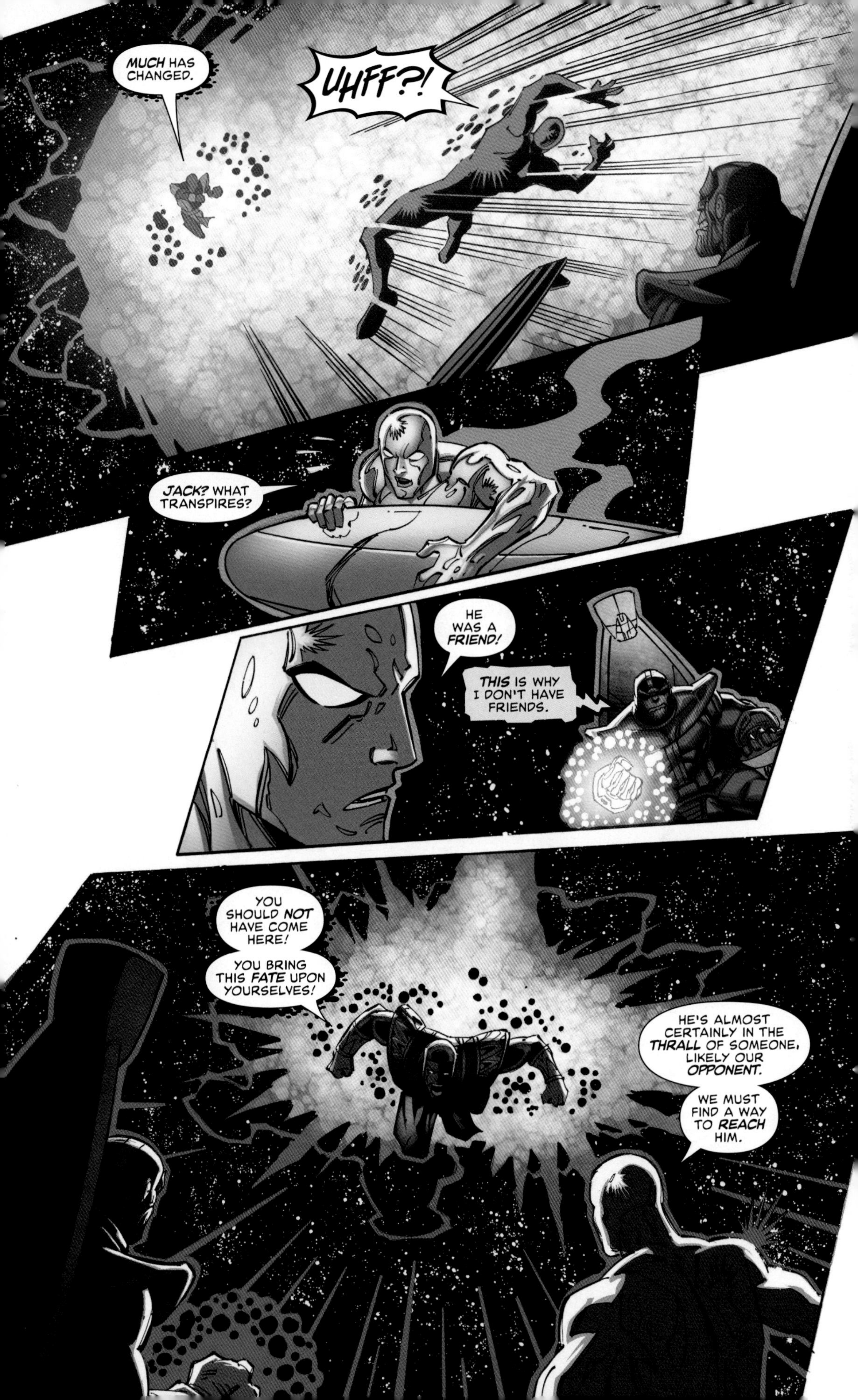
MUCH HAS CHANGED.
UHFF?!
JACK? WHAT TRANSPIRES?
HE WAS A FRIEND!
THIS IS WHY I DON'T HAVE FRIENDS.
YOU SHOULD NOT HAVE COME HERE!
YOU BRING THIS FATE UPON YOURSELVES!
HE'S ALMOST CERTAINLY IN THE THRALL OF SOMEONE, LIKELY OUR OPPONENT.
WE MUST FIND A WAY TO REACH HIM.

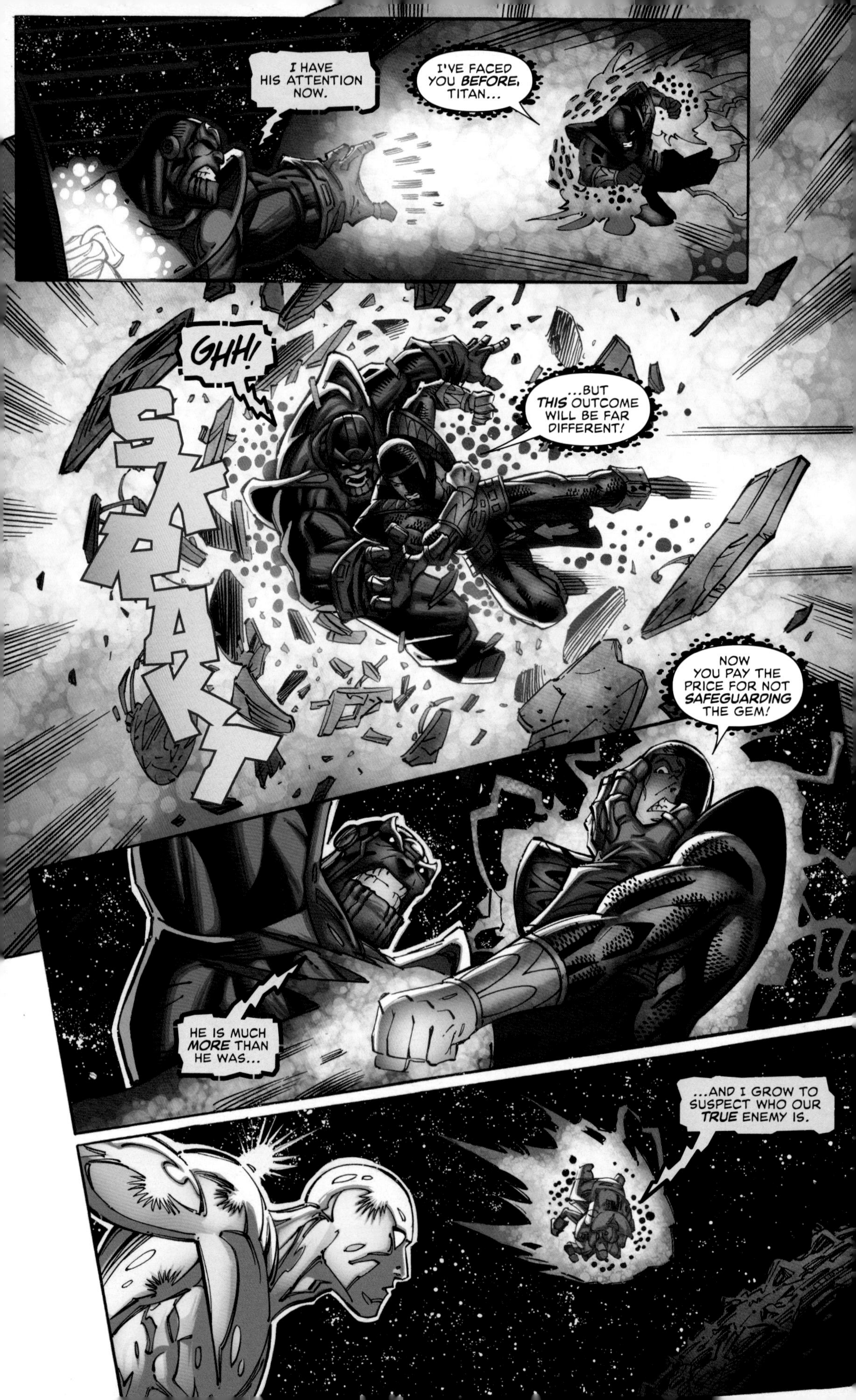
I HAVE HIS ATTENTION NOW.
I'VE FACED YOU BEFORE, TITAN...
GHH!
SKRAKT
...BUT THIS OUTCOME WILL BE FAR DIFFERENT!
NOW YOU PAY THE PRICE FOR NOT SAFEGUARDING THE GEM!
HE IS MUCH MORE THAN HE WAS...
...AND I GROW TO SUSPECT WHO OUR TRUE ENEMY IS.

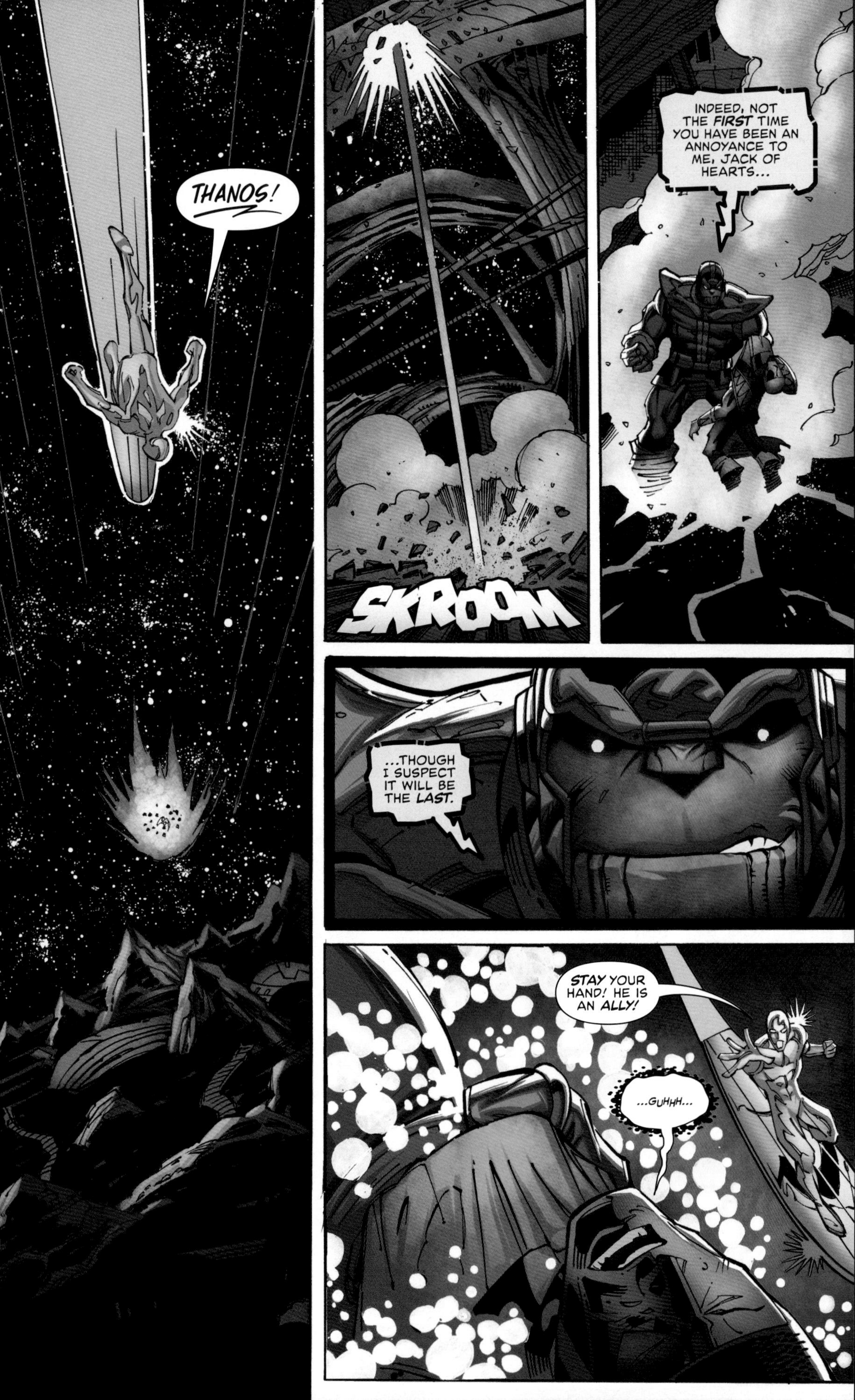
THANOS!
SKROOM
INDEED, NOT THE FIRST TIME YOU HAVE BEEN AN ANNOYANCE TO ME, JACK OF HEARTS...
...THOUGH I SUSPECT IT WILL BE THE LAST.
STAY YOUR HAND! HE IS AN ALLY!
...GUHHH...

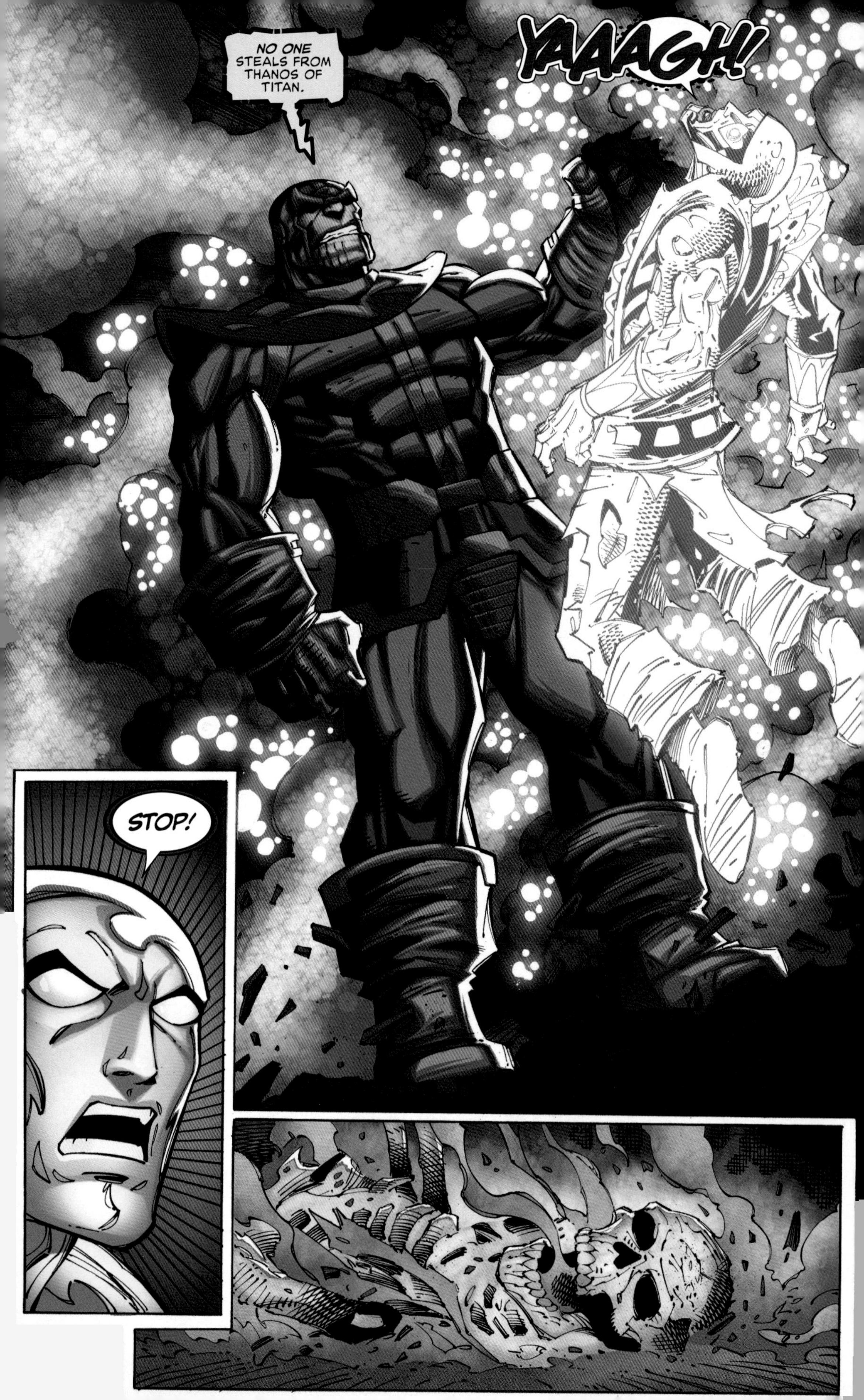
NO ONE STEALS FROM THANOS OF TITAN.
YAAAGH!
STOP!

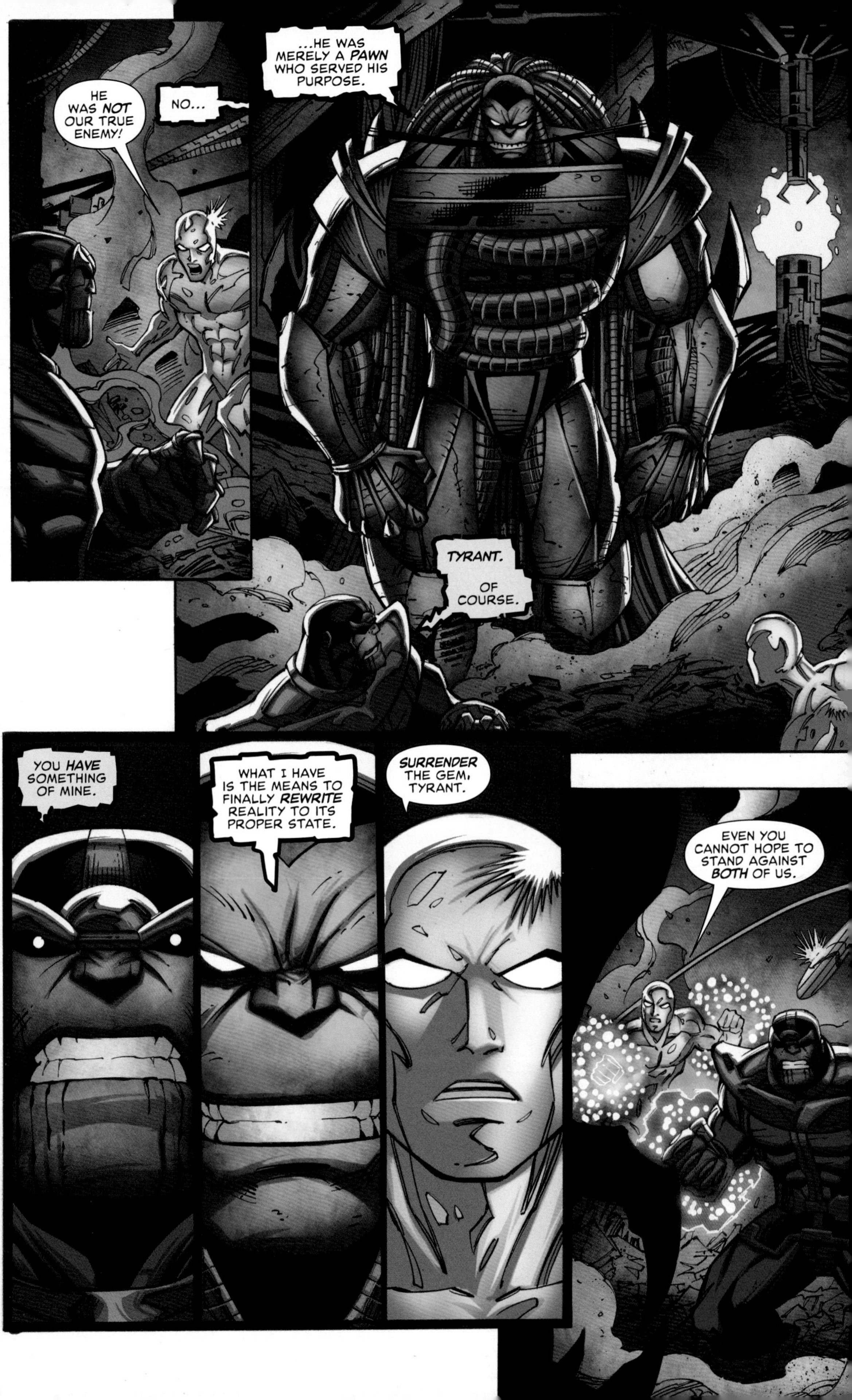

HE WAS NOT OUR TRUE ENEMY!
NO...
...HE WAS MERELY A PAWN WHO SERVED HIS PURPOSE.
TYRANT.
OF COURSE.
YOU HAVE SOMETHING OF MINE.
WHAT I HAVE IS THE MEANS TO FINALLY REWRITE REALITY TO ITS PROPER STATE.
SURRENDER THE GEM, TYRANT.
EVEN YOU CANNOT HOPE TO STAND AGAINST BOTH OF US.

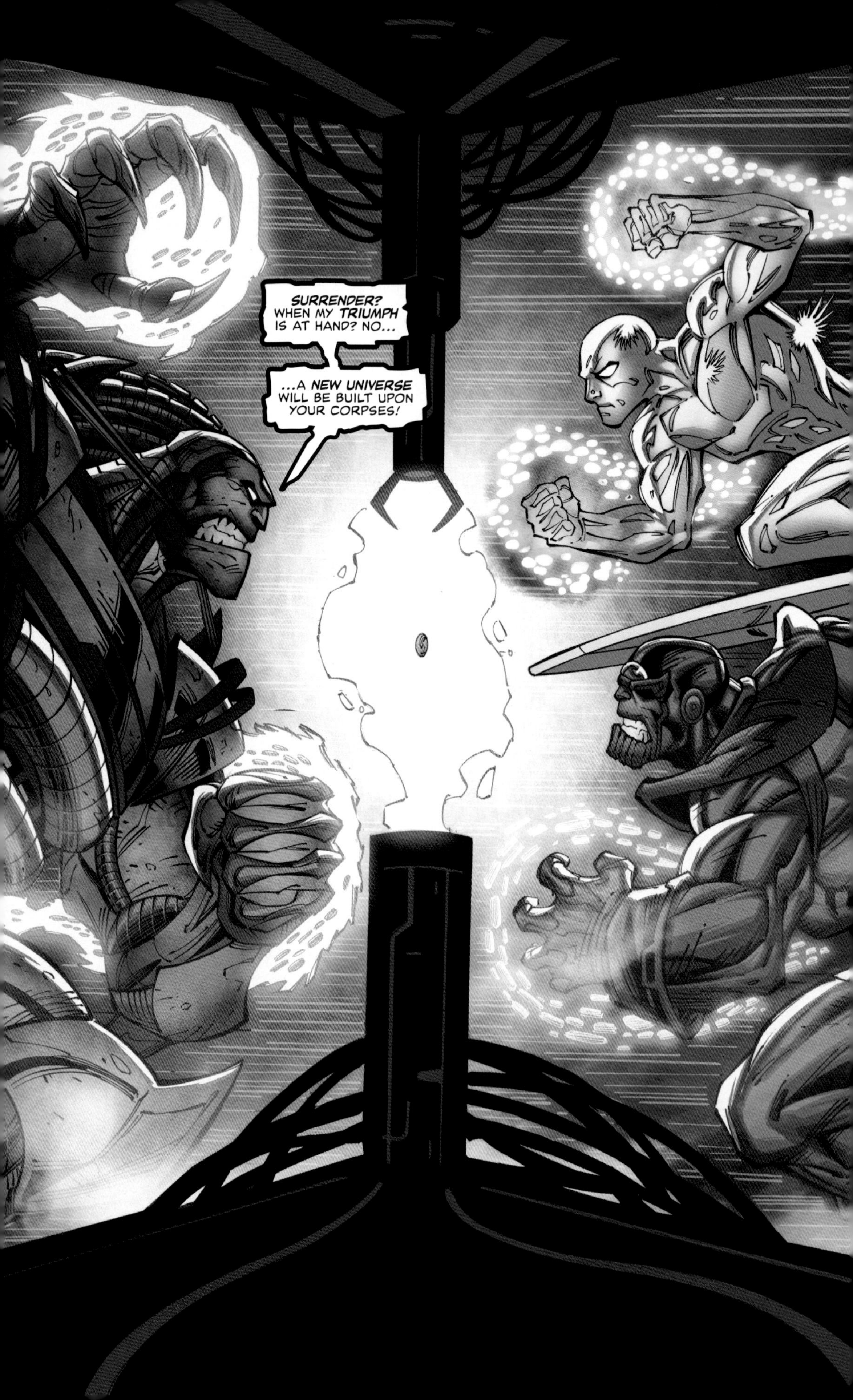
SURRENDER? WHEN MY TRIUMPH IS AT HAND? NO...
...A NEW UNIVERSE WILL BE BUILT UPON YOUR CORPSES!

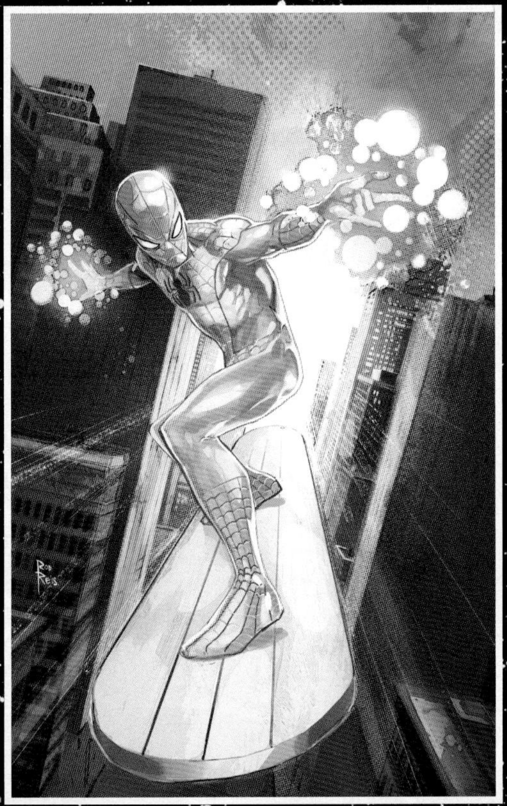

#4 SPIDER-MAN 60TH ANNIVERSARY VARIANT BY
ROD REIS

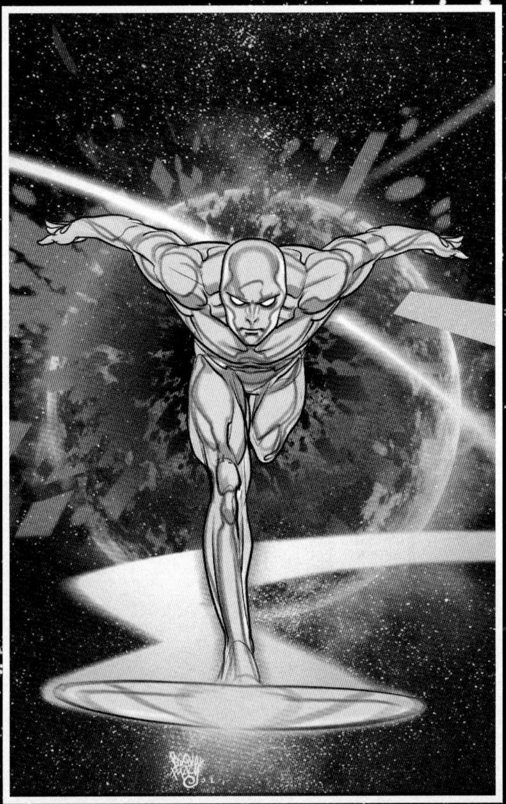

#4 VARIANT BY
PASQUAL FERRY

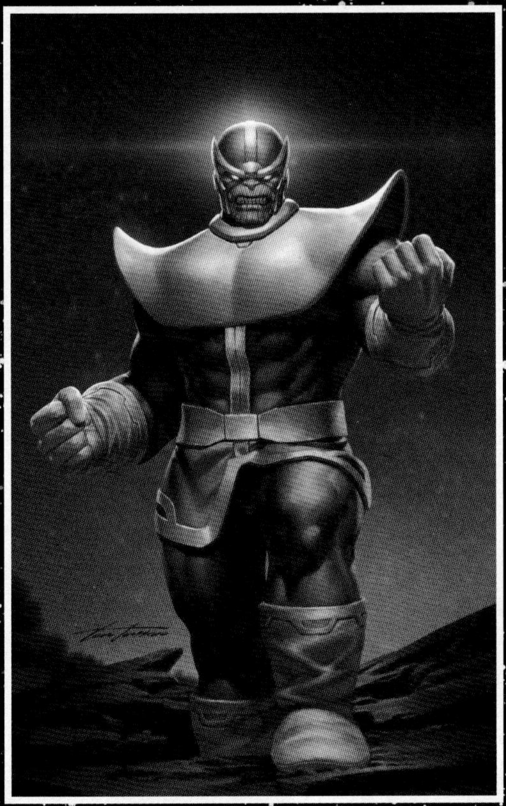

#5 VARIANT BY
JUNGGEUN YOON

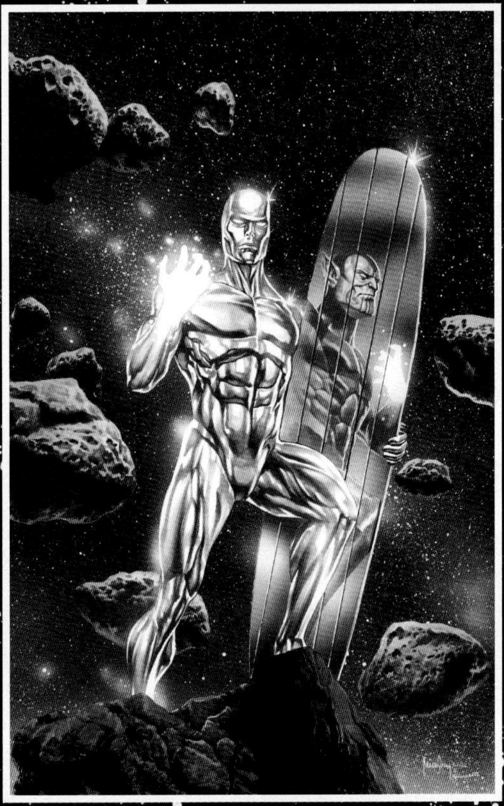

#5 SKRULL VARIANT BY
MICO SUAYAN & ALEX GUIMARÃES

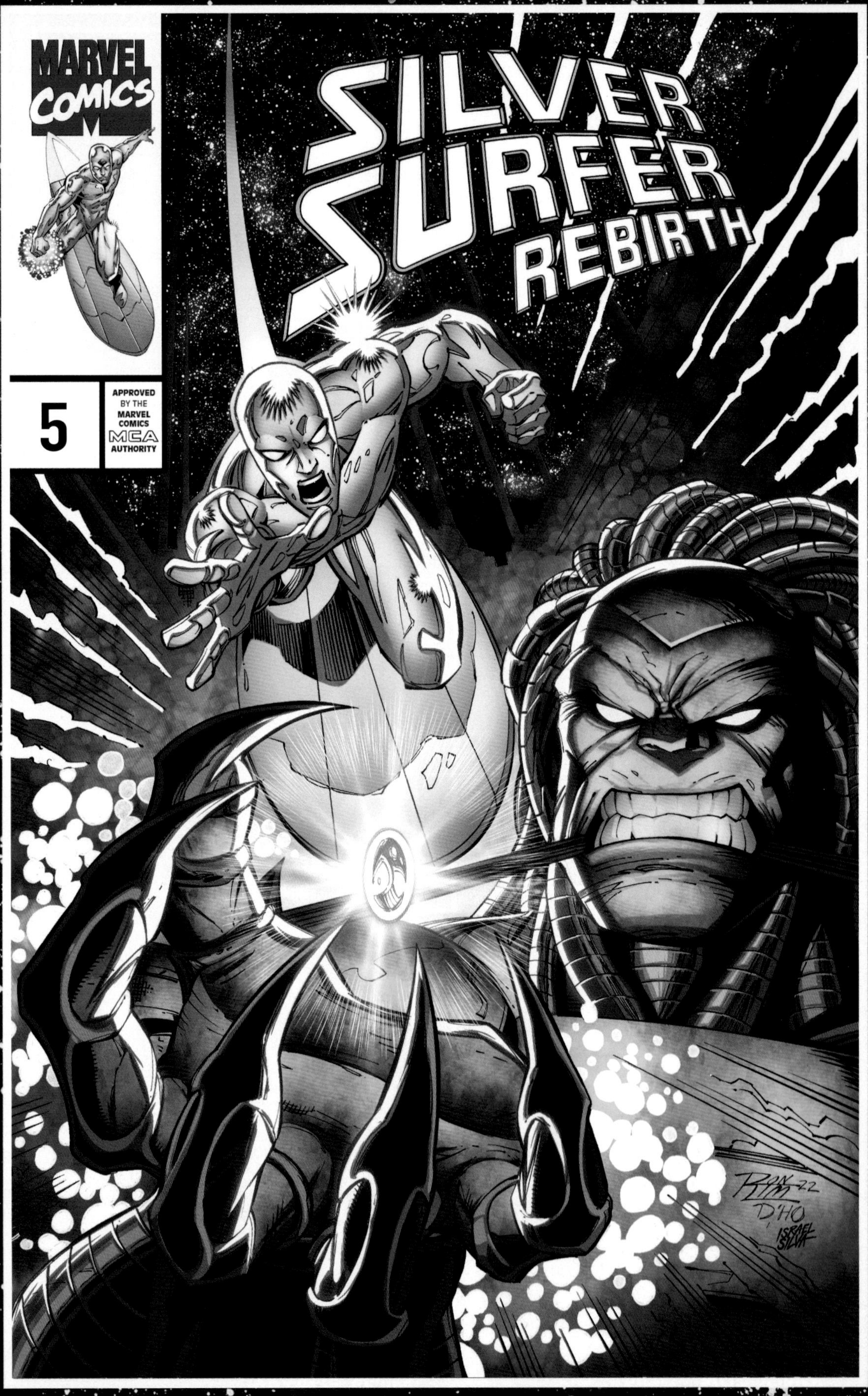

MARVEL COMICS
SILVER SURFER
REBIRTH
5
APPROVED BY THE MARVEL COMICS MCA AUTHORITY
RON LIM '22
D'HO
ISRAEL SILVA

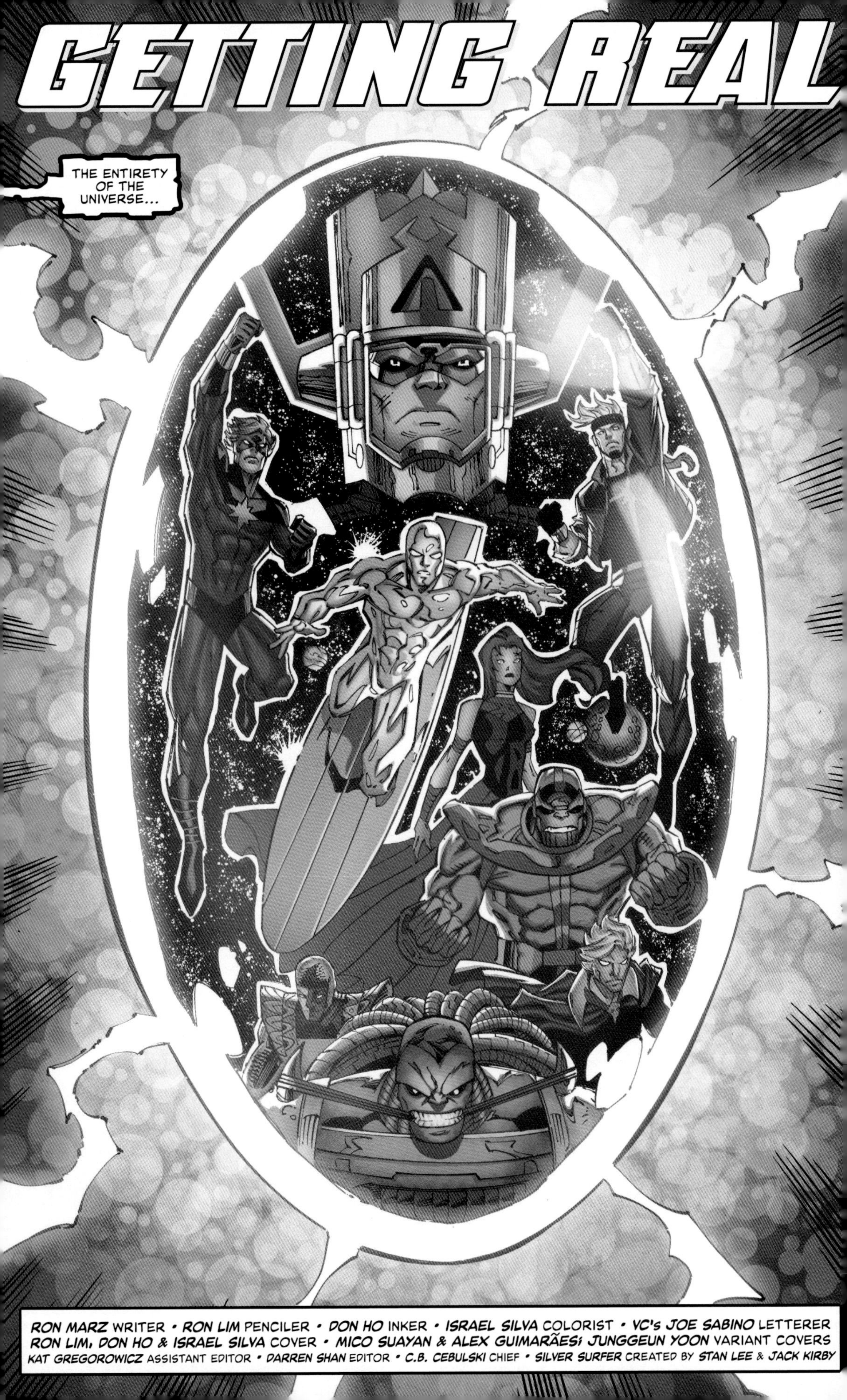
GETTING REAL
THE ENTIRETY OF THE UNIVERSE...
RON MARZ WRITER • RON LIM PENCILER • DON HO INKER • ISRAEL SILVA COLORIST • VC's JOE SABINO LETTERER
RON LIM, DON HO & ISRAEL SILVA COVER • MICO SUAYAN & ALEX GUIMARÃES; JUNGGEUN YOON VARIANT COVERS
KAT GREGOROWICZ ASSISTANT EDITOR • DARREN SHAN EDITOR • C.B. CEBULSKI CHIEF • SILVER SURFER CREATED BY STAN LEE & JACK KIRBY

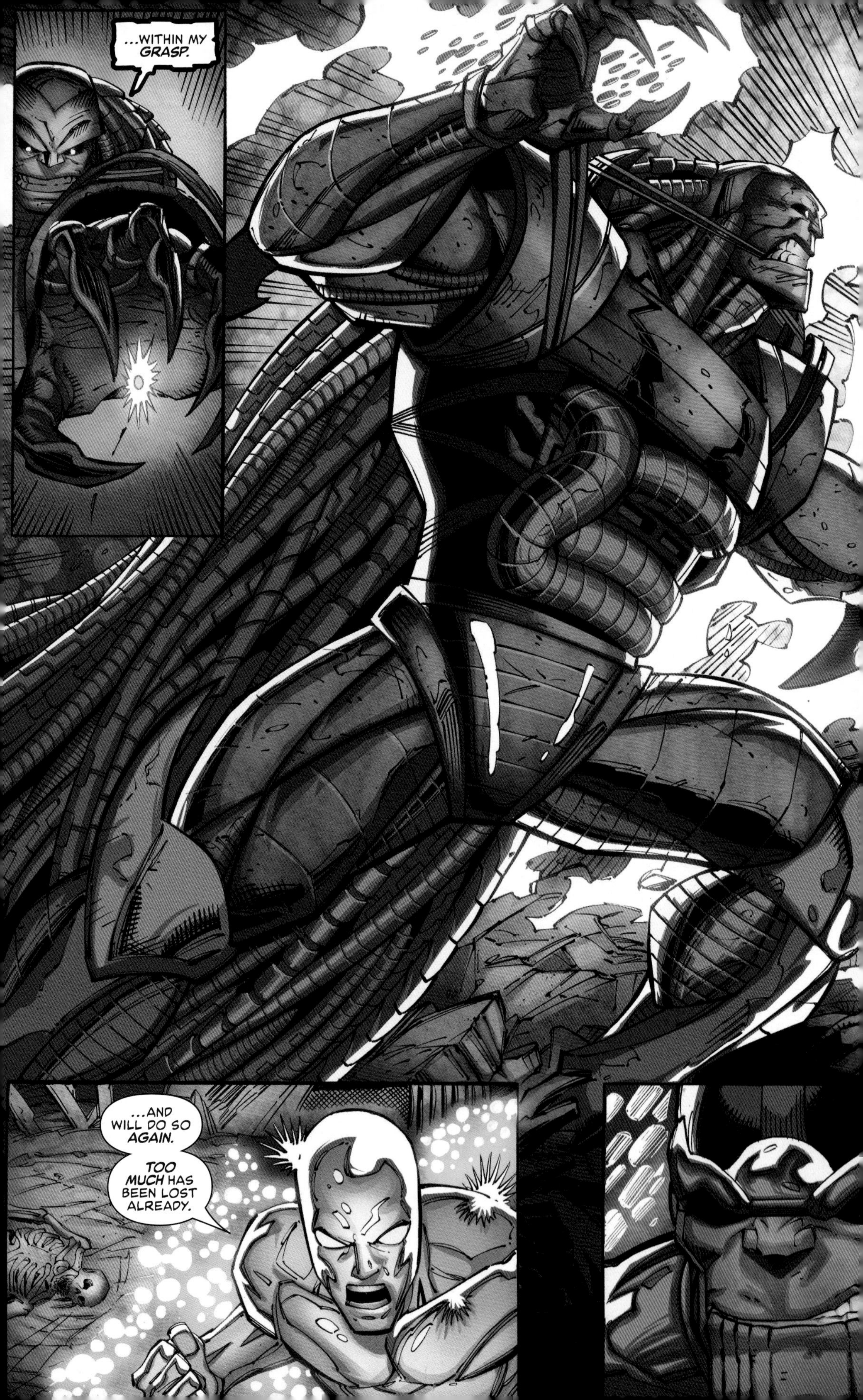
...WITHIN MY GRASP.
...AND WILL DO SO AGAIN.
TOO MUCH HAS BEEN LOST ALREADY.

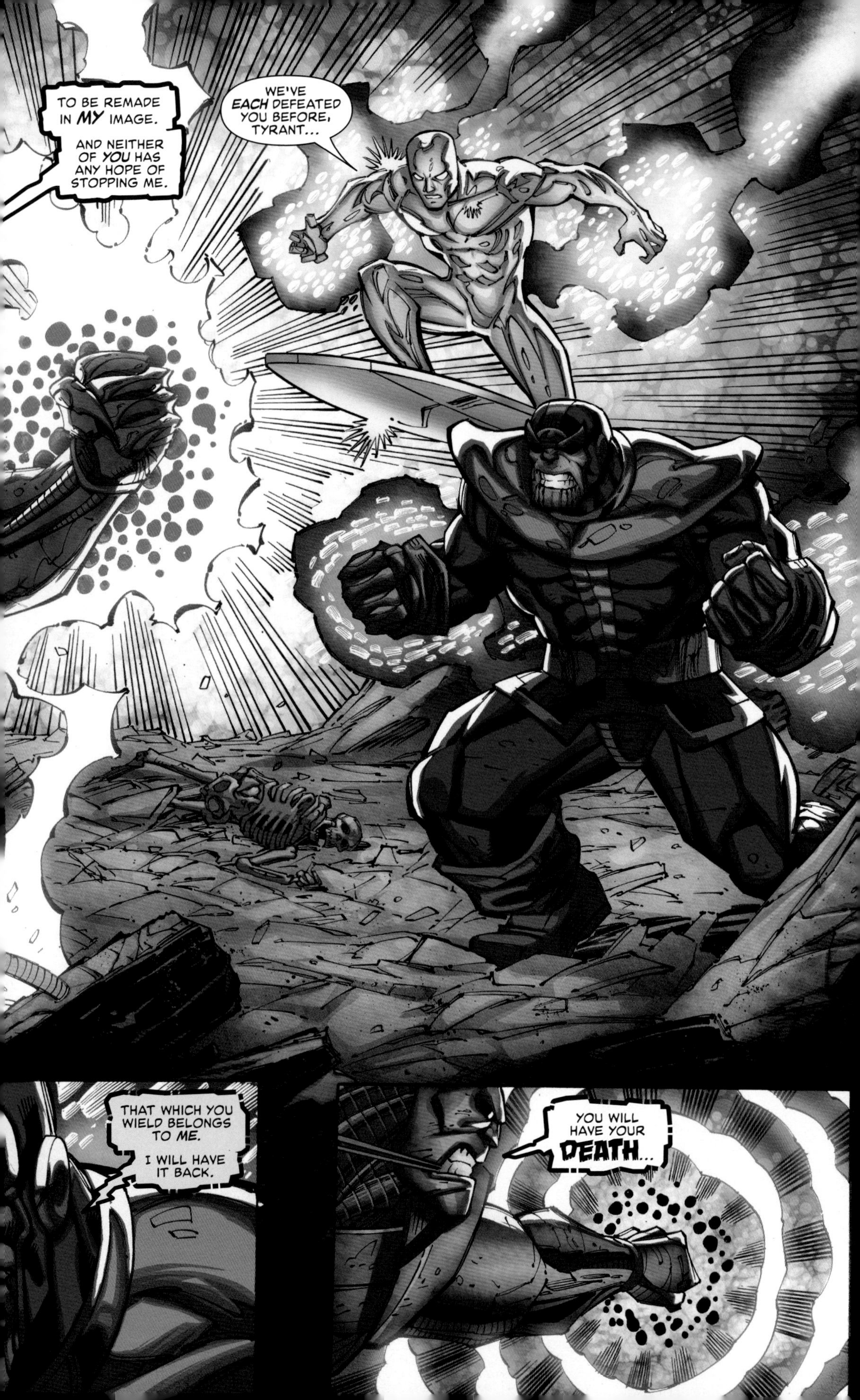
TO BE REMADE IN MY IMAGE.
AND NEITHER OF YOU HAS ANY HOPE OF STOPPING ME.
WE'VE EACH DEFEATED YOU BEFORE, TYRANT...
THAT WHICH YOU WIELD BELONGS TO ME.
I WILL HAVE IT BACK.
YOU WILL HAVE YOUR DEATH...

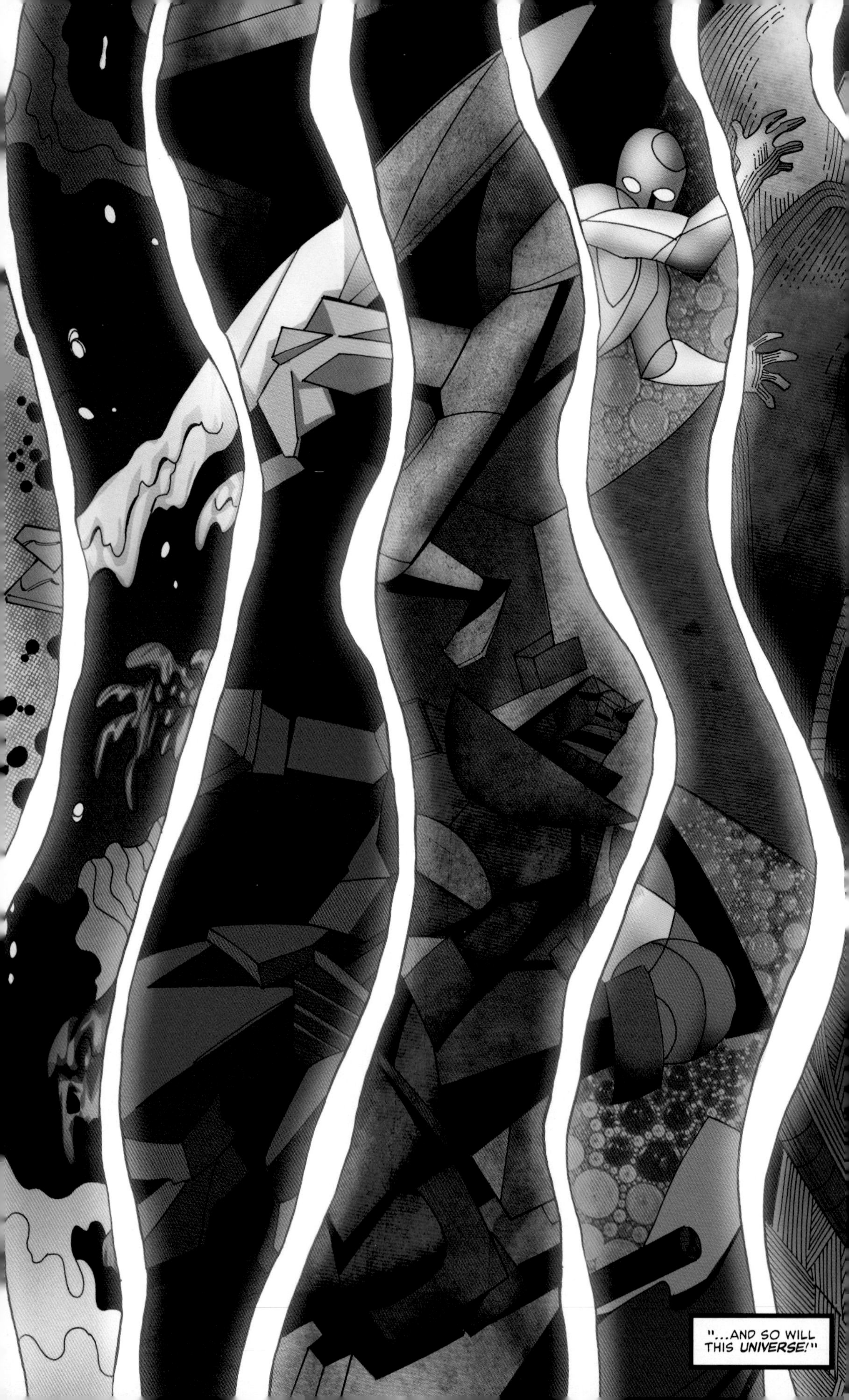
"...AND SO WILL
THIS UNIVERSE!"

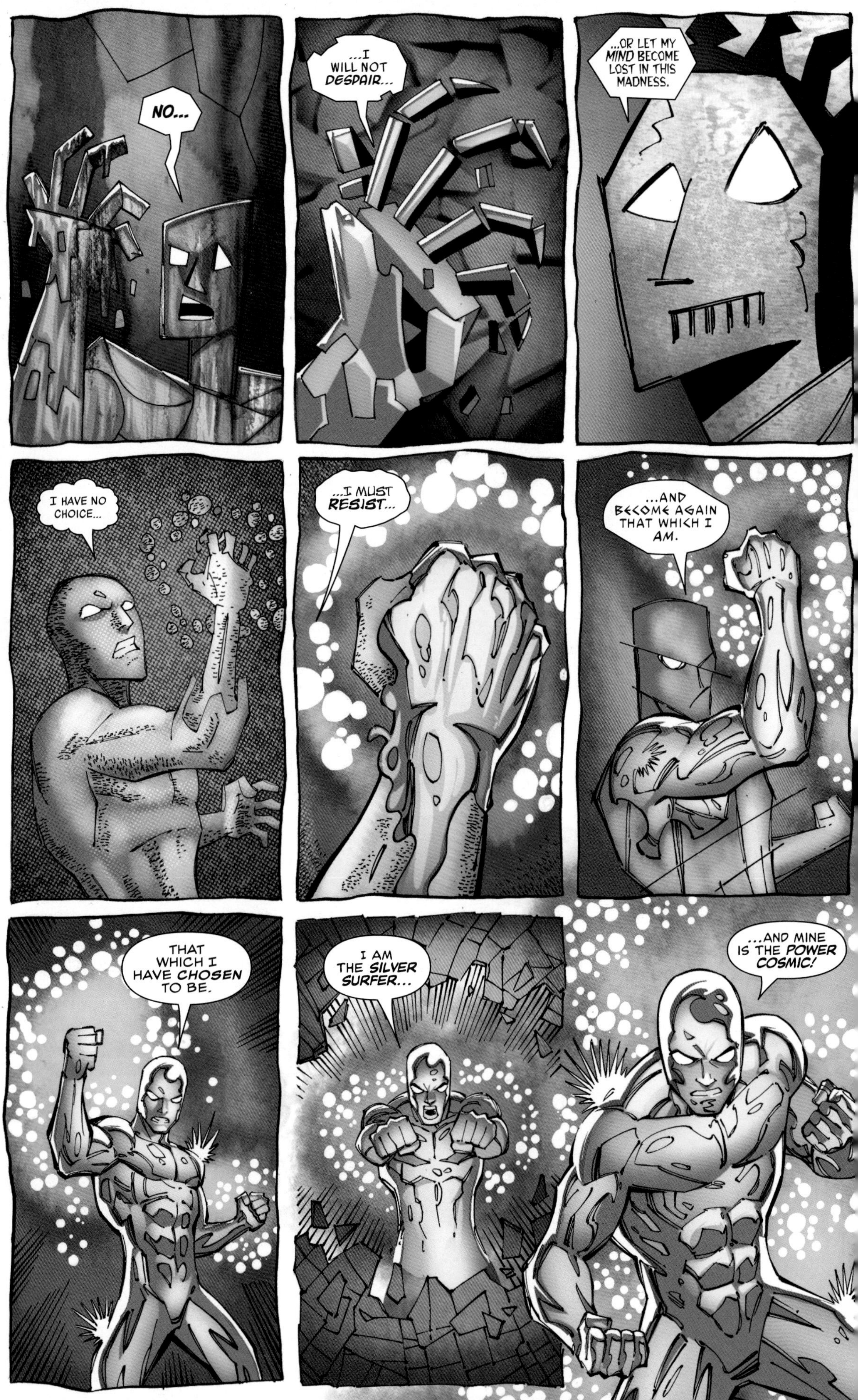
NO...
...I WILL NOT DESPAIR...
...OR LET MY MIND BECOME LOST IN THIS MADNESS.
I HAVE NO CHOICE...
...I MUST RESIST...
...AND BECOME AGAIN THAT WHICH I AM.
THAT WHICH I HAVE CHOSEN TO BE.
I AM THE SILVER SURFER...
...AND MINE IS THE POWER COSMIC!

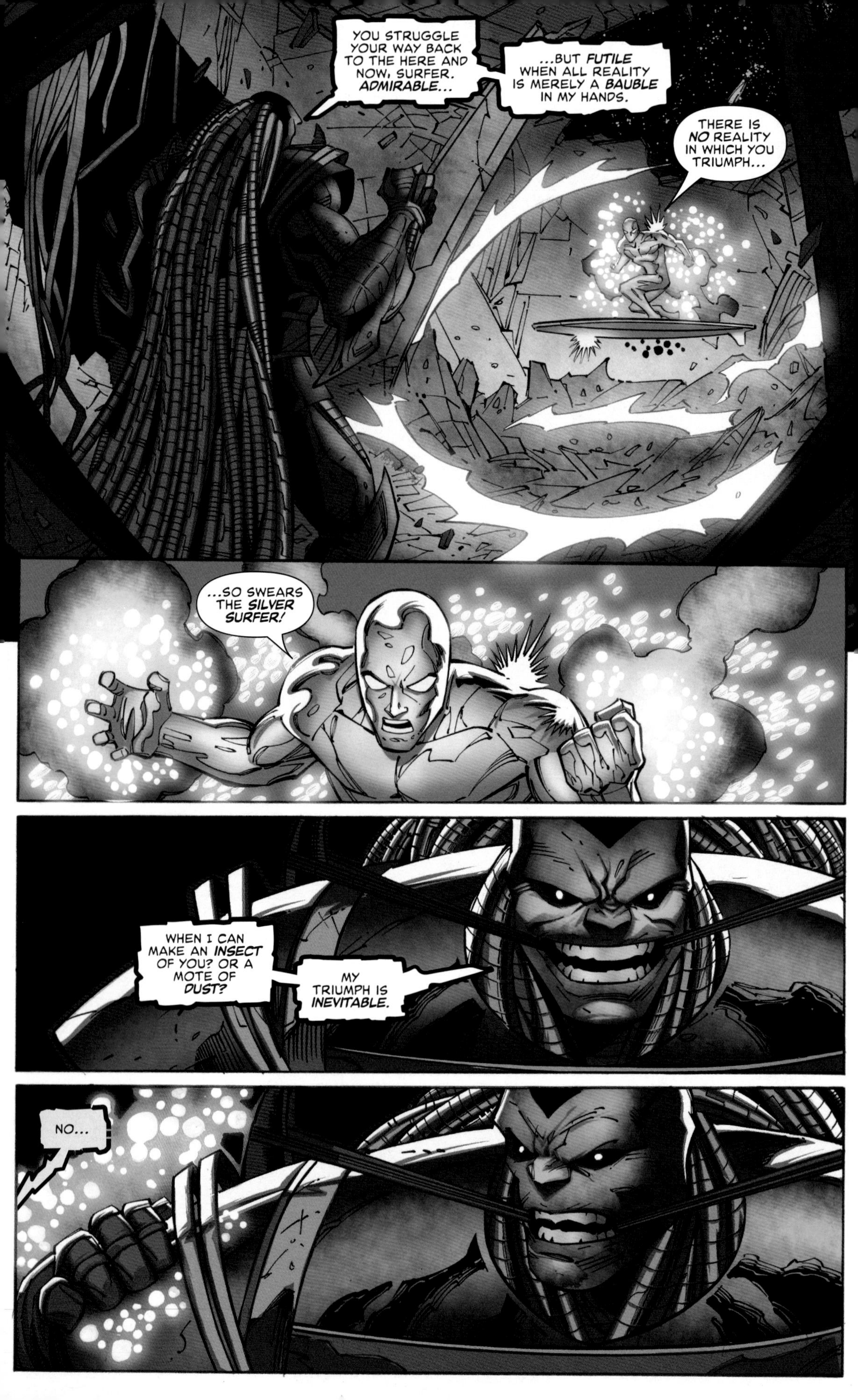
YOU STRUGGLE YOUR WAY BACK TO THE HERE AND NOW, SURFER. *ADMIRABLE*...
...BUT *FUTILE* WHEN ALL REALITY IS MERELY A *BAUBLE* IN MY HANDS.
THERE IS *NO* REALITY IN WHICH YOU TRIUMPH...
...SO SWEARS THE *SILVER SURFER!*
WHEN I CAN MAKE AN *INSECT* OF YOU? OR A MOTE OF *DUST?*
MY TRIUMPH IS *INEVITABLE.*
NO...

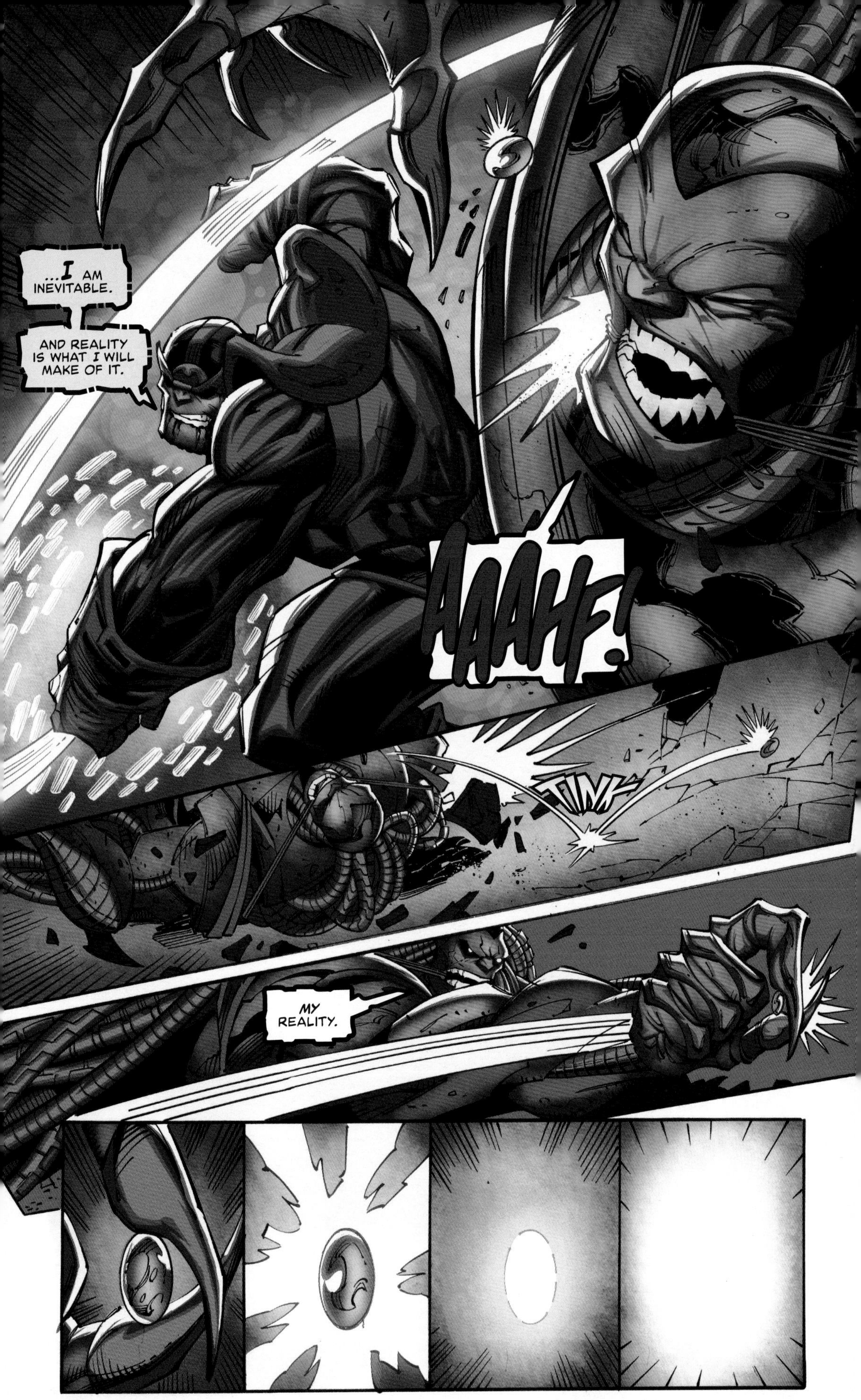
...I AM INEVITABLE.
AND REALITY IS WHAT I WILL MAKE OF IT.
AAAHF!
TINK
MY REALITY.

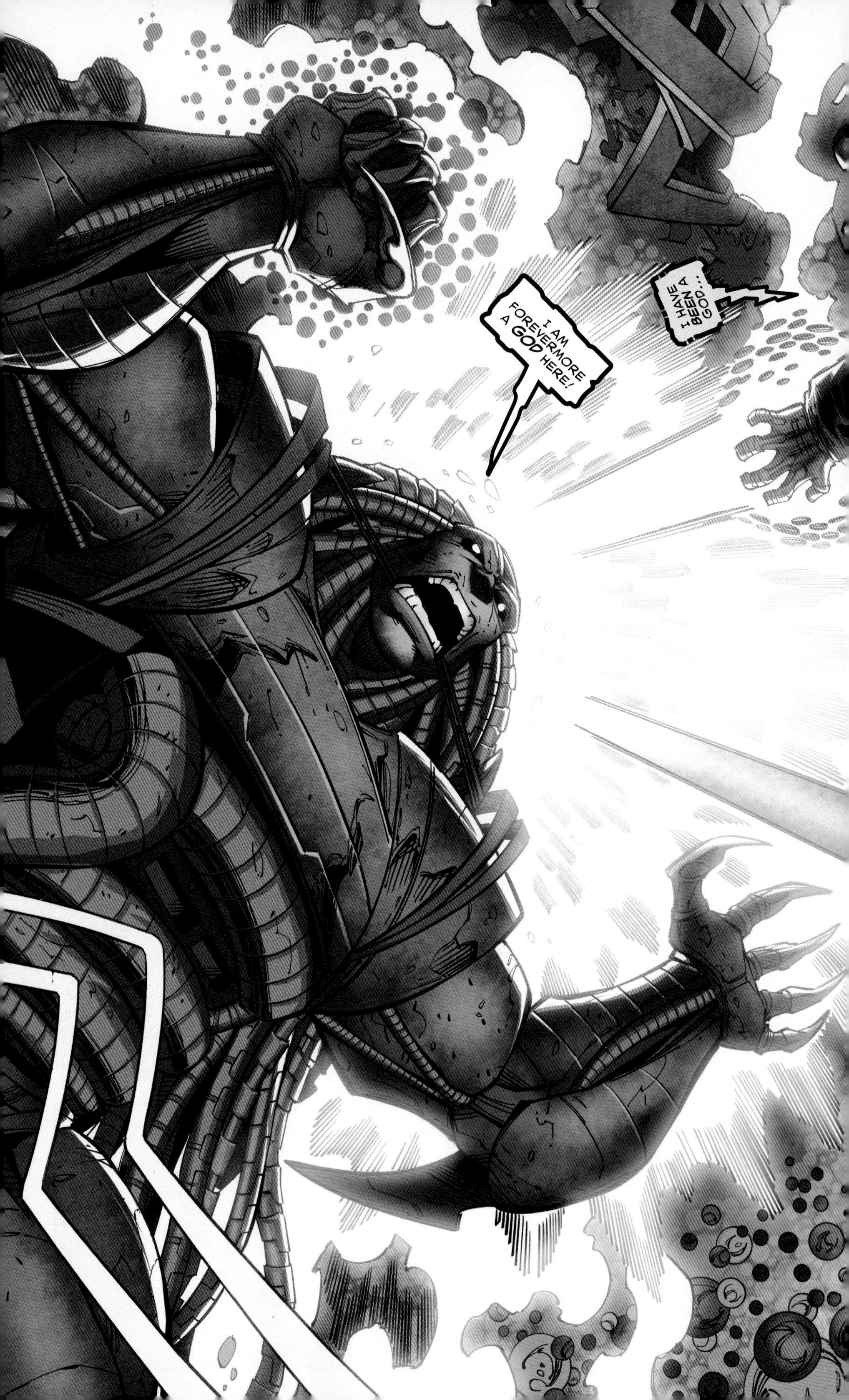
I HAVE BEEN A GOD...
I AM FOREVERMORE A GOD HERE!

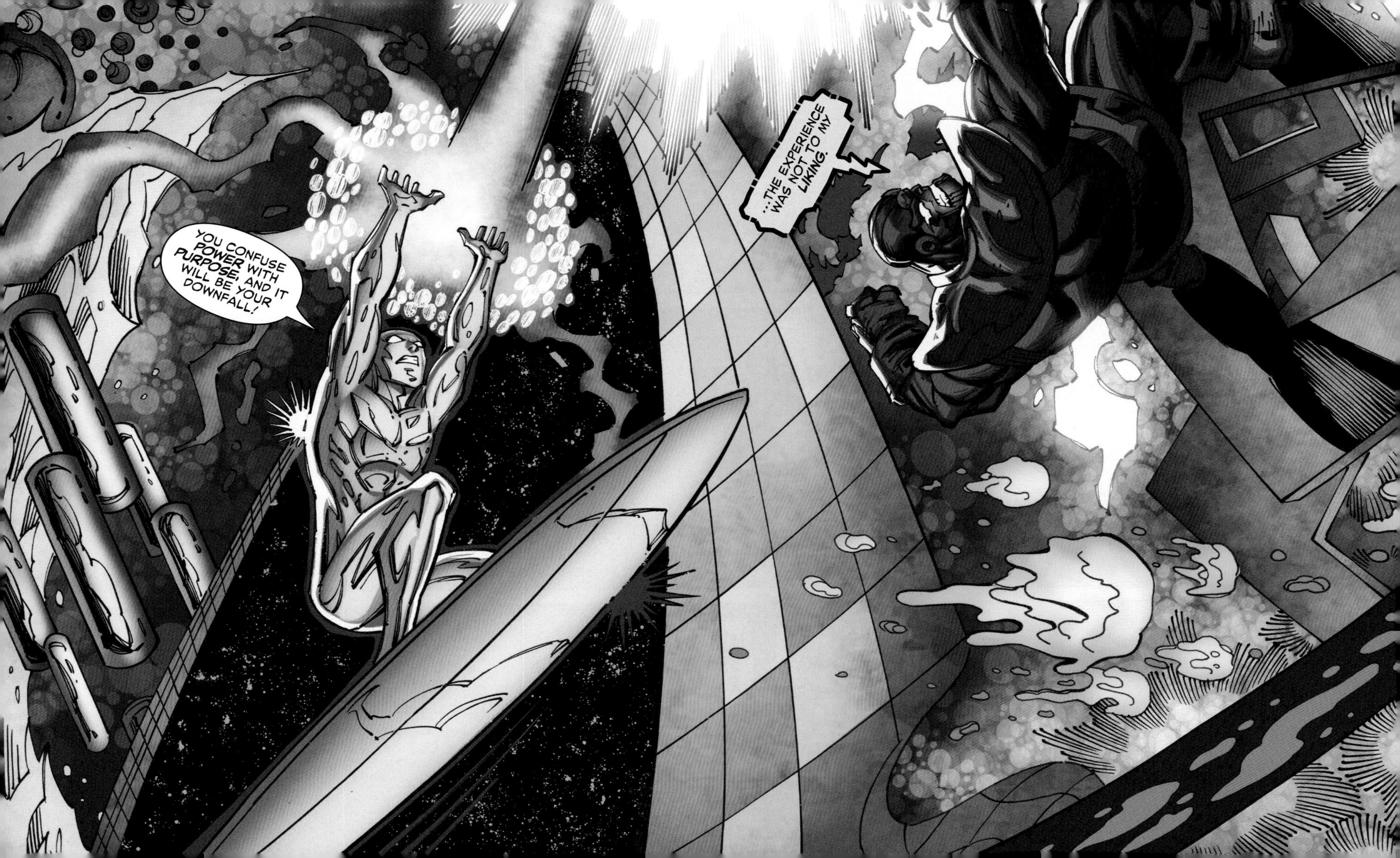
YOU CONFUSE POWER WITH PURPOSE, AND IT WILL BE YOUR DOWNFALL!
...THE EXPERIENCE WAS NOT TO MY LIKING.

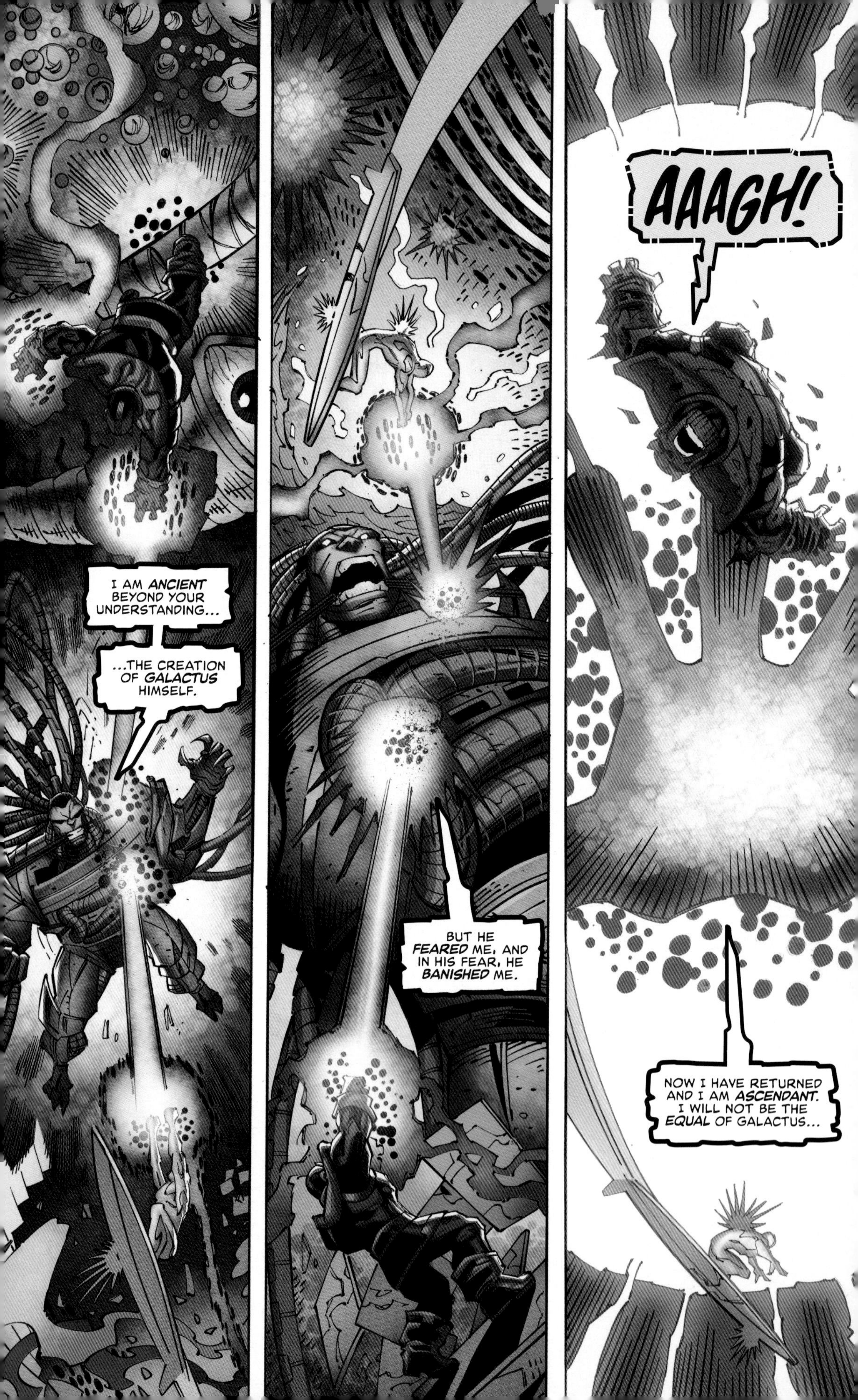
I AM ANCIENT BEYOND YOUR UNDERSTANDING...
...THE CREATION OF GALACTUS HIMSELF.
BUT HE FEARED ME, AND IN HIS FEAR, HE BANISHED ME.
AAAGH!
NOW I HAVE RETURNED AND I AM ASCENDANT. I WILL NOT BE THE EQUAL OF GALACTUS...

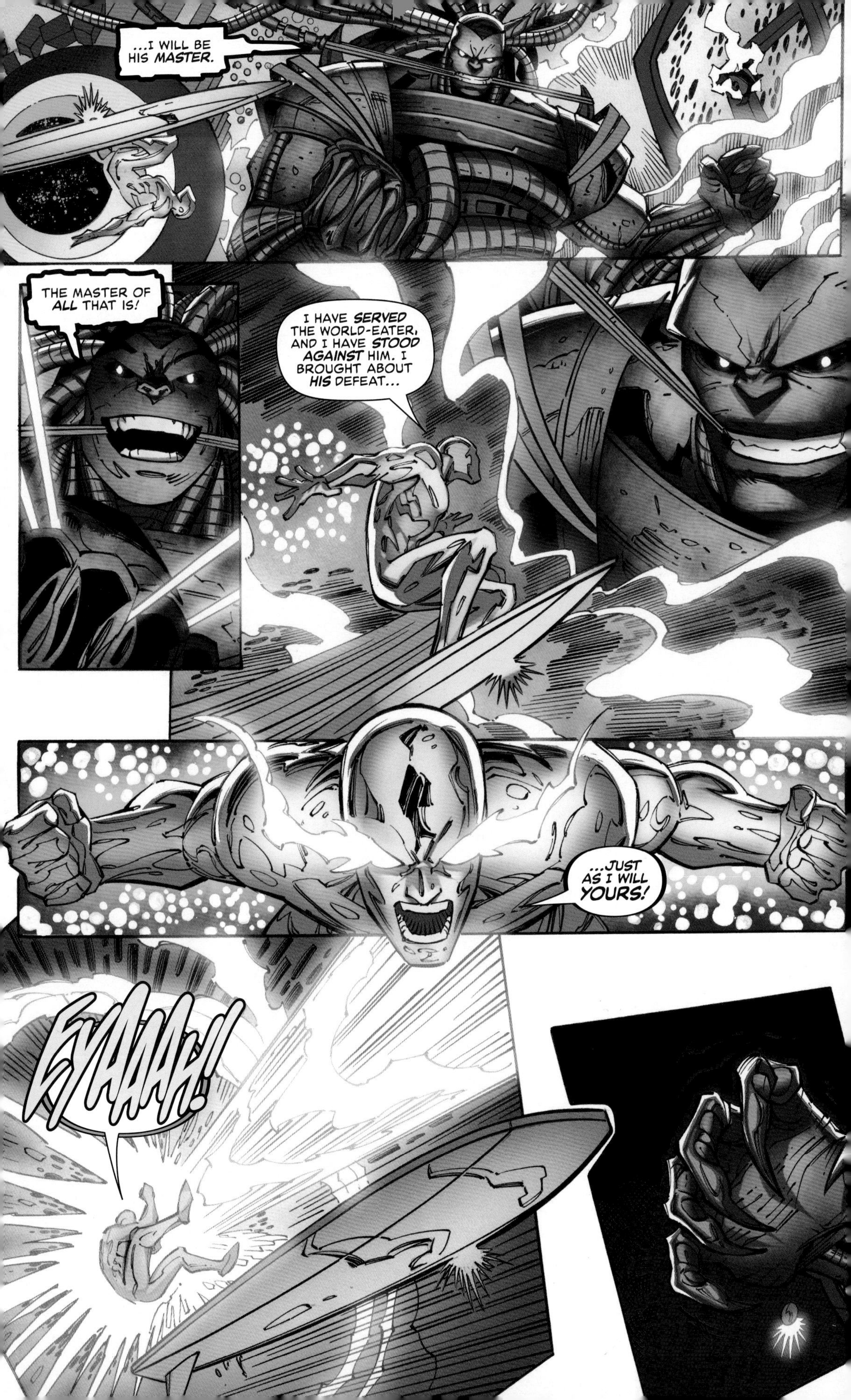
...I WILL BE HIS MASTER.
THE MASTER OF ALL THAT IS!
I HAVE SERVED THE WORLD-EATER, AND I HAVE STOOD AGAINST HIM. I BROUGHT ABOUT HIS DEFEAT...
...JUST AS I WILL YOURS!
EYAAAH!!

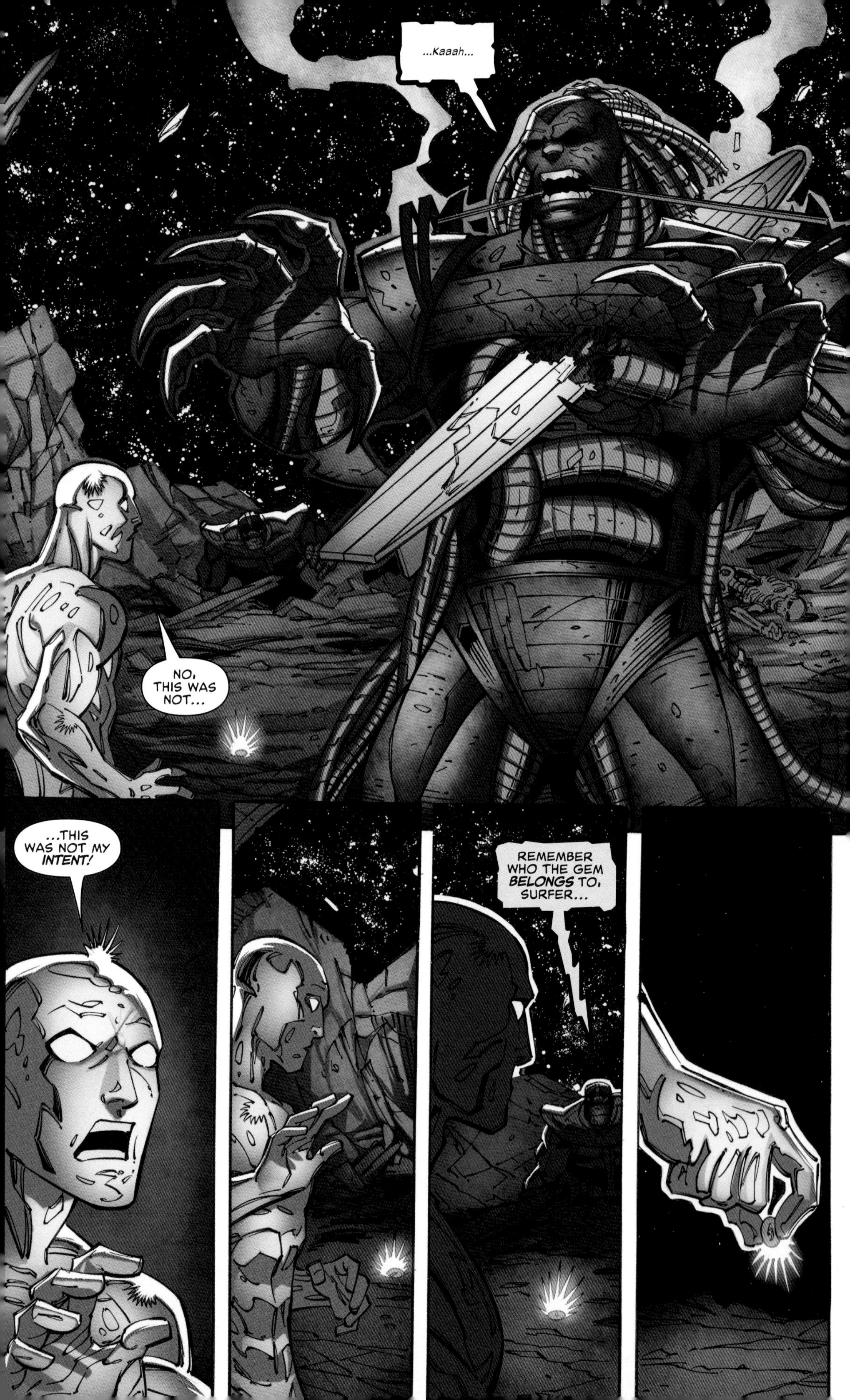
...Kaaah...
NO, THIS WAS NOT...
...THIS WAS NOT MY INTENT!
REMEMBER WHO THE GEM BELONGS TO, SURFER...

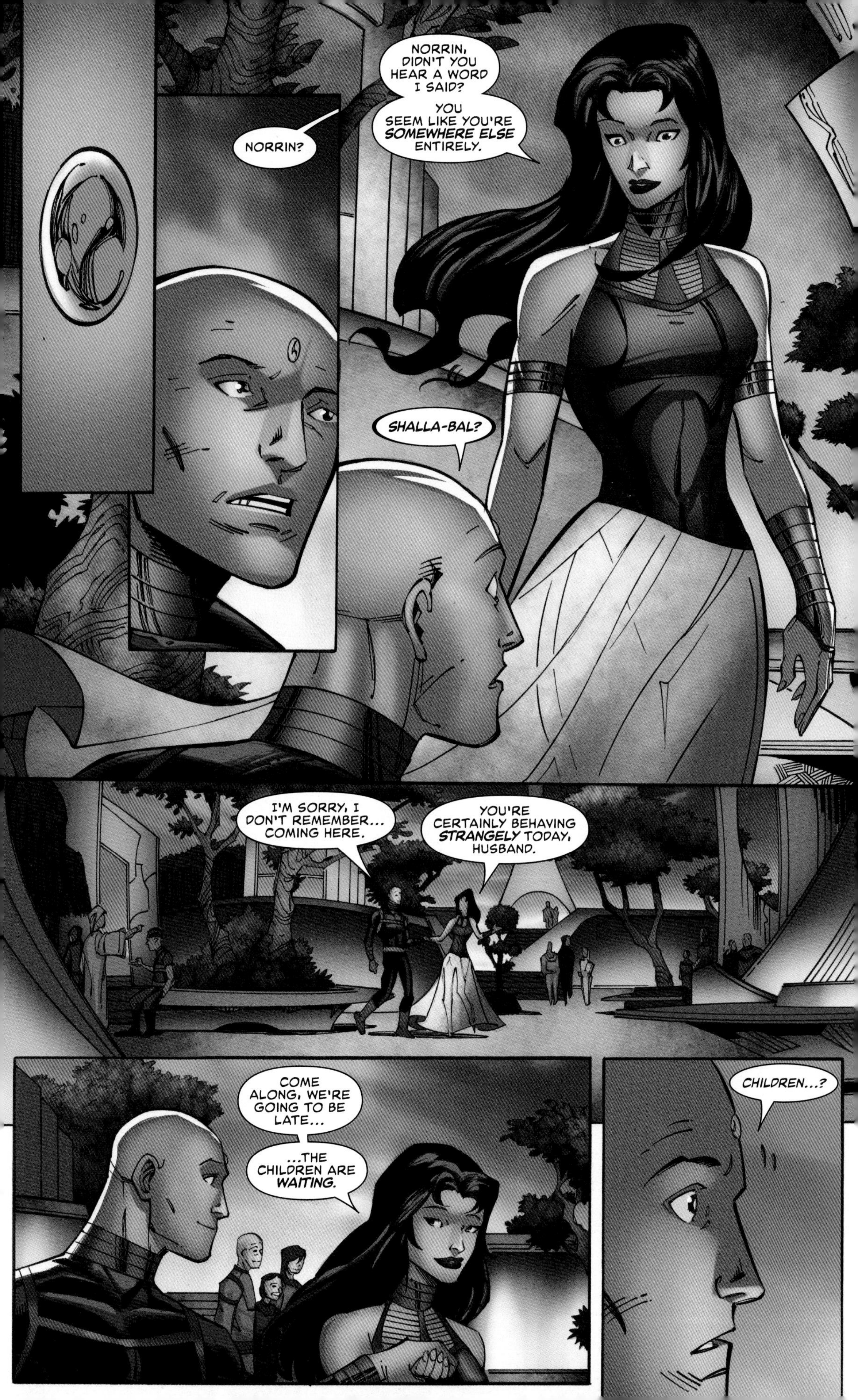
NORRIN?
NORRIN, DIDN'T YOU HEAR A WORD I SAID?
YOU SEEM LIKE YOU'RE *SOMEWHERE ELSE* ENTIRELY.
SHALLA-BAL?
I'M SORRY, I DON'T REMEMBER... COMING HERE.
YOU'RE CERTAINLY BEHAVING *STRANGELY* TODAY, HUSBAND.
COME ALONG, WE'RE GOING TO BE LATE...
...THE CHILDREN ARE *WAITING.*
CHILDREN...?

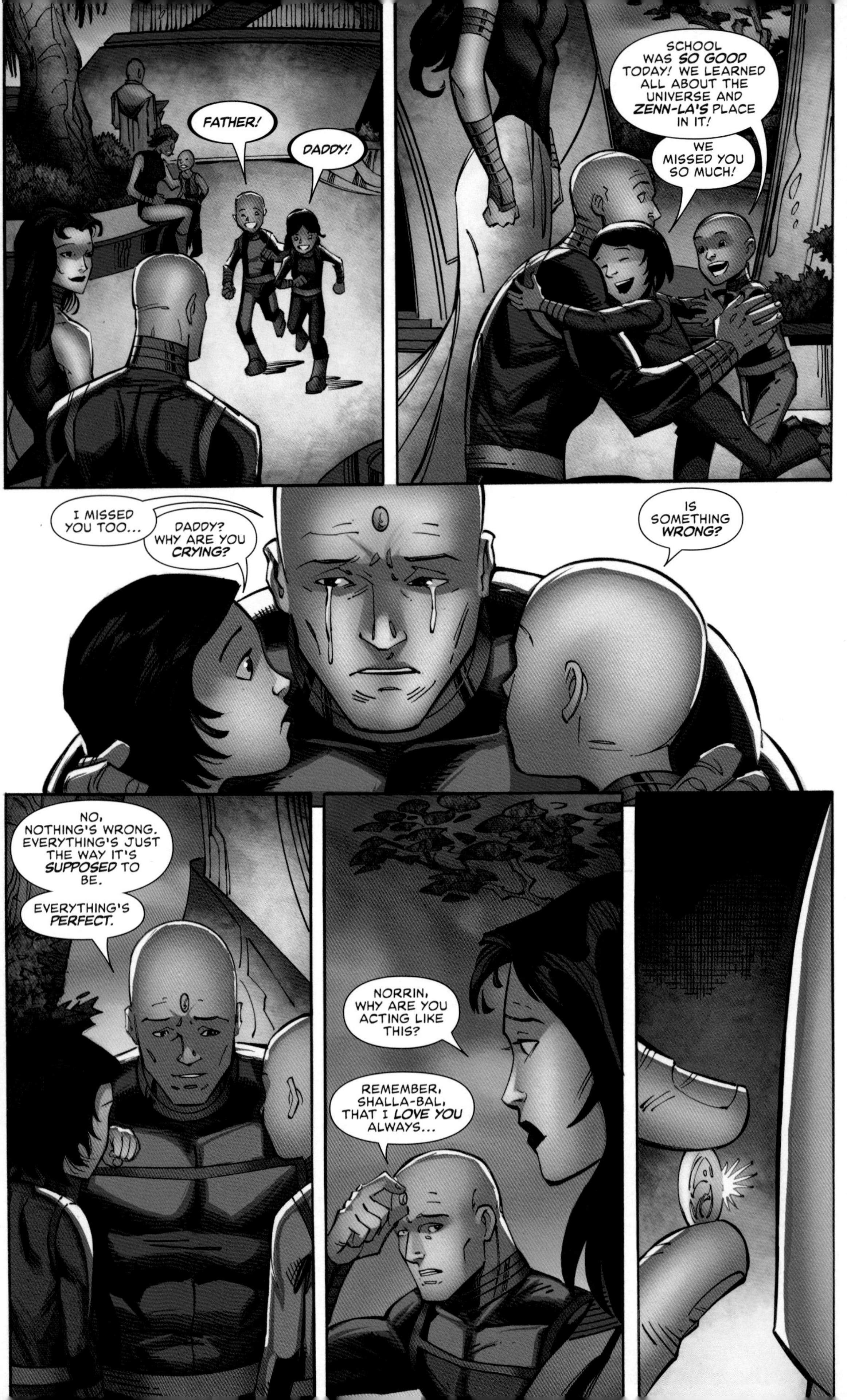
FATHER!
DADDY!
SCHOOL WAS SO GOOD TODAY! WE LEARNED ALL ABOUT THE UNIVERSE AND ZENN-LA'S PLACE IN IT!
WE MISSED YOU SO MUCH!
I MISSED YOU TOO...
DADDY? WHY ARE YOU CRYING?
IS SOMETHING WRONG?
NO, NOTHING'S WRONG. EVERYTHING'S JUST THE WAY IT'S SUPPOSED TO BE.
EVERYTHING'S PERFECT.
NORRIN, WHY ARE YOU ACTING LIKE THIS?
REMEMBER, SHALLA-BAL, THAT I LOVE YOU ALWAYS...

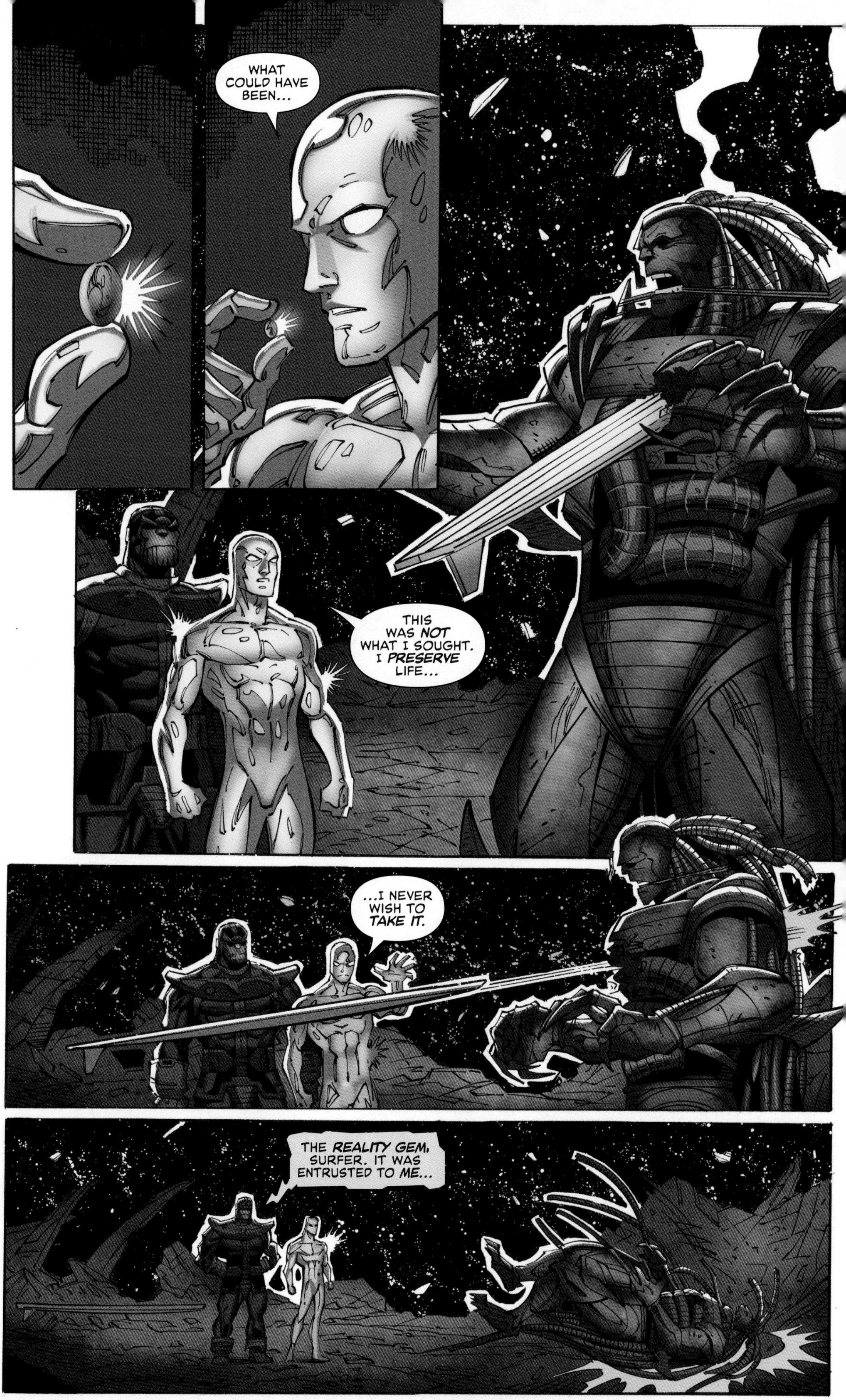
WHAT COULD HAVE BEEN...
THIS WAS NOT WHAT I SOUGHT. I PRESERVE LIFE...
...I NEVER WISH TO TAKE IT.
THE REALITY GEM, SURFER. IT WAS ENTRUSTED TO ME...

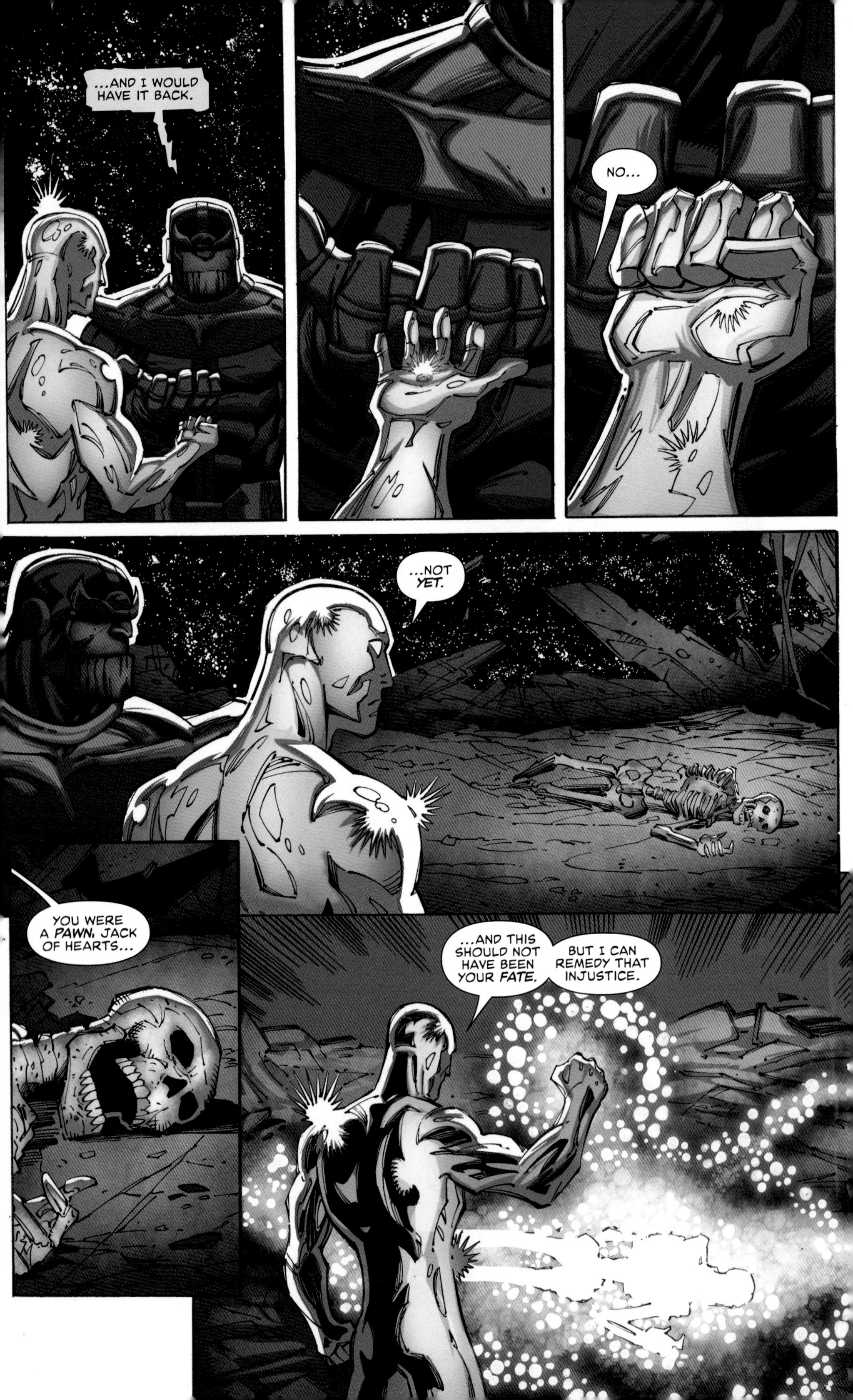
...AND I WOULD HAVE IT BACK.
NO...
...NOT YET.
YOU WERE A PAWN, JACK OF HEARTS...
...AND THIS SHOULD NOT HAVE BEEN YOUR FATE.
BUT I CAN REMEDY THAT INJUSTICE.

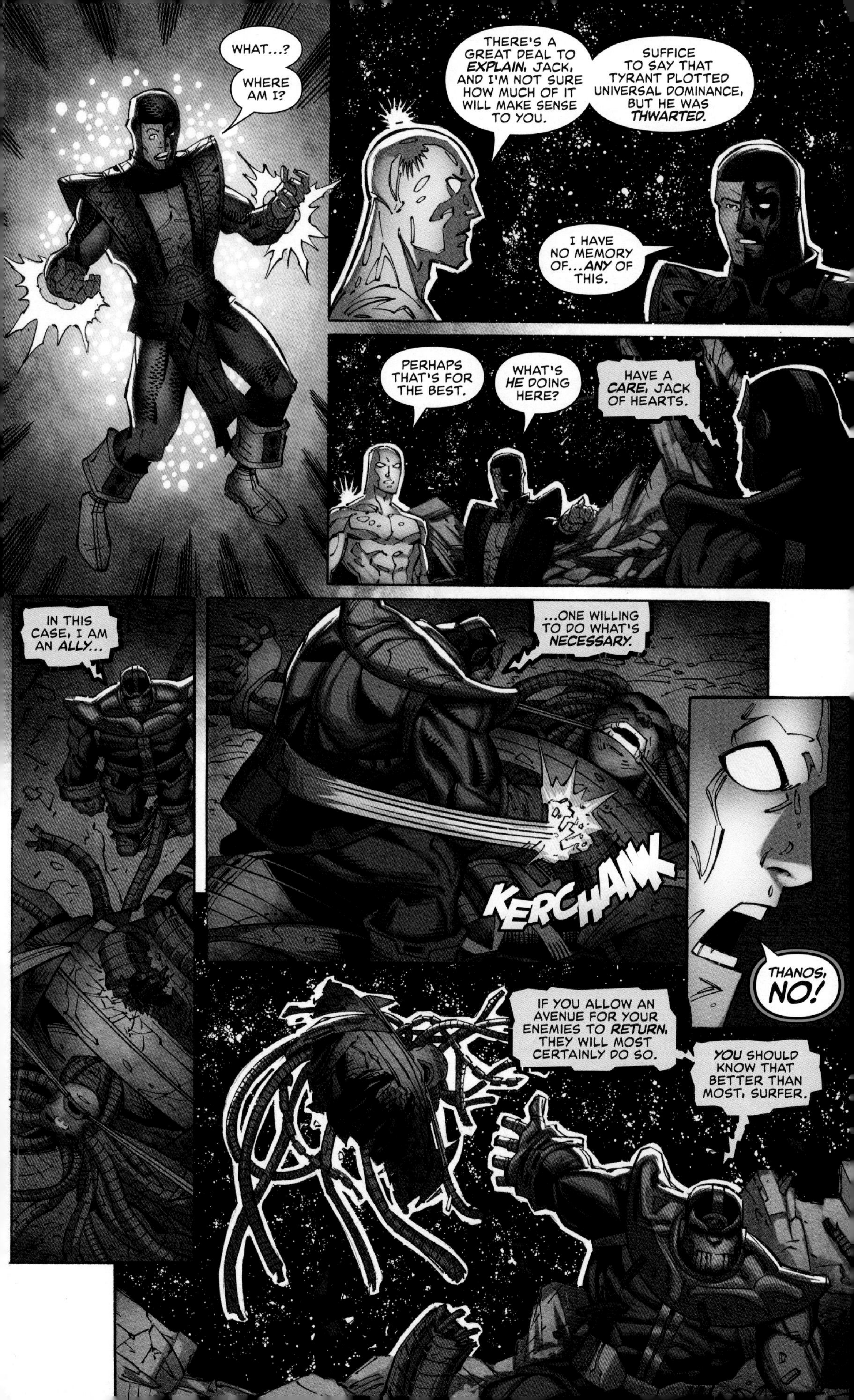
WHAT...? WHERE AM I?
THERE'S A GREAT DEAL TO EXPLAIN, JACK, AND I'M NOT SURE HOW MUCH OF IT WILL MAKE SENSE TO YOU.
SUFFICE TO SAY THAT TYRANT PLOTTED UNIVERSAL DOMINANCE, BUT HE WAS THWARTED.
I HAVE NO MEMORY OF...ANY OF THIS.
PERHAPS THAT'S FOR THE BEST.
WHAT'S HE DOING HERE?
HAVE A CARE, JACK OF HEARTS.
IN THIS CASE, I AM AN ALLY...
...ONE WILLING TO DO WHAT'S NECESSARY.
KERCHANK
THANOS, NO!
IF YOU ALLOW AN AVENUE FOR YOUR ENEMIES TO RETURN, THEY WILL MOST CERTAINLY DO SO.
YOU SHOULD KNOW THAT BETTER THAN MOST, SURFER.

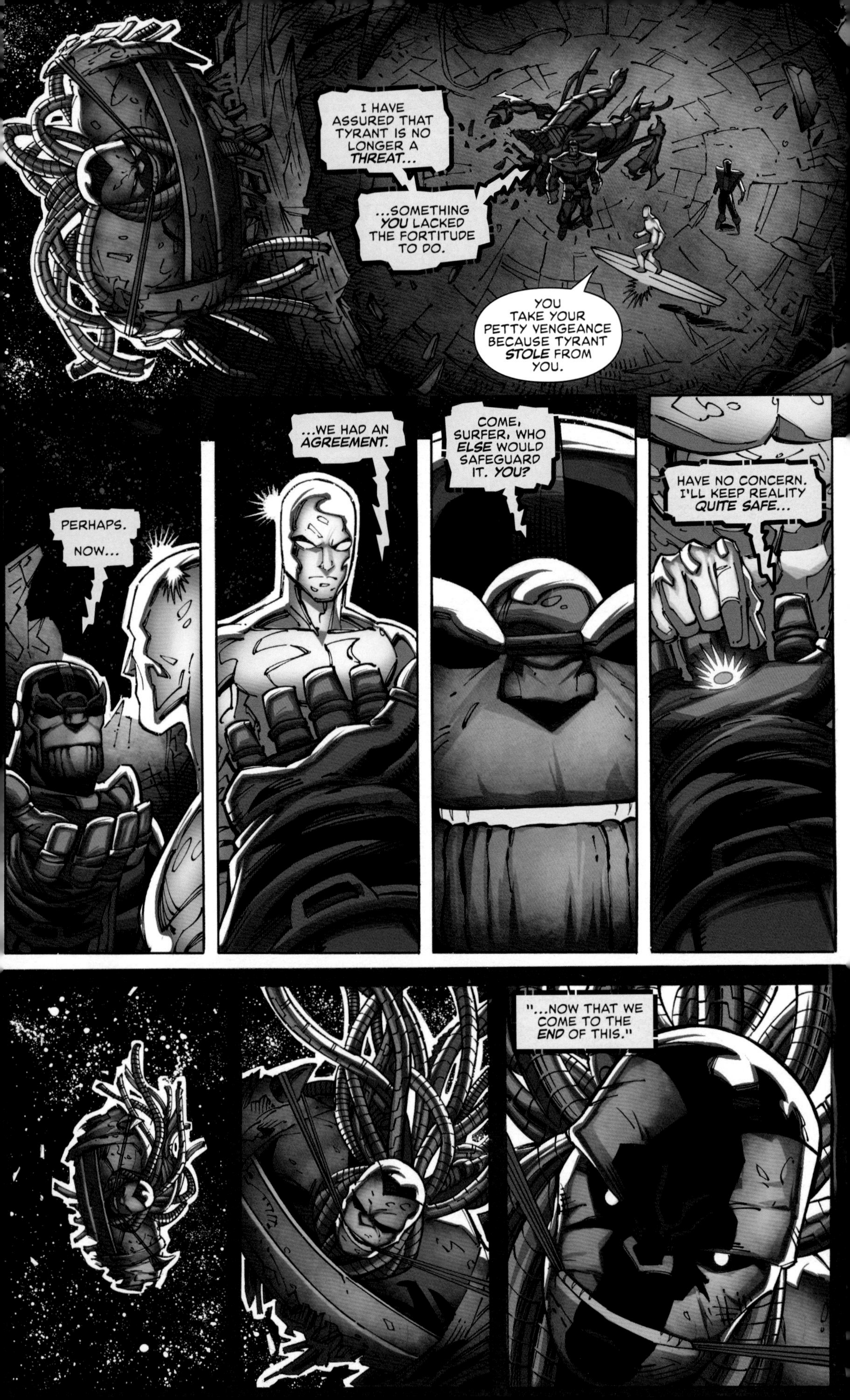
I HAVE ASSURED THAT TYRANT IS NO LONGER A THREAT...
...SOMETHING YOU LACKED THE FORTITUDE TO DO.
YOU TAKE YOUR PETTY VENGEANCE BECAUSE TYRANT STOLE FROM YOU.
PERHAPS. NOW...
...WE HAD AN AGREEMENT.
COME, SURFER, WHO ELSE WOULD SAFEGUARD IT. YOU?
HAVE NO CONCERN. I'LL KEEP REALITY QUITE SAFE...
"...NOW THAT WE COME TO THE END OF THIS."

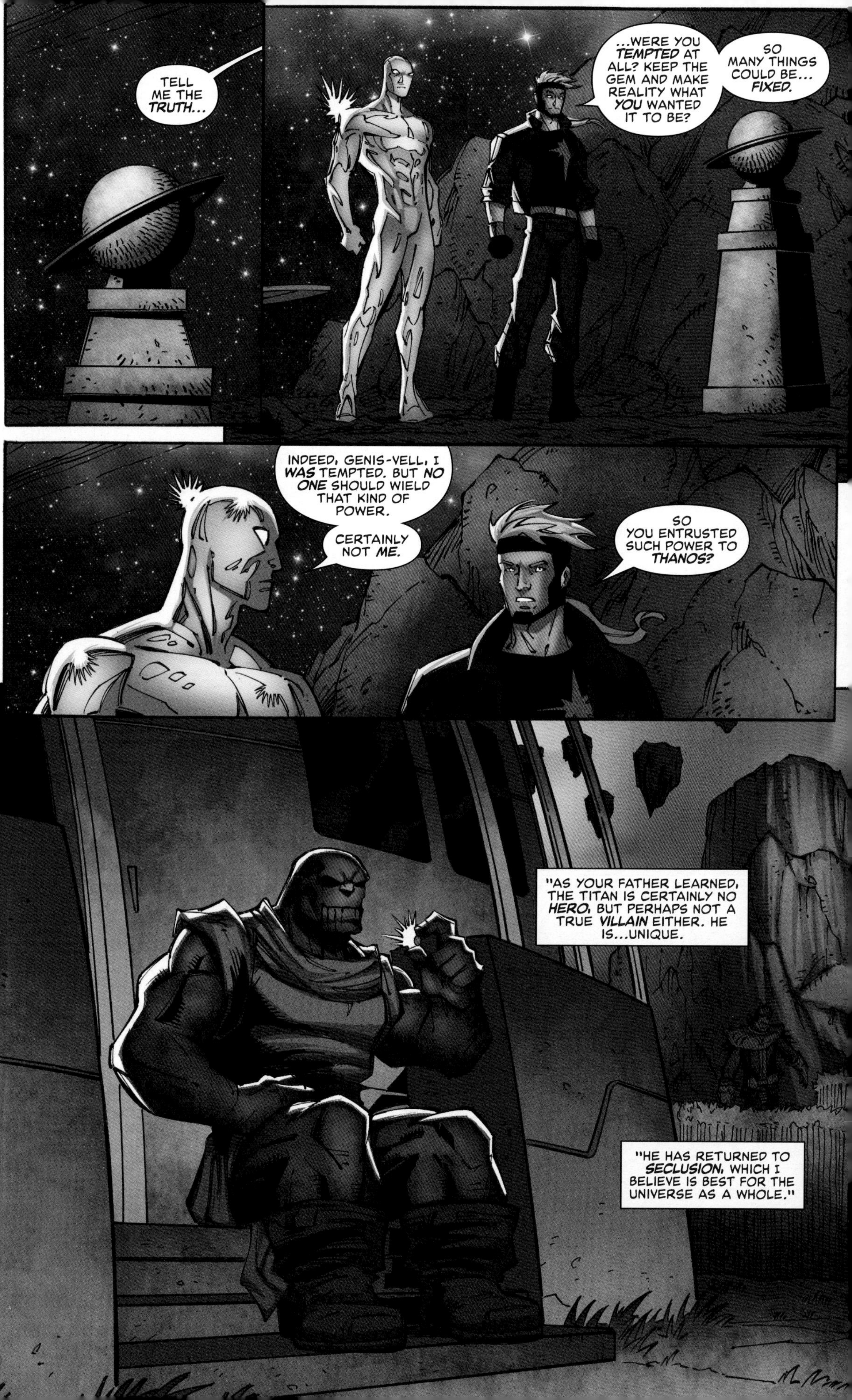
TELL ME THE TRUTH...
...WERE YOU TEMPTED AT ALL? KEEP THE GEM AND MAKE REALITY WHAT YOU WANTED IT TO BE?
SO MANY THINGS COULD BE... FIXED.
INDEED, GENIS-VELL, I WAS TEMPTED. BUT NO ONE SHOULD WIELD THAT KIND OF POWER.
CERTAINLY NOT ME.
SO YOU ENTRUSTED SUCH POWER TO THANOS?
"AS YOUR FATHER LEARNED, THE TITAN IS CERTAINLY NO HERO, BUT PERHAPS NOT A TRUE VILLAIN EITHER. HE IS...UNIQUE.
"HE HAS RETURNED TO SECLUSION, WHICH I BELIEVE IS BEST FOR THE UNIVERSE AS A WHOLE."

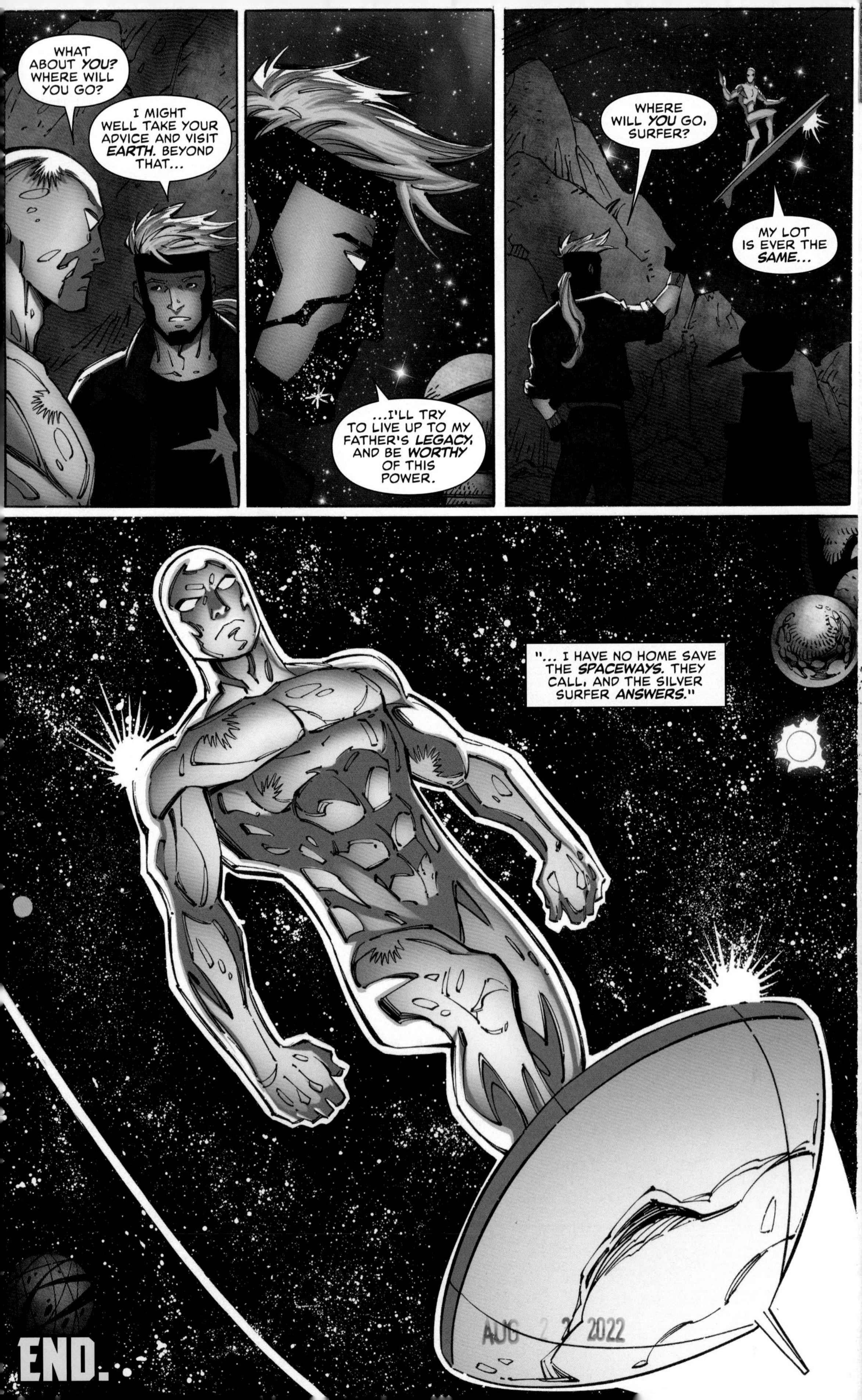
WHAT ABOUT YOU? WHERE WILL YOU GO?
I MIGHT WELL TAKE YOUR ADVICE AND VISIT EARTH. BEYOND THAT...
...I'LL TRY TO LIVE UP TO MY FATHER'S LEGACY, AND BE WORTHY OF THIS POWER.
WHERE WILL YOU GO, SURFER?
MY LOT IS EVER THE SAME...
"... I HAVE NO HOME SAVE THE SPACEWAYS. THEY CALL, AND THE SILVER SURFER ANSWERS."
END.